Max-Planck-Institut für ausländisches öffentliches Recht und Völkerrecht

Beiträge zum ausländischen öffentlichen Recht und Völkerrecht

Begründet von Viktor Bruns

Herausgegeben von
Armin von Bogdandy · Rüdiger Wolfrum

Band 164

Rüdiger Wolfrum · Nele Matz

Conflicts in International Environmental Law

Springer
Berlin Heidelberg New York Barcelona
Hongkong London
Mailand Paris Tokio

ISSN 0172-4770
ISBN 3-540-40520-8 Springer-Verlag Berlin · Heidelberg · New York

Bibliografische Information Der Deutschen Bibliothek

Die Deutsche Bibliothek verzeichnet diese Publikation in der Deutschen Nationalbibliografie; detaillierte bibliografische Daten sind im Internet über <http://dnb.ddb.de> abrufbar.

Printed in Germany

Satz: Reproduktionsfertige Vorlagen vom Autor
Druck- und Bindearbeiten: Konrad Triltsch, Print und digitale Medien GmbH,
97199 Ochsenfurt-Hohestadt
SPIN: 10944585 64/3130 x z – 5 4 3 2 1 0 – Gedruckt auf säurefreiem Papier

Table of Contents

Part I

Conflicts between Environmental Agreements

A. Conflicts and the Need for Harmonization in International Environmental Law: an Introduction

(Matz)

Conflicts between regulations within the same legal system are problematic, from a policy point of view, because they interfere with the coherence and, as a result, the efficiency of the respective legal system. This applies to national and supranational legal systems as well as to the network of regulations in international law. The objective of this introductory section is to give an overview of the causes of conflicting international regulation in the context of international environmental law, and to answer the question why the issue of conflicts in this context is relevant from a practical point of view. The different forms of conflicts will also be identified.

The following sections of Part I of this study will then discuss conflicts between international treaties dealing with different aspects of international environmental law, including: (1) dumping, (2) the protection and management of the marine environment, (3) the protection and management of Antarctica, (4) the protection of biological diversity, (5) the protection against climate change and desertification, as well as (5) the rules on the transport of hazardous wastes are covered.

I. The Development and Significance of Conflicts in International Environmental Law

Environmental law has dominated the progressive development of international law since the early 1970s. It developed a variety of specific factors, many of which may still be considered to be unique characteristics of international environmental agreements, while some others seem to have been slowly adopted in other distinct fields of international law-making. In particular, the means of non-confrontational enforcement of international legal obligations that were developed by international environmental agreements have lead to a shift of paradigms in international law in general.[1]

An important feature of the development of international environmental law over the last thirty years has been the growing number of multilateral and bilateral treaties concluded between States. This trend was triggered by the United Nations Conference on the Human Environment (UNCHE) held in Stockholm in 1972, and by the "Earth Summit", as the United Nations Conference on Environment and Development (UNCED) is known, which was held in Rio de Janeiro, in 1992. Today there are about 1000 international instruments that include at least some provisions related to the environment and its protection.[2] These international agreements concern a wide range of environmental issues. They address global threats like global warming, ozone depletion, desertification or the deterioration of biological diversity. They also involve the regulation of environmental problems of a more regional or even local scope, e.g. the protection and management of lakes or rivers shared by two or more States or the protection of a certain species existing only in a specific border region between two States. Many of the existing environmental conventions substantially or partially overlap and are linked to one another by their respective subjects, their scopes, objectives or approaches.

In the absence of a universal legislature or an administration with a comprehensive mandate, most international treaties exist parallel to one another and are further developed without the benefit of consideration being given to potential conflicts with other agreements either during their negotiation or at a later stage of their existence. Insofar as these agreements overlap, this overlap can either take the form of a doubling of efforts concerning a particular problem or as a contradiction or conflict between the objectives, programs or means of the respective agreements. The phenomenon of a multitude of parallel, substantially

---

1 On the development of these mechanisms see R. Wolfrum, "Means of Ensuring Compliance with and Enforcement of International Environmental Law", *RdC* 271 (1998), 7 et seq.

2 E. Brown Weiss, "Understanding Compliance with International Environmental Agreements: The Baker's Dozen Myths", *Univ. Richmond L. R.* 32 (1999), 1555.

or partially overlapping and colliding agreements in international environmental law, exacerbated by the practice of negotiating ever more binding instruments, has been labeled "treaty congestion".[3]

The doubling of efforts can diminish the effectiveness of international environmental law because scarce financial, administrative or technical resources may be wasted. For this reason, conflicts between different international agreements create an even more fundamental problem. The effectiveness of international environmental agreements can be significantly curtailed if conflicts between agreements lead to uncertainty concerning their interpretation and, consequently, their implementation and overall application in the field of international environmental law. The issue of conflicts between international treaties still lacks a satisfactory solution in international law. Generally, both the doubling of efforts and conflicts between environmental agreements require a systematic approach to harmonization and coordination in order to provide for greater coherence and, accordingly, enhanced efficiency of international environmental law.

In regard to conflicting treaties in international law, after an examination is made to determine if and how two treaties collide, the main consideration is the question which, if either, of the agreements enjoys priority. So far, this question has not gained as much attention in international law as it deserves, especially regarding its dogmatic and, particularly, its practical relevance.[4] Not even the international convention that was adopted to regulate questions regarding the law of treaties, the Vienna Convention on the Law of Treaties (VCLT),[5] sheds much light on this matter. The VCLT addresses, in its article 30, only some specific kinds of conflicts, thus leaving the issue to be one of the rather "obscure" matters of international law.[6] Solving conflicts between international environmental agreements pursuant to the law of treaties or by way of institutional cooperation is the subject of Part II of this study.

---

[3] See for example B. Lukitsch Hicks, "Treaty Congestion in International Environmental Law: The Need for Greater International Coordination", *Univ. Richmond L. R.* 32 (1999), 1643 et seq.

[4] See, however, J.B. Mus, "Conflicts Between Treaties in International Law", *NILR* 45 (1998) 208 et seq.; M. Zuleeg, "Vertragskonkurrenz im Völkerrecht – Teil I: Verträge zwischen souveränen Staaten", *GYIL* 20 (1977), 246 et seq.

[5] *UNTS* 1155, 18232.

[6] I. Sinclair, *The Vienna Convention on the Law of Treaties* (1984), 93.

But first, the questions why environmental law is prone to conflicts and what forms of conflicts can be established must be settled. That effort will be followed by an examination of specific instruments, with a view to assessing their overlap and possible contradictions.

II. Ecological Interdependencies: One Reason for Conflicts in International Environmental Law

Besides the enormous number of existing treaties, there are other specific reasons why the problem of treaty congestion is of particular relevance to environmental law. One factor is the interdependence of ecological processes that results in a very close relationship between the subject matter with which international environmental treaties are concerned. This interrelation necessarily leads to a linkage of the problems addressed by treaties. It also necessarily leads to a linkage of the means, provided by the rules of the environmental agreements, which are intended to solve the respective environmental problems. The ecological and, if the matters are regulated by instruments of international law, the legal interdependence of agreements is one of the reasons why international environmental law is prone to conflicts, contradictions and the doubling of efforts. The regulation of one environmental issue almost necessarily touches upon topics subject to other international legal instruments.

All environmental processes are based upon the linkage of different factors. Human interference with these processes can trigger unpredictable environmental changes. The same applies to the solutions humans apply to certain environmental problems, since these solutions can also lead to impacts on the environment not predicted or only later discovered by environmental science. A lack of scientific understanding of ecological interdependencies makes it more difficult to detect, avoid and solve potential conflicts that are based upon linked ecological factors.

It is known, for example, that some ozone depleting substances, e.g. halocarbons, are also greenhouse gases. Consequently, the approaches taken by the respective legal treaties concerned with the protection of the ozone layer and the prevention of climate change must be coordinated to take account of this overlap.[7] Another example of the legal im-

---

[7] In this specific case the international community has not only identified the overlap but reacted to it by explicitly excluding the regulation of the re-

plications of a close relationship between ecological, chemical, biological and physical interactions involves research that shows that some of the chemicals that might substitute banned ozone depleting substances in industrial processes happen to be greenhouse gases. Although a shift from ozone depleting substances to these substitutes would be in accordance with the obligations under the Montreal Protocol banning these substances, it would be contrary to the aims of and efforts under the international legal instruments on the prevention and abatement of climate change processes.

Various interactions and close links between the phenomena of desertification, climate change and the loss of biological diversity also demonstrate the need to address all possible causes of an environmental problem in an integrated and holistic manner. Climate change, for example, can increase land degradation of sensitive dry-lands and promote desertification, while desertification also leads to a loss of biodiversity. International agreements on the regulation of these issues already exist but, as is typical, only one of them, the Convention to Combat Desertification (CCD),[8] explicitly refers to a linkage to the other phenomena and the respective legal instruments.[9] This demonstrates the need, in order to enhance efficiency, to promote a means of cooperation and coordination between these instruments with a view towards taking the interdependencies into account and avoiding contradictions between the regimes.

In regard to the regulation of environmental protection, only an integrated and holistic approach can avoid both the shifting of different kinds of damage from one environmental medium to another and the conflict of the respective approaches to regulation. The need for better integration, to avoid the shifting of environmental damage and conflicts between instruments, concerns all levels of law-making: national, regional and international. The variety of linkages between ecological processes is an integral part of the variety of potential conflicts that can

---

spective ozone depleting substances that are addressed by the Montreal Protocol on Substances Depleting the Ozone Layer, *ILM* 26 (1987), 1550 et seq. from the scope of the Framework Convention on Climate Change (FCCC), *ILM* 31 (1992), 849 et seq. and its Kyoto Protocol, *ILM* 37 (1998), 32 et seq.; see e.g. the paragraphs and subparagraphs of article 4 FCCC. These provisions refer to the reduction of greenhouse gases "not controlled by the Montreal Protocol". See also articles 2, para. 1, lit. (a) (ii) and (vi) Kyoto Protocol.

8 *ILM* (1994), 1328 et seq.

9 See the Preamble and article 8, para. 1 CCD.

arise between legal instruments aiming at the regulation of a specific threat to the global environment.

III. Different Kinds of Conflicts: an Approach to Categorization

Conflicts can arise between: (1) instruments of a different legal nature; (2) instruments with different geographical scopes; (3) agreements with different point of views or with different objectives; (4) original and modified agreements; and (5) treaties that, in principle, regulate the same subject matter but have different parties.[10] As a result, conflicts and contradictions between international environmental agreements can take a variety of forms, not all of which have traditionally been considered conflicts in a legal sense.

A conflict, in the strict sense, relates to the incompatibility of two legal norms. That is to say, that one obligation cannot be fulfilled without necessarily violating the other.[11] In the case of international treaties, and according to this definition, only two regulations of international law that establish incompatible obligations would be considered to be in conflict with one another. In the field of international environmental law the collisions and overlap that lead to the assumption of treaty congestion do not necessarily take this incompatible form, but rather establish divergences or inconsistencies without establishing contradicting, absolute obligations. Theoretically, these inconsistencies or divergences could be made compatible without abolishing the substantive content of either of the regulations. Compared to incompatibilities, these collisions represent "conflicts" in a broader sense. Even these more broadly defined conflicts, particularly if the number of potential collisions is taken into account, may have the same negative effects as the more narrowly defined conflicts. Since contradictions can, due to the uncertainties involved in the application of the respective regulations, diminish the potential effectiveness of international environmental law, all divergences shall be included in the following examination of conflicts.

With respect to the occurrence of contradictions between international environmental treaties, different categories of conflicts can be distin-

---

[10] See C.W. Jenks, "The Conflict of Law Making Treaties", *BYIL* 30 (1953), 401 et seq. (418).

[11] H. Kelsen, *General Theory of Norms* (1991), 123.

guished. The different categories of conflicts developed in the following paragraphs are very closely linked to one another and interrelate to some extent, making it difficult to draw clear distinctions between them. Still, the approach taken to categorizing conflicts can demonstrate where the main, collision-generating differences between agreements lie. If different categories of potential conflicts can be identified, it may be easier in future intergovernmental negotiations to avoid the establishment of yet more contradicting international environmental agreements.

1. Conceptual Conflicts between Different Approaches or Programs

One kind of conflict can arise out of the different approaches or underlying programs adopted by instruments, e.g. concerning the incorporation of the environmental principles or philosophical considerations upon which a convention is based. Conflicts with other agreements can, for example, result from the application of disparate approaches: (1) the ecosystem approach, (2) the precautionary approach, (3) the integrated approach to the regulation of environmental problems or the introduction of sustainability, or (4) the exploitation oriented management criteria for environmental resources. These and comparable approaches are important not only for the general guidance they provide but also in the way they inform the interpretation of an agreement by its States Parties; divergent approaches can thereby lead to contradictions in relation to other agreements. The approach a treaty takes is often also of significance with respect to its objectives and aims as well as for its more specific mechanisms. A single treaty can be based upon several of the above identified (or other) approaches, e.g. an ecosystem approach, a precautionary approach as well as the integrated protection of the environment. A mix of approaches is possible, provided of course that the different approaches followed by one single instrument are compatible with one another.

Since a treaty's approach documents only the controlling underlying concepts and considerations, it is possible that two agreements, although following the same approach, differ with regard to their aims or political priorities. A result of such dissimilarity, in spite of the common approach employed, is that the agreements will be in conflict with each other. The incorporation of the same approach, therefore, does not guarantee that two treaties will not collide. If, however, two agreements are not even based upon similar fundamental approaches, the probability that they conflict with one another rises and, because of the lack of a common basis, they may be particularly difficult to harmonize. While many of the modern environmental agreements are based upon similar concepts, e.g. sustainable development, there can still be significant differences between them and, especially, older agreements.

One example may serve as an illustration of this generally described phenomenon. The Convention on the Conservation of Antarctic Marine Living Resources, 1980 (CCAMLR),[12] follows an ecosystem-based approach. The Convention makes reference to this underlying concept in the first paragraph of the Preamble. However, article I, para. 1 is even more explicit in this respect. It reads:

> "The Convention applies to the Antarctic marine living resources of the area south of 60 South latitude and to the Antarctic marine living resources of the area between that latitude and the Antarctic convergence which form part of the marine ecosystem."

The rules concerning the exploitation of living resources are modeled on this approach.

In comparison, article 119 UN Convention on the Law of the Sea (UNCLOS)[13] obligates States to observe standards:

> "...which are designed, on the best scientific evidence available to the States concerned, to maintain or restore populations of *harvested* species at levels which can produce the maximum sustainable yield, as qualified by relevant environmental and *economic* factors..." (emphasis added).

The reference in article 119 UNCLOS to "harvested species" rather than "harvested and associated species" as in article II, para. 3 CCAMLR, clearly indicates that the Convention on the Law of the Sea follows a utilitarian approach whereas the Convention on the Protection of Antarctic Marine Living Resources pursues an ecosystem approach. The difference in approaches taken by the two Conventions, particularly with respect to non-harvested species like seals, has significant consequences.

2. *Conflicting Objectives*

Apart from differences in the respective approach that informs a treaty, conflicts can result form the distinct objectives or aims of agreements. A

---

[12] *ILM* 19 (1980), 841 et seq.

[13] *ILM* 21 (1982), 261 et seq.

collision of objectives, due to the different purposes and fields of regulation, is a very likely scenario in international environmental law. Although a treaty's objectives also reflect the approaches and programs, which are considered the philosophical basis of an agreement, objectives are more concrete and can substantially contradict the aims of other agreements. A frequently cited example of conflicting approaches, as well as conflicting aims, is the distinction between the protection of the environment, on the one hand, and the promotion of free trade, on the other hand.[14] Conflicting objectives can also occur in relation to different environmental conventions, especially if the objectives of one convention do not take the aims of other agreements into consideration. It goes without saying that, to take an extreme example, the objective of the Convention Designed to Ensure the Conservation of Various Species of Wild Animals in Africa, Which Are Useful to Men or Inoffensive, 1900,[15] is hardly reconcilable with the Convention on Biological Diversity (CBD), 1992.[16]

Contradicting aims of international environmental agreements usually do not establish incompatible conflicts. While the objectives of agreements characterize the detailed obligations laid down in the treaty, the objectives themselves do not, in most cases, incorporate clear enough provisions such that they establish regulations that are incompatible with the aims of other agreements. It is the concrete duties and obligations established by a treaty in order to pursue its objectives that can initiate conflicts with another agreement. Thus, it is often the case that a conflict does not materialize directly but rather emerges as a conflict between obligations or as a conflict in the implementation, i.e. on a sub-

---

[14] While the relationship between the environment and free trade is outside the scope of this study, see the following articles on the relationship between multilateral environmental agreements and trade agreements: N. Matz, "The Relation Between International Agreements for the Protection of the Environment and the GATT", in: T. Zhenghua/ R. Wolfrum (eds.), *Implementing International Environmental Law in Germany and China* (2001), 163 et seq.; D. Brack, "Reconciling the GATT and Multilateral Environmental Agreements with Trade Provisions: the Latest Debate", *RECIEL* 6 (1997), 112 et seq.; J. Cameron/ J. Robinson, "The Use of Trade Provisions in International Environmental Agreements and their Compatibility with the GATT", *YIEL* 3 (1992), 3 et seq.; S. Charnovitz, "Multilateral Environmental Agreements and Trade Rules", *Environmental Policy & Law* 26 (1996), 163 et seq.

[15] *IPE* IV, 1542 et seq.

[16] *ILM* 31 (1992), 818 et seq.

sequent level. Accordingly, conflicting objectives, with their influence on the obligations created by different agreements, can also be the basis for subsequent conflicts and are of special importance for the potential inconsistency between agreements.

3. Conflicting Obligations

Conflicting obligations are a traditional example of conflicting legal regulations. If obligations come into conflict they can, though they need not, appear as conflicts in the more strict sense, i.e. as incompatible duties. Conflicting obligations arise if the duties imposed or behavior required by the provisions of one agreement collide with an obligation owed under the rules of another treaty. In order for a conflict between obligations, in the strict sense, to be established, the scenario requires further that an agreement clearly and unambiguously formulate the duties of the States Parties. If duties are vague and in need of interpretation, a conflict in the strict sense is less likely because a clear incompatibility will not automatically be established. Although two vague obligations could, in the end, also be interpreted as being incompatible with one another, interpretation is rather seen as a means of harmonizing colliding agreements. This is particularly so, if the colliding obligations are formulated only in rather soft terms.

In contrast to, e.g. conflicting approaches, potentially conflicting obligations are easier to identify during the negotiation phase of the promulgation of modern multilateral environmental agreements. For this reason, the chances of avoiding conflicting obligations are better than the chances of avoiding other conflicts, which are usually more difficult to detect or only manifest themselves in the implementation of an agreement. The practical relevance of this category of conflicts shall, therefore, not be overemphasized. Furthermore, since environmental agreements typically formulate obligations in a vague manner, at least to the degree that they more typically lay down positive duties instead of prohibitions, conflicts of obligations may often not occur directly. Conflicts between vague obligations are more likely, emerging only after the interpretation of vague obligations by the States Parties and then taking the form of conflicting means of implementation or as political conflicts.

4. *Conflicts in the Implementation Phase*

Even if the objectives or obligations of agreements do not directly collide, the means to pursue these aims and duties can initiate another category of conflicts. Although conflicts are generally rooted in the instruments themselves, they can realize their potential in a later phase involving the implementation of obligations derived from international environmental agreements in national law. As already mentioned, it can be difficult to draw a line between the different categories because they are closely interrelated. Conflicts between agreements can be seen in all of these categories in a single set of circumstances, without the existence of a clear distinction between whether a conflict arises out of the approach, the objectives or the implementation.

The category of conflicts that emerge in the implementation phase, and not on the level of objectives or obligations, can be illustrated by the following example, which is again taken from the interrelation of the means used to combat ozone depletion and global warming. The protection of the ozone layer does not, per se, collide with the aim of preventing and mitigating global warming. A conflict with the international instruments for the protection of the global climate can emerge, however, if efforts to protect the ozone take the form of obligations to substitute ozone-depleting substances with chemicals that are also greenhouse gases. A similar conflict results if States, even in the absence of a clear obligation requiring them to do so, pursue the protection of the ozone by requiring or promoting the use of such substitutes.

The category of conflicts occurring at the implementation phase is particularly relevant if duties and obligations, e.g. in framework conventions, are deliberately cast in vague terms, thus granting States Parties a wider margin of interpretation and discretion in the adoption of mechanisms to pursue the objectives of an agreement. Such conflicts might eventually be avoided if a harmonized interpretation of treaties is favored and if the harmonized interpretation is made binding for the States Parties involved. However, such a proceeding would reduce flexibility, which is often employed as a tool to enhance compliance and efficiency.

5. *Political Conflicts*

The final category of conflicts to be described here digresses even further from traditional legal conflicts and refers, instead, to political conflicts. Political contradictions are closely related to each of the other categories of conflicts that can arise between international environmental agreements. In this respect the political aims and underlying considerations can lead to tensions between agreements, if political priorities are promoted by either a favorable national interpretation or by means of compliance to the disadvantage of another agreement.

A State's political vision and practice are particularly closely related to the implementation of an agreement and the respective potential for conflicts. A State does not expect to give up its political sovereignty in favor of international environmental decision-making, but if international processes have led to an international decision on environmental governance, any conflicts between international instruments must be regulated by similar international decision-making. Any other approach significantly diminishes the viability of international governance and international law. Such considerations, however, necessarily reduce the discretion for formulating national policy in the respective fields of environmental governance and might, despite their potential viability, face resistance from States fearing a further loss or transfer of their sovereignty.

While political conflicts cannot be avoided in all cases, conformity between agreements achieved through interpretation and cooperation can further decrease the freedom to justify certain political priorities. Furthermore, streamlining international environmental politics, e.g. by the establishment of international policies and principles, can help to diminish the significance of this category of conflicts. It must be recognized, however, that streamlining the variety of interests involved in this field of international relations will be very difficult.

6. Conclusions Concerning the Categorization of Conflicts

An approach to categorizing potential conflicts must acknowledge the fact that clear-cut distinctions between different types of conflicts cannot be established. While the categories described above have mainly been grouped as genuine types, e.g. as either conflicts between two approaches or conflicts between two obligations, a broad range of cross-cutting conflicts may also occur: obligations can conflict with approaches, approaches can conflict with implementation measures, and objectives can conflict not only with other aims but also with approaches or obligations. Yet, the categories of different kinds of potential conflicts, or rather, the different starting points for conflicts, may help to identify contradictions when two agreements are examined with a view towards their conformity. Throughout the examination of colliding agreements of international environmental law in Part I of this study, reference will be made to the above-described categories of different types of conflicts.

B. The Law of the Sea and International Environmental Law

I. Introduction

(Matz)

The world's oceans serve various vital ecological, logistical and other functions, e.g. food security or climate stabilization. Their continuing existence in good condition and normal functioning is not only a matter of human luxury, but rather a major factor for sustaining all life on the planet. Furthermore, it is possible to recognize an intrinsic value of the marine environment and to pursue the protection of the oceans for their own sake.[17] Judged by the number of international and regional instruments and the general international attention attached to the issue, e.g. by international conferences and by different UN institutions, protecting the seas from pollution and the depletion of their biological resources plays a central role in global environmental concern and international law-making.

Due to the broad variety of human uses, the oceans have for a long time been subject to severe pollution and the depletion of their resources. As a result, the legal regulation of the marine environment has become an important part of international environmental law, mainly consisting of

---

[17] In contrast to the scientific, aesthetic, recreational, cultural, social or economic value attached to environmental resources or features, the intrinsic value relates to none of these anthropocentric considerations but considers environmental components valuable *per se*. The recognition of an intrinsic value (parallel to anthropocentric value) of environmental features is promoted by some modern instruments of international environmental law, e.g. in the first preambular paragraph of the Convention on Biological Diversity or article 3 of the 1991 Protocol on Environmental Protection to the Antarctic Treaty (Environmental Protocol), *ILM* 30 (1991), 461 et seq.

regional international treaties[18] and (parts of) the Convention on the Law of the Sea. In regard to marine environmental issues addressed by international agreements, two broad and equally important categories of regulations can be distinguished: (1) the prevention of pollution, and (2) the protection and management of biological resources. Both categories have their basis in the desire to protect marine ecosystems from adverse effects while pursuing the sustainability of human uses of the seas.

The protection of the marine environment from damage is, however, only one aspect of the law of the sea. While many environmental treaties and parts of the Convention on the Law of the Sea are concerned with the prevention of pollution and the protection of the marine environment, other aspects of the law of the sea are concerned with: (1) the regulation of shipping and related issues; (2) the exploitation and management of marine biological resources, particularly fishing; (3) marine scientific research; and (4) the exploitation of mineral resources and other uses of the sea and the sea-bed by different actors.

Conflicts in the realm of the regulation and protection of the seas can result from the various and at times fundamentally different interests and uses concerning the marine environment and its components. Two examples of such conflicts involve: (1) the collision of interests between fisheries and the exploitation of mineral resources, and (2) the collision of interests between the seas' recreational functions and accidental pollution resulting from the use of the oceans for logistical and transportation purposes.[19] Of growing significance, particularly in northern European countries, is the issue of potential conflicts between the production of energy in offshore wind parks and the impact these projects may have on the safety of shipping as well as the protection of the

---

[18] E.g. the Convention on the Protection of the Marine Environment of the North-East Atlantic (OSPAR), *ILM* 32 (1993), 1068 et seq., the Helsinki Convention for the Protection of the Marine Environment of the Baltic Sea, 1992, *BGBl.* II (1994), 1397 et seq., English version accessible at <http://www. helcom.fi>, last visited 23 January 2002; see also Ph. Sands, *Principles of International Environmental Law* (1995), Vol. I, 296 et seq. on the treaties and protocols concluded as parts of the UNEP Regional Seas Programme.

[19] See B.A. Vestal, "Dueling with Boat Oars, Dragging through Mooring Lines: Time for More Formal Resolution of Use Conflicts in States' Coastal Waters?", *Ocean & Coastal L. J.* 4 (1999), 1 et seq. (2).

oceans' fauna from sound and vibration disturbances connected with the wind parks.[20]

The following section of this study covers two issues which give rise to potentially colliding fields of regulations applicable to the seas. First, conflicts related to marine pollution and the dumping of installations and ships at sea is considered. Second, problems regarding the protection and management of biological resources and the ecosystem under the Convention on the Law of the Sea, on the one hand, and the Convention on Biological Diversity, on the other hand, will be discussed.

II. Conflicts between the Convention on the Law of the Sea and the Convention on Biological Diversity

(Matz)

The last decade has seen growing interest in the protection and sustainable use of marine biological and genetic diversity, *inter alia*, due to the discovery of marine life in deep-sea areas and the genetic capabilities of the newly discovered microorganisms to adapt to their adverse living conditions. The Convention on the Law of the Sea and the Convention on Biological Diversity are global treaties that are applicable to the protection of marine life. Consequently, the relationship between the Convention on the Law of the Sea and the Convention on Biological Diversity is crucial for a coherent approach to the protection of marine life in general. Generally, if an agreement like the Convention on the Law of the Sea regulates a variety of uses of the oceans, addressing environmental but also economic and other issues, the risk that provisions of this treaty collide with environmental agreements applicable to the marine environment rises.[21] This applies also to the specific relationship

---

[20] Some European countries like Sweden, the UK and Denmark are already experimenting with offshore wind parks, while other States' administrations, e.g. the German Federal Maritime and Hydrographic Agency are still considering applications for permission to pursue those projects.

[21] Not only because of the variety of issues regulated by the agreement, but also because of an exploitation orientated approach to marine living resources, the Convention on the Law of the Sea cannot be considered an explicit agreement for the protection of the marine environment, R. Wolfrum, "The Protection of the Marine Environment after the Rio Conference: Progress or Stale-

between the Convention on the Law of the Sea and the Convention on Biological Diversity, which can be in conflict with respect to issues like the protection and management of marine biological resources and other uses of the seas.[22]

Concerning the relationship between the Convention on the Law of the Sea and the Convention on Biological Diversity, differences between the two agreements primarily have their basis in the different approaches each adopts towards the protection and use of marine living and genetic resources. The Convention on Biological Diversity, in respect to marine living as well as genetic resources, generally follows a more protective approach than the management orientated approach of the Convention on the Law of the Sea. Furthermore, priorities concerning legal concepts or principles established by the Convention on the Law of the Sea, e.g. the freedom of shipping, innocent passage and transit passage, can collide with the approaches the Convention on Biological Diversity takes towards the protection of marine biodiversity. The relationship between the Convention on the Law of the Sea and other agreements was the subject of political difficulties during the negotiations and has, at least with respect to the CBD, found its solution in article 22 CBD.[23] The extent and viability of conflict clauses like article 22 CBD is subject to a discussion in Part II. First, it is necessary to more clearly articulate the potential overlap and conflicts between these treaties.

1. The Scope and Application of the Convention on Biological Diversity in Regard to the Marine Environment

According to the definition of biological diversity in article 2 CBD, biodiversity also includes the variety of marine ecosystems. While States mainly concentrated on terrestrial biodiversity during the negotiation of the agreement and did not discuss the significance of marine

---

mate?", in: U. Beyerlin et al. (ed.), *Recht zwischen Umbruch und Bewahrung – Festschrift für Rudolf Bernhardt* (1995), 1003 et seq. (1009).

22 See also R. Wolfrum/ N. Matz, "The Interplay between the UN Convention on the Law of the Sea and the Convention on Biological Diversity", *UNYB* 4 (2000), 445 et seq.

23 On the respective negotiations see also M. Chandler, "The Biodiversity Convention: Selected Issues of Interest to the International Lawyer", *Colo. J. Int'l Env. L. & Policy* 9 (1993), 141 et seq. (149).

ecosystems extensively,[24] the second Conference of the Parties (COP) to the Convention on Biological Diversity, which met in 1995, adopted a work-program on the issue called the Jakarta Mandate on Marine and Coastal Biological Diversity.[25] The Jakarta Mandate was prepared by the Subsidiary Body of Scientific, Technical and Technological Assistance (SBSTTA) and addresses, *inter alia*, the physical modification and destruction of marine habitats, pollution, the introduction of non-native species and the exploitation of natural resources.[26]

Regarding the scope of the Convention on Biological Diversity with respect to biological diversity of the oceans, there exists a close interrelation between this agreement and the Convention on the Law of the Sea. The Convention on the Law of the Sea establishes maritime zones, which differ in regard to the rights a State has and the duties a State owes in these zones. With respect to the oceans' waters, the Convention on the Law of the Sea distinguishes between internal waters,[27] the territorial sea,[28] archipelagic waters,[29] the exclusive economic zone (EEZ),[30] and the high seas.[31] Concerning the ocean floor, the Convention distinguishes between the continental shelf[32] and the deep sea-bed[33] (the Area). The distinction between different maritime zones gains relevance also in regard to the regulation of the management of living resources and marine scientific research under the rules of the Convention on the Law of the Sea. Particularly important in relation to the applicability of the Convention on Biological Diversity is the degree of

---

24 G. Verhoosel, "Prospecting for Marine and Coastal Biodiversity: International Law in Deep Water", *Int'l J. Marine & Coastal L.* 13 (1998), 91 et seq.

25 See Report of the 2nd Conference of the Parties to the Convention on Biological Diversity, Annex II, Decision II/10, Doc.UNEP/CBD/2/19.

26 The programme has remained on the agenda of the Conference of the Parties since then, see for example the Report of the Executive Secretary on the implementation of the programme of work on marine and coastal biological diversity on the occasion of the 4th COP, 1998, Doc.UNEP/CBD/COP/4/5.

27 E.g. Article 8, para. 1 and article 10, para. 4 UNCLOS.

28 See Part II UNCLOS, i.e. articles 2 et seq.

29 E.g. article 49 UNCLOS.

30 Part V UNCLOS, i.e. articles 55 et seq.

31 Part VII UNCLOS, i.e. articles 86 et seq.

32 Part VI UNCLOS, i.e. articles 76 et seq.

33 Part XI UNCLOS, i.e. articles 133 et seq.

sovereignty assigned to States in maritime zones by the Convention on the Law of the Sea, because the Convention on Biological Diversity, in its article 4, distinguishes between the applicability of its regulations within and beyond zones of national sovereignty.

According to article 4, lit. (a) CBD, the Convention is applicable to components of biological diversity within zones of national sovereignty. For areas outside national sovereignty the agreement is applicable only to processes and activities under the control of a State Party regardless of where the effects of these activities occur (article 4, lit. (b) CBD).[34] This establishes the provisions of the Convention on the Law of the Sea regarding the extent of national sovereignty over different parts of the oceans as a precondition for the scope and applicability of the Convention on Biological Diversity.

It follows that, in connection with the provisions of the Convention on the Law of the Sea, the Convention on Biological Diversity is applicable to components of biological diversity within the territorial waters of a State (article 4, lit. (a) CBD together with article 2, para. 1 UNCLOS) and to archipelagic waters (article 4, lit. (a) CBD together with article 49, para. 1 UNCLOS). The exclusive economic zone of a coastal State is, according to article 55 UNCLOS, the subject of a special regime concerning rights and jurisdiction particularly characterized by a limited grant of sovereignty. However, article 56 UNCLOS establishes exclusive rights of the coastal States concerning the exploration, exploitation, protection and management of marine biological and other resources in the exclusive economic zone. For this reason the exclusive economic zone is considered a zone of national jurisdiction in the light of article 4, lit. (a) CBD, although the sovereign rights of the coastal States in the EEZ are not as far reaching as in the territorial sea or archipelagic waters. Still, the Convention on Biological Diversity is applicable to components of biodiversity.[35]

---

[34] The distinction between the application of the Convention on Biological Diversity to components according to article 4, lit. (a) CBD on the one hand and to activities under the control of a State according to article 4, lit. (b) CBD has been considered arbitrary, see L. Glowka *et al.*, *A Guide to the Convention on Biological Diversity* (1994), 27.

[35] G. Henne, *Genetische Vielfalt als Ressource* (1998), 327.

2. *The Conservation and Management of Living Resources*

Two issues must be distinguished with respect to the contradictory approaches taken by the two conventions, represented by the protection, on one hand, and the sustainable use of marine living resources, on the other hand. The first issue concerns the criteria and standards regarding the degree of and approach to the exploitation of living resources. The second issue concerns the establishment of protected areas for living resources and ecosystems. In order to discuss and contrast different attitudes as to the first of these issues, that is, an approach to the use of certain marine species and the respective criteria for their protection, the Agreement for the Implementation of the Provisions of the United Nations Convention on the Law of the Sea of 10 December 1982 relating to the Conservation and Management of Straddling Fish Stocks and Highly Migratory Fish Stocks (1995 Agreement on Fish Stocks)[36] must be considered along with the Convention on the Law of the Sea and the Convention on Biological Diversity.

(a) Criteria for the Exploitation of Living Resources

A conflict between the Convention on the Law of the Sea and the Convention on Biological Diversity may exist, with respect to the exploitation of marine living resources, with respect to the incorporation of an ecosystem approach into the fisheries regime. While both agreements call for the conservation of populations on a sustainable level, the Convention on Biological Diversity also pursues an ecosystem approach that might go further than the criteria for conservation of stocks in the fisheries regime of the Convention on the Law of the Sea.

According to the Convention on the Law of the Sea, States exercise exclusive sovereignty over the management of the respective living resources in the territorial as well as in archipelagic waters.[37] Since the relevant provisions of the Convention on the Law of the Sea concerned with the exploitation of living resources in the territorial waters do not indicate a specific fisheries policy that is to be pursued by the coastal States, in principle, more strict conservation measures based on the Convention on Biological Diversity could be controlling.

---

[36] *ILM* 34 (1995), 1547 et seq.

[37] Internal waters are treated in a manner similar to terrestrial areas and are, therefore, not specifically referred to in this study.

The situation is different as far as the exclusive economic zone is concerned. According to article 56 UNCLOS, coastal States have sovereign rights in the exclusive economic zone. This sovereignty extends to exploring and exploiting, conserving and managing natural resources, whether living or non-living. However, there are specific management criteria concerning straddling stocks and highly migratory species,[38] and further management standards in articles 61 and 62 UNCLOS. In general, these provisions require States to protect marine living resources against overexploitation (paragraph 2) and to maintain and restore populations of harvested species at levels that can produce the maximum sustainable yield (paragraph 3). This aim, in principle, resembles the provision in the Convention on Biological Diversity requiring the maintenance of viable populations of species (article 8, lit. (d) CBD). However, the maintenance of viable populations is only one aspect of the *in situ* conservation of biological diversity under article 8, lit. (d) CBD. This aim is further qualified by the additional requirement that viable populations be maintained "in their natural surroundings." This additional requirement hints at an ecosystem approach. Of equal importance, on this point, are the provisions in the same article requiring the protection and conservation of ecosystems. The far-reaching provision in article 8, lit. (f) CBD, which requires the rehabilitation and restoration of degraded ecosystems, is also significant.

In defining the maximum sustainable yield according to the Convention on the Law of the Sea the relevant environmental and economic factors may be taken into account. The environmental factors referred to in paragraph 3, and further specified in paragraph 4, are the interdependence of stocks (i.e. the effect exploitation has on species associated with or dependent upon harvested species) and generally recommended international minimum standards. Generally, fisheries have a considerable effect on other species and marine ecosystems because of ecological interdependency; stock depletion affects, *inter alia*, coral reefs, mangroves,

---

[38] See articles 63 and 64 UNCLOS, respectively. These provisions place a duty on the coastal State and States fishing the high seas to seek agreement on the management of the respective fish stocks. This embraces an obligation to negotiate. The ICJ, *ICJ Reports* (1969), 3, 47 at para. 85 (a), has emphasized in the North Sea Continental Shelf Cases that "the Parties are under obligation to enter into negotiations with a view to arriving at an agreement ... they are under an obligation so to conduct themselves that the negotiations are meaningful." Thus the regime on highly migratory species and straddling stocks under the Convention on the Law of the Sea provides a solution through procedural means rather than by establishing substantive standards.

estuaries as well as mammal species and turtles.[39] By taking into account the effect exploitation has on dependent and associated species, the Convention on the Law of the Sea has taken a first step towards an ecosystem approach without fully actualizing this tendency in the fisheries regime.

The protection of the diversity of ecosystems described above can be distinguished from the mere protection of species, encompassing not only the community of species but also the interactions between the species and the physical structures of the ecosystem.[40] The ecosystem approach as applied *vis-à-vis* marine living resources means, in general, that the following points must be addressed by a fisheries policy: (1) biological and ecological interactions between species as well as such interactions between stocks, in the same as well as in neighboring jurisdictional zones, and (2) the ecological conditions of the physical. Species dependent upon and associated with other species that are protected for human exploitation are addressed by the Convention on the Law of the Sea. These categories, however, represent only a small percentage of all living organisms that build the marine community in an ecosystem. Article 61 UNCLOS does not, for example, refer to the physical structures and conditions of ecosystems. Since fishing alters the relative abundance of species in marine communities and, additionally, fishing gear can physically destroy or alter habitats and disrupt bottom-dwelling communities,[41] ecosystems can be significantly changed even if policies comply with the provisions of the Convention on the Law of the Sea that refer to the interdependence of species.

Article 194, para. 5 of the Convention on the Law of the Sea does, however, refer to the protection of marine ecosystems. That regulation provides for the protection of fragile marine ecosystems. Yet, there is no indication that, apart from permitting the protection of certain particularly fragile ecosystems, an ecosystem approach must be incorporated into the regime on fisheries in the exclusive economic zone. From its systematic

---

[39] A. Rengifo, "Protection of Marine Biodiversity: A New Generation of Fisheries Agreements", *RECIEL* 6 (1997), 313 et seq.

[40] S. Iudicello/ M. Lytle, "Marine biodiversity and international law: instruments and institutions that can be used to conserve marine biological diversity internationally", *Tulane Env. L. J.* 8 (1994), 124 et seq.

[41] A. Rieser, "International Fisheries Law, Overfishing and Marine Biodiversity", *Georgetown Int'l Env. L. R.* 9 (1997), 251 et seq., (254); G. Rose, "Marine Biodiversity Protection through Fisheries Management - International Legal Developments", *RECIEL* 8 (1999), 284.

position, article 194 UNCLOS deals with measures that may be taken to prevent or mitigate pollution. While, in principle, the general rules on environmental protection must also be respected as far as fishing activities are concerned, it is doubtful that a general ecosystem approach will be introduced into the regulation of daily fishing activities as a result of article 194, para. 5 UNCLOS. The 1995 Agreement on Fish Stocks, which implements articles 63 and 64 UNCLOS, is more clearly based upon the ecosystem approach. However, it mitigates the situation for specific species or stocks only and does not consider all components of the marine ecosystems in its main provisions.

In this respect, the regime on fisheries established by the Convention on the Law of the Sea and the Convention on Biological Diversity differ. The sustainable use of biological diversity refers not only to some species that are relevant for human use but, by its definition and according to the conservation measures in its article 8 CBD, requires the protection and conservation of ecosystems as one part of a viable strategy to conserve biodiversity. While States are relatively free to abolish the minimum standards of the Convention on the Law of the Sea in order to pursue a more strict ecosystem-based approach, in accordance with the guidelines of the Convention on Biological Diversity, they are, at least under the rules of the Convention on the Law of the Sea, not required to do so. Although the two conventions do not create incompatible obligations or objectives on this point, the fundamental differences in the approaches taken by the two conventions might prevent the establishment of a coherent system of environmental standards applicable to the marine environment.

(b) The Establishment of Protected Areas

The differences between the approaches taken by the conventions and their potential consequences become even more clear in the context of the establishment of protected areas and the conservation of and access to genetic resources found in those areas. Regarding protected areas, another potential conflict between the objectives and obligations of the Convention on Biological Diversity and the fundamental principles of the Convention on the Law of the Sea becomes apparent. The implementation of the obligations in article 8, lit. (d) and (f) CBD (to provide for protected areas; to promote the protection of ecosystem and natural habitats; and to rehabilitate and restore degraded ecosystems) may come into conflict with the coastal States' obligations created by the Convention on the Law of the Sea, including the obligation: (1) to allow innocent passage in the territorial sea or in archipelagic waters, (2) to respect the right of archipelagic sea lanes passage, (3) to respect the right of transit passage, and (4) to respect the freedom of navigation in the exclusive economic zones. The conflict between the establishment of areas of environmental protection (pursuant to the Convention on Biological Diversity) and the freedom of navigation (pursuant to the Convention on the Law of the Sea) is a prominent example of competing uses of the sea and coastal waters.

According to the Conference of the Parties to the Convention on Biological Diversity, the selection of marine and coastal protected areas, within the framework of integrated marine and coastal area management, shall focus on critical habitats for marine living resources.[42] Specific areas of environmental protection are not explicitly envisioned by the Convention on the Law of the Sea. States can take measures

> "... necessary to protect and preserve rare or fragile ecosystems as well as the habitat of depleted, threatened or endangered species and other forms of marine life" (article 194, para. 5 UNCLOS).

Such measures, however, must not be an

> "unjustifiable interference with activities carried out by other States in the exercise of their rights and in pursuance of their duties in conformity with this Convention" (article 194, para. 4 UNCLOS).

Whether the establishment of areas in which navigation is controlled or prohibited in order to protect a specific habitat constitutes an "unjustifiable interference" with specific navigational freedoms is subject to interpretation. However, given the importance that the right of innocent passage through the territorial sea of another coastal State claims throughout the Convention on the Law of the Sea, it is unlikely that areas in national territorial waters that exclude ships from innocent passage can be established. The same applies in principle to potential protected areas in the exclusive economic zone. On the high seas, States Parties to the Convention on the Law of the Sea, in cooperation with one another, could agree upon protected areas as a means to provide for the protection of living resources. The effect of such an agreement, however, would be limited by the principle that third parties cannot be bound by treaties to which they have not ascented or become a party.[43] Because of the freedom of the high seas such non-parties could still perform a multitude of

---

[42] Annex I to Decision II/10, Doc.UNEP/CBD/COP/2/19.

[43] The principle of *pacta tertiis nec nocent nec prosunt* is incorporated into article 34 of the Vienna Convention on the Law of Treaties, which also reflects customary international law.

potentially harmful activities in areas recognized by some States as protected areas. Such agreements concerning the high seas would not, however, represent a conflict between UNCLOS and the CBD because the Convention on Biological Diversity does not apply to components of biological diversity beyond areas of national jurisdiction. The establishment of protected areas on the high seas is not, therefore, part of the scope of the Convention on Biological Diversity. The Convention on Biological Diversity does, however, oblige States Parties to cooperate with respect to areas beyond their respective national jurisdiction (article 5 CBD).

The practical relevance of the conflict between the two conventions associated with the CBD's provisions regarding protected areas is further limited by the fact that the Convention on Biological Diversity, given its vaguely formulated obligations, does not require States Parties to establish protected areas in areas of national jurisdiction which are free from all use. It is also questionable whether it is necessary, pursuant to the Convention on Biological Diversity, to exclude all shipping from a protected area since the normal operation of a ship might not be considered a disturbance of the marine ecosystem. Still, the different approaches, objectives and priorities of the two conventions, represented by the CBD's protected areas provisions, clearly demonstrate the difficulties that can arise if two agreements address a problem from different points of view. The States Parties to the Convention on Biological Diversity are, to a wide extent, free to adopt policies in order to protect marine biological resources that are more strict than obligations regarding the protection of the marine environment arising out of the Convention on the Law of the Sea. The fundamental freedoms guaranteed under the Convention on the Law of the Sea can, however, limit the policy choices available for the achievement of the protection of the marine environment under the Convention on Biological Diversity.

3. Marine Genetic Resources: Different Concepts of Access and Conservation

The issue of the exploration and exploitation of marine genetic resources is a result of the discovery of marine living organisms that have genetic dispositions of potentially high value for industrial and commercial uses. In particular, the organisms discovered in the realm of hydrothermal vents on the ocean floor possess certain characteristics, e.g. heat resistance, which are of potential economic value.[44]

While Part XII of the Convention on the Law of the Sea formulates general rules regarding the protection of the marine environment, these provisions are not suitable to specifically promote the sustainable use of biological and, particularly, genetic resources, because they are too general. Neither are the provisions on the protection of living resources of the high seas, articles 117 – 120 UNCLOS, intended to protect genetic resources. To protect genetic resources, the protection of the living organism in its ecosystem is indispensable. Still, a comprehensive system regarding protection and the sustainable use of genetic resources in areas outside national jurisdiction calls for different regulations than the regime which aims only for the protection against overfishing. A system that aims at the sustainable use of fishery resources is fundamentally different compared to a scheme on bioprospecting and the sustainable use of microorganisms and their genetic particularities. While a protective element is essential in regulations concerning marine genetic resources, an elaborate system on their sustainable use and a potential sharing of the benefits derived therefrom is also crucial with regard to the yet unknown commercial potential of marine genetic resources.[45]

The collection of samples for marine genetic research does not take the form of exploitation as in the context of fishing. In this respect, it more closely resembles scientific research activities than commercial fishing, although both activities are undertaken for commercial purposes. As a consequence, it is proper to consider whether the provisions of the Convention on the Law of the Sea concerned with scientific research offer applicable and appropriate mechanisms for the management of genetic

---

[44] On hydrothermal vents and their legal protection see L. Glowka, "The Deepest of Ironies: Genetic Resources Marine Scientific Research and the Area", *Ocean Yearbook* 12 (1996), 154 et seq. and, particularly on human threats to these ecosystems, the same author, "Bioprospecting, Alien Invasive Species, and Hydrothermal Vents: Three Emerging Legal Issues in the Conservation and Sustainable Use of Biodiversity", *Tulane Env. L. J.* 13 (2000), 329 et seq. (349 et seq.).

[45] A system for sharing the benefits drawn from the genetic resources of the high seas and the deep sea-bed could be based upon a common heritage approach, supported by an institutional regime comparable to the regulations on mineral resources of the Area, see N. Matz, "Marine Biological Resources: Some Reflections on Concepts for their Protection and Sustainable Use" (2001), Presentation given at the Ladenburger Diskurs Marine Biodiversität/Marine Biodiversity, February 2001, manuscript with the author.

research on marine living resources and to what extent such an approach is consistent with the Convention on Biological Diversity's regime providing for the conservation and use of genetic resources, including the CBD's elaborate system of access and benefit sharing.

According to article 238 UNCLOS, all States have the right to conduct marine scientific research subject to the rights and duties of other States. In general terms, the expression "marine scientific research" is most often used to describe activities to expand scientific knowledge of the marine environment and its processes and includes, *inter alia*, oceanography, marine biology, marine chemistry, scientific ocean drilling and coring, geological and geophysical surveying.[46]

The authority coastal States can exercise over foreign marine scientific research depends on the maritime zone in which it is conducted as well as on the nature of the research activity. The Convention on the Law of the Sea vests in coastal States particular rights to exercise authority over marine scientific research in accordance with the distribution of jurisdictional powers in the territorial sea, the exclusive economic zone and the continental shelf.[47] In the territorial sea the coastal States have the exclusive right to regulate, authorize and conduct marine scientific research. Any marine scientific research conducted by other States or international organizations or nationals of other States may be conducted only with the express consent and subject to the conditions imposed by the coastal State concerned (article 245 UNCLOS). The coastal States are under no obligation to provide access to marine resources of the territorial sea for genetic research and they are not under an obligation to facilitate such access. Further, the Convention on the Law of the Sea explicitly provides that passage through territorial waters for the purpose of carrying out research activities does not qualify as innocent passage (article 19, para. 2, lit. (j) UNCLOS). The Convention on Biological Diversity, while affirming sovereign rights over biological resources, is based upon a facilitation of access to genetic resources on mutually agreed

---

[46] J.A. Roach, "Marine Scientific Research and the New Law of the Sea", *ODILA* 27 (1996), 59 et seq., (60).

[47] For the drafting history of the regime on marine scientific research see A.H.A. Soons, *Marine Scientific Research and the Law of the Sea* (1982), 154 et seq.; as to an assessment of the regime see, amongst others, W. Plessmann/ V. Röben, "Marine Scientific Research: State Practice v. Law of the Sea?", in: R. Wolfrum (ed.), *Law of the Sea at the Crossroads: The Continuing Search for a Universally Accepted Regime* (1991), 373 et seq.; R. Wolfrum, "Der Schutz der Meeresforschung im Völkerrecht", *GYIL* 19 (1976), 99 et seq.

terms. The respective coastal States could also incorporate such an approach into the regime on marine scientific research in territorial waters without conflicting with the general rules or approaches of the Convention on the Law of the Sea.

With respect to the exclusive economic zone and the continental shelf, the coastal State concerned has jurisdiction with respect to marine scientific research. The coastal State's authority in these areas is, however, subject to limitation. It is true that Marine scientific research may only be conducted with the express consent of the coastal State concerned but, as opposed to the provisions concerning the territorial waters, coastal States may be obliged to grant this consent. Article 246, paragraphs 3 to 5 UNCLOS distinguishes between scientific research which aims to increase knowledge of the marine environment (purely scientific research) and scientific research which is of direct significance for the exploration and exploitation of the natural resources of the given exclusive economic zone or the continental shelf. In the latter case the coastal State may withhold its consent subject to State discretion, whereas in the former case, under normal circumstances, the State is obligated to grant permission.

Since bioprospecting does not have, as its exclusive aim, the addition to the general scientific knowledge on the environment of a given zone, but is rather oriented toward commercial use, it should come under article 246, para. 5 UNCLOS. As a consequence the coastal States concerned may withhold their consent and are under no obligation to facilitate access to genetic resources in their exclusive economic zone.[48] The same is true with respect to access to genetic resources located on the continental shelf, as long as this area does not extend/to the limit of 200 nautical miles from the baselines. It follows from this rule, laid out by the Convention on the Law of the Sea, that the degree of State discretion to withhold or grant access to genetic resources for bioprospecting in the exclusive economic zone and the continental shelf may collide with the objective of the Convention on Biological Diversity to facilitate and mutually agree upon the terms of access to marine genetic resources in areas of national sovereignty.

---

[48] Henne (note 35), 328; different Verhoosel (note 24), 100 et seq. who seems to qualify bioprospecting as purely scientific research. The whole issue is, however, somewhat futile since coastal States enjoy considerable discretion in characterizing research as application oriented or purely scientific. The means to challenge the exercise of this discretionary power is limited (article 297, para. 2, lit. (b) UNCLOS).

The provisions of the Convention on the Law of the Sea on marine scientific research predominantly aim for a distribution of jurisdictional powers rather than for the protection of the object of research and at the equitable distribution of the benefits resulting from such research. The only general duty States Parties to the Convention on the Law of the Sea have is to promote and facilitate marine scientific research as such according to article 239. This obligation in no way permits the conclusion that research by foreign national scientists must be facilitated. Regulations for the promotion of marine scientific research can be focused on conditions for national scientists and still comply with article 239 of the Convention on the Law of the Sea. There is no customary law of the sea that deals with genetic resources or access thereto. Therefore, these rules cannot cover the scope covered by the Convention on Biological Diversity.

The approach of the Convention on Biological Diversity to the conservation and use of genetic resources is fundamentally different. In fact, the rules on access to genetic resources and a sharing of benefits derived from their use are a central part of the convention. To achieve its various objectives concerning the protection and sustainable use of biological diversity the Convention on Biological Diversity provides for a network of trade-offs. States hosting genetic resources within their territory may offer grants of access to genetic resources in exchange for a share of the benefits[49] derived from their use. Article 15, para. 2 CBD is one of the essential structural elements in the framework for biodiversity protection. The article calls for the facilitation of access providing that States

> "…. shall endeavor to create conditions to facilitate access to genetic resources for environmentally sound uses by other Contracting Parties and not to impose restrictions that run counter to the objectives of this Convention".

---

[49] See articles 15, 16 and 19 CBD; such benefits may, for example, include participation in scientific research (article 15, para. 6); the fair and equitable sharing of research results (article 15, para. 7); participation in commercial and other benefits derived from genetic resources (article 15, para. 7); access to, and transfer of, technology making use of the genetic resources provided (article 16, para. 3) and access to the results and benefits arising from biotechnologies based upon genetic resources provided (article 19, para. 2). Access to and transfer of technology that is relevant to the conservation and sustainable use of biological diversity (article 16, para. 1) shall be provided for, not as a matter of benefit sharing, but rather as an undertaking under the common responsibility of all States Parties to promote the protection of biological diversity.

However, due to the vague wording, article 15 CBC does not oblige States Parties to grant access to genetic resources and leaves room for them to impose conditions concerning the protection of resources, e.g. on the methods of sampling, etc. The possibility of benefiting from the utilization of genetic resources is established as an incentive for the conservation of biological diversity and ensuring that biological resources under the jurisdiction of the host State are used in a sustainable manner. National sovereignty over genetic resources and the obligation to facilitate access are necessary elements of the incentive-based system established by the Convention on Biological Diversity. This incentive-based system could be threatened if resources, for which access and benefit sharing would have to be negotiated in a zone of national jurisdiction, were freely accessible on the high seas, as is presently the case. Similarly, the CBD's incentive-based system could be threatened if States were obligated to grant access to resources in the exclusive economic zones.

Neither the rules on access to genetic resources and benefit sharing under the Convention on Biological Diversity nor the specific rules on scientific research under the Convention on the Law of the Sea are applicable outside those zones for which coastal States exercise some degree of national jurisdiction, i.e. the high seas and the deep sea-bed. Scientific research on the high seas knows no limits. In principle, the same is true of scientific research activities in the Area, if concerned with biological resources.[50] Yet, article 143 UNCLOS, concerning marine scientific research in the Area, cooperation shall be promoted and research shall be carried out for the benefit of humankind as a whole.

The establishment of a regime on the protection and sustainable use of genetic resources in the deep sea-bed, which would seem to be in accord with the aims of the Convention on Biological Diversity, is not possible under the current terms of the system of the Convention on the Law of the Sea dealing with mineral resources in the deep sea-bed. International cooperation must develop a regime for the protection of genetic resources and the sharing of the results of the research, particularly coordinating the respective approaches of the Convention on Biological Diversity and the Convention on the Law of the Sea in order to prevent further conflicts. As far as zones of national jurisdiction are concerned, the more protective approach the Convention on Biological

---

[50] The prospecting, exploration and exploitation of mineral resources is subject to the regime of Part XI under UNCLOS, particularly article 153 UNCLOS in connection with Annex III.

Diversity takes with regard to genetic resources could supplement the regime of marine scientific research provided by the Convention on the Law of the Sea. This aim, however, calls for a clarification and harmonization of the respective regulations to promote coherence in international law.

4. *Conclusions*

An examination of conflicts between the two agreements does not show any incompatible contradictions. Yet, the differences concerning the conservation of marine living and genetic resources differ fundamentally. States that are parties to both conventions are relatively free to supplement the law-of-the-sea approach with more strict, ecosystem-based standards or criteria governing access to genetic resources. The later would be in line with the approach taken by the Convention on Biological Diversity. Furthermore, the absence of absolute obligations under the Convention on Biological Diversity (many obligations are qualified by the phrase "as far as possible and as appropriate"[51]) reduces the possibility of establishing incompatible conflicts. The implementation of more strict protective criteria for the sustainable management of biological resources and ecosystems especially applies to the territorial sea, for which the Convention on the Law of the Sea does not establish management criteria, but also to the exclusive economic zone as a supplement to the minimum management standards established by the Convention on the Law of the Sea.

Although the Convention on the Law of the Sea pursues a more exploitation-orientated approach within the terms of the management criteria for the exclusive economic zone, the incorporation of a farther reaching ecosystem approach (like that of the CBD) would not necessarily be contradictory to its provisions, which only establish minimum standards. The Fish Stocks Agreement, 1995, for example, established more strict but compatible standards for the protection and management of certain fish stocks and is more clearly based upon an ecosystem approach. Such an approach could be further supplemented by criteria for *in situ* protection according to article 8 CBD. Depending on the will of the States Parties the different approaches could be bridged by respective means of implementation.

---

[51] See e.g. article 8 CBD but also articles 5, 7, 9, 10, 11 and 14 CBD.

An issue that again raises the specter of conflict is: (1) whether States Parties to the Convention on Biological Diversity are obliged to implement more strict standards, despite the fact that most duties are not of an absolute nature, or (2) whether they can set aside more strict approaches with a view to the minimum standards established by the Convention on the Law of the Sea. This issue should not be subject to a decision based on political discretion but calls instead for a systematic approach to its solution. The same applies to a new regime, yet to be negotiated, on genetic resources of the high seas and, particularly, the deep sea-bed.

III. The Regime Governing Polar Regions in Relation to the Law of the Sea

(Wolfrum)

1. Introduction

The relationship between the regimes governing Polar Regions (the Arctic and Antarctica) and the law of the sea is anything but clear. This is particularly problematic because the regimes on the Polar Regions as well as part of the Convention on the Law of the Sea serve the same objective, as far as the protection of the environment is concerned. It has often been argued that the territorial scope of the Third UN Conference on the Law of the Sea, due to the delicate situation resulting from claims to the Polar Regions, particularly the rejection of the validity of claims and overlapping claims, was purposefully not expanded to cover the Antarctic waters.[52] If this view were correct, a regulatory gap would exist as far as Antarctic waters are concerned because article VI Antarctic Treaty[53] states that the provisions of the Antarctic Treaty are without prejudice to the rights of States regarding the use of the

---

[52] This view is based upon a statement made by Hamilton Shirley Amerasinghe, the President of UNCLOS III, although he spoke as the representative of Sri Lanka: "I should make it clear that the question of the status of Antarctica is in no way linked with the issues before the United Nations Conference on the Law of the Sea and, therefore, this question should not delay agreement on a new Convention on the Law of the Sea."; United Nations General Assembly, Official Records, 30th Session, 2380th Meeting., para. 36.

[53] *UNTS* 402, 71.

high sea. For a long time the Consultative Parties of the Antarctic Treaty, 1959, refrained from extending their regulations (so-called measures) to the high seas. This was one of the reasons why they felt it necessary to draft a Convention for the Conservation of Antarctic Seals, 1972,[54] instead of providing for their protection under the Agreed Measures of article IX of the Antarctic Treaty[55] as was possible.

The situation concerning Arctic Polar Regions is equally complex. However, concerning the relation between the Convention on the Law of the Sea and the implementation of the Arctic Environmental Protection Strategy (AEPS) adopted by the First Ministerial Conference on the Protection of the Arctic Environment in Rovaniemi, Finland, on 14 June 1991, the Strategy states that:

> "the implementation of the Strategy will be carried out through national legislation and in accordance with international law, including customary international law as reflected in the 1982 United Nations Convention on the Law of the Sea."[56]

The participants, bearing in mind that the UN Convention on the Law of the Sea is a framework treaty, further concluded, in the Arctic Environmental Protection Strategy, that the preventive measures taken would be "consistent in particular with the 1982 United Nations Convention on the Law of the Sea."[57] They agreed to apply

> "the principles concerning the protection and preservation of the marine environment as reflected in the 1982 United Nations Convention on the Law of the Sea."[58]

In this respect the Arctic Environmental Protection Strategy could serve to fill in the framework of the Convention on the Law of the Sea with regard to a region that, due to its specific geographic and climate characteristics, requires equally specific regulation. Still, these specific regulations would, according to the Strategy, be guided by the respective principles of the Convention on the Law of the Sea.

---

[54] *ILM* 11 (1972), 251 et seq. (417).

[55] A. Watts, *International Law and the Antarctic Treaty System* (1992), 148 et seq.

[56] Arctic Environment Protection Strategy, Chapter 1, *ILM* 30 (1991), 1624 et seq.

[57] Ibid, Chapter 7.

[58] Ibid, Chapter 7 (i).

It is of interest to note that another instrument relevant to the environmental protection of Polar Regions, namely the 1991 Protocol on Environmental Protection to the Antarctic Treaty (Environmental Protocol),[59] is more obtuse regarding the interrelation between it and the law of the sea, in particular the Convention on the Law of the Sea. Neither the Protocol nor its Annex IV, dealing specifically with the prevention of marine pollution in the Antarctic Treaty area, contains a reference to the UN Convention on the Law of the Sea.[60]

The issue may also be considered from the point of view of the Convention on the Law of the Sea. As already indicated the Convention on the Law of the Sea is considered to constitute a framework of regulations applicable to different issues concerning the various uses of the oceans. Part XII deals with the protection and preservation of the marine environment. Apart from the rules laid down in this part, other regulations regarding the protection of the marine environment are contained in various parts of the Convention as well. The Convention on the Law of the Sea, in contrast to many other treaties applicable to (parts of) the oceans,[61] does not contain any limitation as to its territorial scope. Instead, the drafters of the Convention intended to cover the whole ocean space, thereby not only including all waters but also the sea-bed.[62] The statement of Hamilton Shirley Amerasinghe, to which reference is made above, only exempts the question of the status of Antarctica from the Convention on the Law of the Sea. This exemption clearly does not address the issue of protecting the Antarctic marine environment. As a consequence, the application of the Convention on the Law of the Sea to Polar Regions must be subject to further discussion with the objective of establishing the extent of the applicability and the content of the respective regulations. In addition to the Convention on the Law of the Sea other relevant international instruments will also have to be discussed in this context.

---

[59] See note 17.

[60] The interrelation with other instruments on the law of the sea will be addressed later.

[61] E.g., as discussed above, the Convention on Biological Diversity but also agreements like the OSPAR-Convention or the agreements on polar regions subject to this section.

[62] B. Vukas, "United Nations Convention on the Law of the Sea and the polar marine environment", in: D. Vidas (ed.), *Protecting the polar marine environment* (2000), 34 et seq. (36).

Generally, the Convention on the Law of the Sea and other relevant instruments, e.g. on fishing, differ in one important aspect from the instruments governing activities in Polar Regions. The former are primarily utilitarian oriented, whereas the latter follow an essentially ecosystem-oriented approach. Hence, in this respect, a divergence as to the approach, comparable to the contradicting approaches of the Convention on Biological Diversity and the Convention on the Law of the Sea, can be identified. However, before it is possible to establish in detail whether and to what extent the regimes for the environmental protection of the polar regions and the regulation of the seas differ, it is necessary to establish whether those parts of the Convention on the Law of the Sea, which are relevant for the protection of the marine environment, may be applied to polar regions. However, only an overview can be provided in this context.

2. *The Convention on the Law of the Sea and Polar Regions*

(a) Application of the Provisions on Enclosed and Semi-enclosed Seas

The UN Convention on the Law of the Sea, pursuant to article 122 UNCLOS, makes it possible for States to give special treatment to enclosed or semi-enclosed seas. As article 123, lit. (a) UNCLOS indicates, the States bordering such seas may provide for a particular regime concerning the management of living resources and the protection of the marine environment therein. The wording of article 122 UNCLOS, however, does not give much assistance in clarifying the notion of enclosed and semi-enclosed seas.[63]

While the provision was meant to cover seas like the Black Sea or the Baltic Sea, one may also extend it to Arctic and Antarctic waters, if the wording of the provision is taken literally. This would be particularly true if the rudimentary provisions on enclosed or semi-enclosed seas were meant to cover such marine spaces which, due to their special geographical characteristics, require a regime concerned with resource management and environmental protection that takes specific account

---

[63] Article 122 UNCLOS reads: "For the purpose of this Convention, 'enclosed or semi-enclosed seas' means a gulf, basin or sea surrounded by two or more States and connected to another sea or the ocean by a narrow outlet or consisting entirely or primarily of the territorial seas and exclusive economic zones of two or more coastal States."

of the respective particularities of the marine region in question.[64] Another element to be considered in that respect is that the management of such specific marine regions requires particular cooperative efforts from the littoral States concerned, although article 123 UNCLOS refers to such cooperation only in hortatory terms.

Starting from this point of view it could be well assumed that the polar and the Antarctic marine areas should be considered semi-enclosed seas, since a respective close cooperation exists amongst – in the case of the Arctic sea – the littoral States and, as far as Antarctic waters are concerned, among littoral States and States which have shown a substantive interest in the scientific research of this area and its environmental protection. However, such argumentation would put the cart before the horse. Cooperation is meant to be the result of the qualification of a particular area to constitute a semi-enclosed sea, not a precondition as to its identification. Consequently, cooperation cannot be used to justify the qualification of a marine area as a semi-enclosed sea. Otherwise, States could, by cooperating in the management of particular marine areas, change the characterization of a marine region and thereby grant themselves the possibility of imposing their rules regarding the marine region in question upon other States. As a result, with respect to the qualification of the polar marine areas, one has to reconsider the legislative history of article 122 UNCLOS and the meaning attached to it at the III. UN Conference of the Law of the Sea. According to this legislative history, as already indicated above, the provisions were meant to cover marine areas such as the Black Sea and the Baltic Sea, but not, however, the polar marine spaces.[65]

(b) Part XII UNCLOS and its Application to Polar Regions

Perhaps even more important is the question whether Part XII of the Convention on the Law of the Sea extends to polar marine areas. This Part of the Convention provides for, in a comprehensive way, the protection and preservation of the marine environment, including standard setting, implementation and enforcement. Part XII does not, however, provide for a complete, ready-for-direct-application regime. It is, as can be seen from article 211, para. 1 UNCLOS, designed as a legal frame-

---

64 Vukas (note 62), 40.

65 A. van der Essen, *The Arctic and Antarctic Regions*, 525; different probably Vukas (note 62), 41 et seq.

work which must be perfected by the enactment of additional regulations.[66] This concept makes it easier to extend Part XII UNCLOS to polar marine areas, as the supplemental regulations can be adapted to regional particularities.

The over-arching provision, which spells out the general obligation of States, has been formulated without limitation as to its territorial scope. States, pursuant thereto, are under the obligation to protect and to preserve the marine environment. This provision has been considered a major advancement in international environmental law, although it has to be taken into account that article 193 balances this general obligation of States by referring to their sovereign rights "to exploit their natural resources pursuant to their environmental policies." As the latter part of article 193 UNCLOS indicates both provisions have to be read together. States have to find a proper balance between their economic interests and the interest the community of States has in the protection of the marine environment. The respective balancing of environmental and sovereignty interests is considered to constitute customary international law; its content has already been expressed in the Principles issued by the Stockholm Conference on the Human Environment[67] as well as in the principles enshrined in the Rio Declaration on Environment and Development.[68]

As such, the provisions of articles 192 and 193 UNCLOS may well be extended to marine Polar Regions. Since, however, the protection of the marine environment in these areas is already the dominant policy principle for the States involved, articles 192 and 193 UNCLOS lack normative content that would add to and/or enhance their existing obligation to protect the environment in these areas. This may change the moment the concerned States begin again to express interest in the exploration or exploitation of natural, in particular, mineral resources in Polar Regions. If, because of such economic interests, environmental considerations for the protection of Polar Regions are threatened, the balancing of interests as reflected by the provisions in Part XII of the Convention on the Law of the Sea might gain importance.

---

[66] Article 211, para. 1 UNCLOS refers to "the competent international organisation", which means IMO or a "general diplomatic conference" as the appropriate institutions to establish rules and standards to prevent, reduce and control pollution of the marine environment from vessels.

[67] Declaration of the United Nations Conference on the Human Environment, UN Doc. A/CONF.48/14/Rev. 1.

[68] UN Doc. A/CONF.151/5/Rev.1.

(c) Article 194 UNCLOS and the Protection of the Polar Marine Environment

The application of the rules laid down in article 194 UNCLOS concerning the prevention, reduction and control of pollution of the marine environment in the context of the polar marine environment represents a more specific, and therefore, more interesting question. Pursuant to article 194 UNCLOS, States must take all necessary measures to carry out their basic duties to protect and preserve the marine environment. To this end, they shall use "the best practicable means at their disposal", taking measures "in accordance with their capabilities."[69] In particular, the reference to "best practicable means" may become relevant. Furthermore, States are under an obligation to take all measures to ensure that "activities under their jurisdiction and control are so conducted as not to cause damage by pollution to other States and their environment, and that pollution arising from incidents or activities under their jurisdiction or control does not spread beyond areas where they exercise sovereign rights." Proceeding from its wording, which is quite general, the provision could also be applied to polar marine areas.[70] This view is supported by article 194, para. 5 UNCLOS in particular, according to which, measures taken in compliance with article 194 UNCLOS shall include those necessary to protect fragile ecosystems. There can be no doubt that polar marine areas are particularly fragile ecosystems.

However, a closer examination of article 194, paragraphs 1 and 2 UNCLOS reveals that the extension of their rules to polar marine areas would not be without difficulties. As far as paragraph 1 is concerned, it is rather vaguely formulated. In particular, the notion of best practical means needs further specification given the special circumstances prevailing in Polar Regions. The main problems, however, rest with paragraph 2. Under this provision only damage caused to the environment of other States is prohibited. Taking into account the sensitive situation concerning territorial claims in Antarctica, the applicability of a provision which is based upon territorial sovereignty might upset the balance achieved in article IV Antarctic Treaty. The same is true with respect to

---

[69] As to the aspect that developing countries may apply different standards see Vukas (note 62), 46 et seq.

[70] C.C. Joyner, "The Antarctic Treaty System and the Law of the Sea – Competing Regimes in the Southern Ocean", *Int'l J. Marine & Coastal L.* 10 (1995), 314.

the prohibition on allowing pollution to spread. Although this provision refers to pollution arising from incidents or activities under the jurisdiction of the State concerned, and therefore would also cover expeditions and activities of ships or from those using ships as a base, one has to take into account the inherent limitation to the rule, which obligates states to prevent the spread of pollution beyond the areas over which they exercises sovereign rights. Thus, the application of that provision in Antarctica, where sovereignty issues remain particularly sensitive, would raise fundamental problems.[71]

The situation is somewhat different for Arctic marine areas. In this context it is possible to speak of damages to other States. Nevertheless, the positive impact article 194 UNCLOS might have on the protection of the Arctic marine environment is limited. The provision does not provide for the protection of the marine environment as such; it only prohibits polluting state territory via the environment. This approach is quite different from the one pursued under the respective regimes for the protection of the Arctic marine environment and the Antarctic. Both provide for the protection of the environment as such. This is clearly expressed by both instruments, the Protocol on Environmental Protection to the Antarctic Treaty, 1992, and the Arctic Environmental Protection Strategy.[72] On this point the two regimes concerned with the protection of the polar marine environments are more advanced than the parallel provisions of article 194 UNCLOS. Since the former are to be considered *leges speciales* they take precedence over the latter.

The general prohibition on polluting marine areas drawn from the Convention on the Law of the Sea can also be considered a part of customary international law. Since the provisions concerning pollution of the marine environment cannot be applied to Polar Regions in detail but only in general, it follows that article 194 UNCLOS does not enhance the protection of polar marine areas against pollution beyond that which customary international law already provides.

---

[71] Vukas (note 62), 51 et seq.

[72] The Protocol of Environmental Protection to the Antarctic Treaty in its Article 3, para. 2 reads in the relevant part: "...activities in the Antarctic Treaty area shall be planned and conducted so as to limit adverse impacts on the Antarctic environment and dependent and associated ecosystems...". The Arctic Environmental Protection Strategy provides as its primary objective in 2, para. 1, subpara. (i) the protection of the "Arctic ecosystem including humans".

In consideration of these points, any differences in the approaches of the two regimes do not seem to indicate the existence of relevant conflicts.

(d) Article 197 UNCLOS and Cooperation on a Regional Basis

Article 197 of the Convention on the Law of the Sea also might be of potential relevance for polar maritime areas. It obliges States to cooperate on a global or a regional basis with a view towards formulating and elaborating international rules, standards and recommended practices and procedures for the protection and preservation of the marine environment. This cooperation is expected to take account of characteristic regional features. Whereas the cooperation on the global level is mandatory, regional cooperation is not. The latter is subject to regional characteristics. Although this provision may be applied in the Polar Regions, it is of a procedural nature and without carrying much substance. In particular, the international rules and standards elaborated must be consistent with the Convention on the Law of the Sea. Hence, this provision makes it possible to elaborate respective rules for polar maritime regions under the umbrella of the UN Convention on the Law of the Sea.

(e) Article 234 UNCLOS: Provisions on Ice-covered Areas

Finally, reference must be made to article 234 UNCLOS, which gives coastal States the right to adopt and enforce particular regulations for the reduction, prevention and control of marine pollution in ice-covered areas. This provision, which was included in the Convention upon the initiative of Canada, reflects the situation prevailing in Arctic but not, however, Antarctic waters. In the latter areas no coastal States, in the proper meaning of the phrase, exist. Apart from that, the provision adds little to the enhancement of the protection of the environment in the Arctic, since the standards to be applied may be decided upon by the coastal State concerned. The only limit such States face is that the respective regulations must not be of a discriminatory nature. It follows that even this provision, which, when considering its potential area of application, is the most specific regulation applicable to Polar Regions, lacks substance.

(f) Conclusion

It appears that the regulatory solutions offered by the Convention on the Law of the Sea, while generally applicable to polar marine areas (with limitations concerning Antarctica), cannot contribute to the improvement of environmental protection in the respective areas. However, while not enhancing environmental protection, neither do the provisions run counter to the more specific rules adopted under the instruments aiming at the protection of the environment in the Arctic and Antarctica. Although the approaches adopted by the Convention on the Law of the Sea and the respective instruments on environmental protection of polar marine regions differ, these differences do not realize their potential in conflicts that could diminish the efforts undertaken according to the specific legal regulations.

3. Universal Environmental Protection Instruments and the Polar Marine Environment

(a) Introduction

The protection of the marine environment has become the subject of numerous universal instruments which cover various aspects, including, among others: (1) the disposal of waste, including dumping; (2) marine pollution; and (3) protection of living resources. Some universal instruments deal explicitly with Polar Regions, or at least one of the Polar Regions. Other universal instruments do not. There has been no harmonization of these universal instruments and the instruments which specifically address the protection of the polar environment, although this issue is receiving increasing attention in the literature.[73]

(b) Pollution from Ships and Installations

The Arctic and the Southern oceans are subject to the existing international legal regimes dealing with pollution of the marine environment. The respective instruments, of which the most important one is the International Convention for the Prevention of Pollution from Ships

---

[73] See in particular N. Krüger, *Anwendbarkeit von Umweltschutzverträgen in der Antarktis* (2000), which contains the most detailed and reliable comparison in this respect.

(1973), as modified by the Protocol of 1978[74] (MARPOL73/78), predate the drafting of the UN Convention on the Law of the Sea, although the latter contains several indirect references to the former. MARPOL 73/78 is designed to prevent the pollution of the marine environment by prohibiting and limiting the discharge of harmful substances and effluents from ships. While the Annexes to the Convention cover different aspects of the pollution from ships, the Convention does not cover pollution arising from the exploration and exploitation of minerals from the sea-bed.

The MARPOL Convention has global territorial scope, but it provides enhanced protection for so-called special areas. Such special areas may include parts of the oceans but also entire oceans. Consequently, as the further discussion will show, polar marine regions might come under enhanced protection due to their sensitivity. The main body of MARPOL 73/78, that is to say the convention itself, is a framework agreement. It determines the scope of application of the MARPOL Convention (article 3) and the obligations of States with regard to violations (article 4). It deals with enforcement actions to be taken (article 5 and 6) and several procedural issues (articles 7 and 8). Its article 9 states that the MARPOL Convention supersedes the International Convention for the Prevention of Pollution of the Sea by Oil. It further states that it does not prejudice the codification and development of the law of the sea by the United Nations Conference on the Law of the Sea. Such a clause, which attempts to establish the compatibility of an existing international instrument with an agreement that still is under consideration (actually, the UNCLOS negotiations had just begun) is unprecedented and clearly demonstrates the priority attributed to the UN Convention on the Law of the Sea from the beginning.

aa) The Applicability of MARPOL 73/78 Provisions to Polar Regions

The six Annexes, which are attached to MARPOL 73/78, cover all aspects of pollution from ships except the disposal of waste into the sea by dumping. They concern: the prevention of pollution by oil (Annex I); the control of pollution by noxious liquid substances in bulk

---

[74] *ILM* 17 (1978), 246 et seq.; MARPOL 73/78 has replaced the International Convention for the Prevention of Pollution of the Sea by Oil, 1954. MARPOL 73 did not enter into force until 1983 following the adoption of an amending Protocol in 1978.

(Annex II); the prevention of pollution by harmful substances in packaged forms (Annex III); the prevention of pollution by sewage from ships (Annex IV); the prevention of pollution by garbage from ships (Annex V) and the prevention of air pollution from ships (Annex VI).[75] States Parties must apply the Convention, including the Annexes to which they are parties, to the vessels flying their flag as well as to violations by ships flying the flag of another State that occur within their jurisdiction.

MARPOL 73/78 and its Annexes constitute the main source for the international rules and standards regarding the pollution from ships to which articles 194, 211, 218 and 220 UNCLOS refer. Under these provisions of the Convention on the Law of the Sea, international rules and standards must not only be applied by the flag States but may also be enforced against foreign vessels by port States and within the exclusive economic zone by the respective coastal States. The MARPOL Convention has been continuously adapted to changing circumstances and new technical or environmental insights.

MARPOL 73/78 prohibits the discharge of the substances referred to in the Annexes. The term "discharge", which is particularly important, since it establishes the core of the prohibition, is defined widely. According to article 2, para. 3, lit. (a) MARPOL 73/78 it includes "any escape, disposal, spilling, leaking, pumping, emitting or emptying". However, a discharge does not constitute a violation of the Convention and the respective Annexes if it takes place in an emergency situation.

Annex I prohibits the discharge into the sea of oil if particular circumstances do not justify a discharge.[76] Within designated "Special Areas," discharges are absolutely prohibited with the exception of ships of less than 400 gross tonnage (other than oil tankers), which may discharge under strict conditions. Exceptions apply in cases where a discharge is necessary to secure the safety of the ship and to save life at sea or where

---

[75] Annex VI prohibits deliberate emissions of ozone-depleting substances, which include halons and chlorofluorocarbons, and sets limits on the emissions of sulphur dioxide and nitrogen oxide on board ships. It sets a cap on the sulphur content of any fuel oil on board ships and provides for the future monitoring of the worldwide average sulphur content of fuel. More stringent control of sulphur emissions can be exercised in special sulphur oxide emission control areas. Finally Annex VI prohibits incineration on board of ships of certain products. This Annex was only adopted in 1998 and has not yet entered into force.

[76] Annex I, Regulation 9.

the discharge resulted from damage to the ship. The Antarctic Treaty area was included as a "Special Area" under Annex I by an amendment in 1990,[77] with the result that any discharge of oil in that area is prohibited. The Arctic sea has not yet been recognized as a "Special Area". This is not due to the fact that States do not realize the particular vulnerability of the Arctic marine areas. The main reason seems to be the lack of sufficient port reception facilities (and therefore the considerably limited volume of ship traffic/and therefore the limited ability to monitor compliance) in the Arctic area.

Annex II, dealing with noxious liquid substances in bulk, complements Annex I. Here again the Southern Ocean was listed as a "Special Area" for the purposes of Annex II by amendments adopted in 1992. Annex III is of equal importance, since it covers ships engaged in Antarctic resupply. Annex IV has not yet entered into force. It is, however, of particular relevance for polar regions. Antarctica has also been listed as a "Special Area" under Annex V, but the Arctic waters have not. Consequently, while Antarctic waters seem to be covered, not only by the specific regime on environmental protection in the area, but also by most of the rules regarding the prevention of pollution from ships (with their prohibitions of discharges of certain substances according to MARPOL 73/78), the protection of Arctic waters does not go as far. It is questionable, however, whether the regulation of pollution from ships as envisaged by MARPOL 73/78 can actually enhance the protection of Antarctic waters provided by the rules existing under the environmental protection regime on Antarctica.

Although the rules against pollution developed under the authority of the IMO have frequently been modified and amended due to new insights or technical developments, generally little attention has been paid to polar regions except listing Antarctica as a "Special Area" under Annexes I, II and V. The IMO has also concluded that the Antarctic "Special Area" under MARPOL 73/78 may be expanded to make it identical with the outer limits of the Convention on the Conservation of Antarctic Marine Living Resources.[78] This would be beneficial since these limits are based upon the ecosystem approach; however, no decision has yet been taken on this point.[79]

---

[77] The amendment entered into force 1992.

[78] See above note 12.

[79] D.R. Rothwell, "Global environmental protection instruments and the polar marine environment", in Vidas (note 62), 57 et seq. (62).

bb) The Law of the Sea and the Environmental Regime for Antarctica: a Comparison

In the following section the rules and standards regarding maritime pollution developed within the context of the law of the sea will be compared with the rules concerning the prohibition of pollution that are contained in the Protocol on Environmental Protection to the Antarctic Treaty and its Annex IV. The Protocol does not explicitly deal with pollution; nevertheless, some of its provisions are relevant in this context. Reference has already been made to article 3, para. 2 of the Protocol, according to which activities in Antarctica are to be undertaken

> "so as to limit adverse impacts on the Antarctic environment and dependent and associated ecosystems."[80]

It is evident that this provision also extends to pollution of the Antarctic marine environment. However, it is also clear that this restriction is not of an absolute nature because it only refers to the limitation of adverse effects. Article 3, para. 2, lit. (b) of the Protocol is somewhat more strict; it formulates an obligation to avoid "significant changes in the atmospheric, terrestrial (including aquatic), glacial and marine environments." Although going further than the obligation to limit adverse impacts and formulated in mandatory language, this obligation only extends to *significant* changes and, accordingly, leaves certain leeway to the States Parties.[81]

An aspect that distinguishes the Protocol from the regulations under the law of the sea that are concerned pollution is that it contains an obligation to plan activities in Antarctica. According to the respective provisions of the Protocol, the planning of Antarctic activities must be undertaken so as to ensure the avoidance of significant pollution. This goes significantly further than regulations on the avoidance and limitation of pollution in the law of the sea. The most important instrument concerned with the obligation to the plan Antarctic activities is the required environmental impact assessment.[82]

---

[80] Para. 2 (a).

[81] C.C. Joyner, "Protection of the Antarctic environment against marine pollution under the 1991 Protocol", in: Vidas (note 62) 104 et seq. (107/108) goes too far when he says that the Protocol "mandates that marine pollution must be prevented ...". This is only so, at least according to the Protocol, if the pollution reaches some magnitude.

[82] See Annex I to the Protocol.

In the realm of activities likely to have adverse effects on the Antarctic marine environment, pollution may not only stem from ships but also from installations engaged in sea-bed activities. The regulations of the Protocol do not directly touch upon this issue, since mining activities in the Antarctic Treaty area are banned according to the current regulation.[83] The moratorium is not necessarily a permanent one as it may come under review if and when the Protocol is reviewed after 50 years or if the Antarctic Treaty Consultative Parties agree on a respective amendment. In particular, article 25, para. 5 of the Protocol makes it quite clear that mineral activities are not permanently excluded. In the case that, after a review or an amendment, mineral resource activities are to become permissible, it will be necessary to establish an appropriate regime on sea-bed activities to avoid or limit harmful effects on the Antarctic environment. This is particularly so since other instruments that would be applicable to the Antarctic region, e.g. MARPOL 73/78, do not cover the issue.

The main rules concerning marine pollution are contained in Annex IV to the Environmental Protocol to the Antarctic Treaty. This Annex is specifically linked to MARPOL 73/78 by its articles 1, 3, 5, 6, 13 and 14. It is one of the relatively far-reaching examples of an attempt to harmonize the standards set by different, overlapping regimes. However, the success of this attempt remains in doubt, as the further discussion and comparison of the two regimes will reveal. There was, particularly, an attempt to harmonize the two instruments through the adoption of several definitions from MARPOL 73/78 by Annex IV, e.g. the notion of "noxious liquid substances" and all emergency clauses. Annex IV has also taken over the definition of "discharge" that is, as discussed above, a crucial term for MARPOL 73/78. Instead of referring to the respective definition in MARPOL 73/78, Annex IV repeats the text. Nevertheless, Annex IV of the Protocol to the Antarctic Treaty is broader than MARPOL 73/78, since it does not refer to or repeat the exception clauses established by MARPOL 73/78 that concern scientific research activities and the clauses that provide for coordination with the London Convention. However, only the extension of the regulations of Annex IV dealing with pollution resulting from marine scientific research activities is of particular relevance.[84] The practical relevance of these provisions may, however, be reduced because Annex IV does not apply to warships, naval auxiliary ships and ships operated

[83] See article 7 of the Protocol.

[84] Krüger (note 73), 78.

or owned by States. In particular article 6 of Annex IV to the Protocol shows that the attempts at harmonizing the two regimes are by no means comprehensive. This provision reads:

> "1. Except where it would unduly impair Antarctic operations: each Party shall eliminate all discharge into the sea of untreated sewage ("sewage" being defined in Annex IV of MARPOL 73/78) within 12 nautical miles of land or ice shelves;
>
> beyond such distance, sewage stored in holding tank shall not be discharged instantaneously but at a moderate rate and, where practicable, while the ship is *en route* at a speed of no less than 4 knots."

This article, finally, makes it evident that the reference system is not dynamic but static. If MARPOL 73/78 is amended, such amendment would not apply to Antarctic waters via Annex IV to the Protocol. From a policy point-of-view, this is regrettable. It significantly weakens the efficiency of Annex IV by not providing its automatic adaptation to new developments and insights.

Annex IV of the Protocol prohibits, in article 3, "any discharge into the sea of oil or oily mixture," save in circumstances permitted under Annex I of MARPOL 73/78. In article 4, it is forbidden to discharge "any noxious liquid substance, and any other chemical or other substance, in quantities or concentrations that are harmful to the marine environment." In addition, article 5 prohibits the disposal of certain categories of substances (e.g. garbage). Here again, a certain link has been established to MARPOL 73/78, Annex V. Finally, Annex IV of the Protocol contains certain pollution abatement rules dealing with prevention. However, the rules on preventive measures, emergency preparedness and response as referred to under article 12 of Annex IV are still missing. In that respect the law-of-the-sea-based rules are more complete but cannot be easily used, as indicated, to fill the lacunae of the system based upon the Antarctic Treaty. It is most likely that such lacuna will remain in existence for the time to come. It proves that the regime on the protection of the Antarctic environment is far from being perfect.

According to Joyner[85]

> "State parties to both instruments [the Protocol and MARPOL 73/78] become linked into mutually reinforcing obligations aimed at preventing marine pollution in Antarctic waters. Thus, based on this interaction, parties are brought into a stronger, more

---

[85] Joyner (note 81), 118.

comprehensive legal regime for suppressing pollution of the high seas in Antarctic waters."

We cannot share this positive assessment. It is true that States Parties to the Protocol, which are not States Parties to MARPOL 73/78, are automatically linked to this regime. However, two issues have to be taken into account. The Protocol does not provide for more stringent rules against pollution in Antarctica except its obligations, which already extend to the planning phase. Therefore it is not possible to say that MARPOL 73/78 embraces the minimal rules whereas the Protocol together with Annex IV prescribes the rules necessary for the Antarctic conditions.[86] Additionally, some of the regulations in Annex IV provide for an escape clause in that they oblige States Parties only if this would not unduly impair Antarctic operations.[87] In one aspect the regime under the Protocol to the Antarctic Treaty exceeds the MARPOL 73/78. It refers not only to the ships under the flag of States Parties but also to ships supporting or engaged in their Antarctic activities.[88] Apart from that, one has to identify at least four areas where MARPOL 73/78 is more stringent than the Protocol to the Antarctic Treaty and its relevant Annexes: (1) discharge of ship-generated sewage which has not been treated; (2) ship-generated sewage which has been treated; (3) sewage which has been treated; and (4) air pollution.[89] Generally speaking, the main deficiency lies in the fact that, after the initial attempt at harmonizing the two regimes, no additional and, especially, no dynamic provisions have been established for a harmonization of the two regimes and, particularly, that no provision exists to accommodate changes in MARPOL 73/78 in Antarctica. In that respect the relationship between Annex IV of the Protocol to the Antarctic Treaty and the regulations and MARPOL 73/78 can serve as a model of how rather not to try to harmonize two regimes covering the same area of environmental protection.

---

[86] See in this respect article 14 of Annex IV to the Protocol which reads: "With respect to those Parties which are also Parties to MARPOL 73/78, nothing in this Annex shall derogate from the specific rights and obligations thereunder."

[87] See, for example, article 6, which has already been referred to.

[88] Article 2 Annex IV to the Protocol, for details see Krüger (note 73), 76.

[89] For a detailed analysis see Krüger (note 73), 84 et seq. with an illustrative overview at 100.

(c) Dumping

aa) The Regulations of the London Convention on the Prevention of Marine Pollution by Dumping of Wastes and Other Matters

Another international agreement of relevance for polar regions, although not specifically designed for their protection, is the Convention on the Prevention of Marine Pollution by Dumping of Wastes and other Matters, 1972[90] (London Convention).[91] It is the objective of the London Convention to ensure that all practicable steps are taken to prevent the pollution of the sea by dumping of waste or the dumping of other matter that is liable to create hazards to human health or to harm living resources and marine life. According to the Convention, States Parties must take measures to prevent pollution caused by dumping. The respective enforcement powers rest with three "types of States": (1) the flag State of the ship undertaking the dumping, (2) the port State in which the ship was loading, and (3) the state having jurisdiction over ships or platforms believed to be engaged in dumping. Dumping embraces any deliberate, at-sea disposal of wastes or other matter from vessels, aircraft, platforms or other man-made structures at sea. It also extends to any deliberate, at-sea disposal of vessels, aircraft, platforms or other man-made structure at sea. However, the at-sea-disposal of wastes that are incidental to the normal operation of vessels, aircraft, platforms, etc., is not considered to be dumping under the terms of the London Convention; still, it is covered by the prohibition of pollution established by this agreement.

The London Convention distinguishes between three types of waste: (1) wastes, the dumping of which is prohibited (Annex I); (2) wastes, the dumping of which require a special prior permit (Annex II); and (3) wastes, the dumping of which require a general prior permit (Annex III). The disposal of substances does not constitute the violation of the London Convention when necessary to secure the safety of human life or the safety of vessels. In this respect, the provisions resemble the parallel provisions of MARPOL 73/78 and the Environmental Protocol to the Antarctic Treaty.

---

[90] *UNTS* 932, 3 et seq.

[91] Formerly London Dumping Convention, since 1992 London Convention; this change of name was intended to avoid the false impression of a treaty facilitating dumping. For details see K. Kummer, *International Management of Hazardous Wastes: The Basel Convention and Related Legal Rules* (1995), 176.

The London Convention has been subject to a permanent review, which has resulted in several amendments. The most important amendment was the prohibition of dumping of radioactive wastes, industrial wastes and the incineration at sea of industrial wastes. A new Protocol adopted in 1996,[92] resulted in considerable limitations on material that may be dumped at sea and radically altered the structure of the regime, reversing the system such that following the 1996 Protocol, only those materials listed in Annex I[93] may be dumped, with the sole exceptions being cases of force majeure or any case which involves a danger to human life or a real threat to vessels.

It can be assumed that the London Convention represents the internationally accepted rules and standards for dumping to which article 210 UNCLOS refers.[94]

The question of dumping of waste in polar regions is a matter of practical relevance. In particular, radioactive waste has been dumped in Russian Arctic waters. This issue was addressed at the 1997 Arctic Environment Protection Strategy Meeting. Regarding Antarctica, for a long period it was quite common that resupply ships dumped the waste which had been generated in Antarctica in Antarctic waters or in waters associated therewith. This practice has come to an end. This, however, is not due to the London Convention. The main weakness of the London Convention from the point of view of protecting polar marine areas is that the objective it pursues is not all encompassing. It only protects marine living resources and does not provide for the protection of the environment as such.[95] Here again, a divergence between the approaches taken by the relevant agreements exists.

---

92 *ILM* 36 (1997), 1 et seq.

93 This includes: (1) dredged material; (2) sewage sludge; (3) fish waste; (4) vessels, platforms and man-made structures; (5) inert inorganic material; (6) organic material of natural origin; and (7) various listed bulky items.

94 Kummer (note 91), 176; P.W. Birnie/ A.E. Boyle, *International Law and the Environment* (1992), 320.

95 For further criticism see D. van der Zwaag, *International Law and Arctic Marine Conservation*, 322.

bb) The Provisions on Dumping under the Environmental Protocol to the Antarctic Treaty and the Law of the Sea

In the following section the obligations arising out of Annex III to the Environmental Protocol to the Antarctic Treaty on waste disposal and waste management shall be compared with the obligations regarding waste disposal that are based on the law of the sea. On this point, fewer attempts have been made to harmonize the rules under the law of the sea, when compared with the attempts at harmonization that have been made with respect to the general rules on pollution prevention and limitation. This is due to the fact that the scope of the regimes concerned with dumping only partially overlap.[96]

The rules pertaining to dumping are mostly contained in Annex III to the Protocol, which has already been discussed. However, account must be taken of the fact that the Protocol only covers wastes that are generated in the Antarctic Treaty area. This is different from the London Convention, which does not contain such a territorial limitation as to the origin of the wastes. For Antarctica one must distinguish between wastes, which originate from the Antarctic territory and those originating from marine activities. The management of the latter is covered by MARPOL 73/74 and Annex IV of the Protocol and not by the London Convention.

The application of the London Convention in Antarctica faces the problems connected with sovereignty questions as already indicated. Accordingly, due to a lack of applicability, the London Convention cannot come into conflict with Annex III to the Protocol. If, however, the London Convention would apply, there could be significant discrepancies, although the regulations concerning the management of wastes from the Antarctic territory are not more strict than those arising out of the London Convention.[97]

---

[96] This Annex was developed from a Code of Conduct for Antarctic Expeditions and Station Activities issued in 1975. Under Annex III, article 8, waste is classified into five main groups: (1) Sewage and domestic liquid wastes; (2) other liquids and chemicals, including fuels and lubricants; (3) solid to be combusted; (4) other solid wastes; and (5) radioactive material. The Annex mandates that all States Parties remove all group 2, 4 and 5 wastes if generated after its entry into force. Moreover, States Parties are under an obligation to remove group (1) wastes to the maximum content possible from the Antarctic Treaty area. This obligation is without precedent in the law of the sea.

[97] Krüger (note 73), 135 et seq. see in particular the comparison on 136/137. It has already been pointed out that the 1996 Protocol to the London Conven-

According to Annex IV of the Protocol, sewage and domestic liquid wastes may be discharged directly into the sea provided that three conditions are met: (1) the capability of the marine environment to assimilate such wastes is taken into account;(2) the discharge is situated wherever practicable under conditions for initial dilution and rapid dispersal; and (3) large quantities of these wastes are treated at least by maceration. The dumping of certain products, i.e. those specified in article 7, is, nonetheless, prohibited.

It has already been stated that some of the law-of-the-sea-based standards are more strict than those established by the Environmental Protocol. Furthermore, Annex III contains numerous qualifying phrases, such as "to the maximum extent practicable," "as far as practicable," and "as soon as practicable." Such provisions further dilute the substantial content of States Parties obligations. The issue generating the most dissatisfaction, however, is that, contrary to the approaches under law-of-the-sea-based instruments, incineration is accepted in article 3, para. 1 of Annex III to the Protocol as a permissible form of waste disposal. Although article 3 of Annex III only covers incineration at land, a clear-cut discrepancy between it and the rules of Annex VI to MARPOL 73/78 exists.[98]

In conclusion, the Antarctic rules on dumping are dispersed and not harmonized with the respective law-of-the-sea-based rules. This is due to the fact that, in contrast to the relation to MARPOL 73/78, it was not possible to refer to the London Convention in the Protocol. As a result the Antarctic Treaty Consultative Meetings had to adopt their own standards, which are not as strict as those arising out of the 1996 Protocol of the London Convention.

(d) Pollution from Land-based Sources

Most marine pollution stems from land-based pollution. Nevertheless, on the universal level, such pollution is the least regulated.[99] Also the respective rules of the UN Convention on the Law of the Sea are less

---

tion changes the attitude towards dumping fundamentally. The Protocol attempts to make dumping in general the exception rather than the rule. This clearly goes beyond the rudimentary Antarctic rules on dumping.

98 Regulation 10(4).

99 A.E. Boyle, "Land-Based Pollution: Current Legal regime", *Marine Policy* 16 (1992), 24.

strict compared with those concerned with pollution having a vessel as its source. This is due to the fact that any international regulation would result in a significant infringement on national sovereignty.[100] Since 1982, the United Nations Environment Programme (UNEP) has taken an active role in the attempt to regulate marine pollution caused by land-based sources. UNEP has sponsored a global program of action designed primarily to assist States in preventing, reducing and controlling the degradation of the marine environment from land-based sources.[101] In November, 1995, the UNEP Intergovernmental Conference to formulate a Global Programme of Action for the Protection of the Marine Environment from Land-Based Activities was convened and has since adopted a Declaration.[102] The Global Programme of Action seeks to enhance the coordination at national, regional and international levels and sets common goals of sustained and effective action to deal with land-based impacts upon the marine environment. Particular action is aimed at persistent organic pollutants, radioactive materials, heavy metals, hydrocarbons, nutrients, sediment mobilization and land litter. If this Programme of Action becomes hard law it may fill some of the lacunae[103] that result from the fact that article 207 UNCLOS is, more or less, devoid of substance. The article merely encourages States Parties to engage in a meaningful cooperation without giving indications as to the standards to be applied.

Two regional agreements must be mentioned in this context: (1) the Convention for the Protection of the Marine Environment of the North-East Atlantic, 1992 (OSPAR),[104] and (2) the Helsinki Convention on the Protection of the Marine Environment of the Baltic Sea, 1992.[105] In the context of the regulation of land-based pollution in polar regions, however, the latter is irrelevant.

---

[100] The problems confronting an effort to draft a global international agreement on land-based pollution are highlighted by D. van der Zwaag, "Land-based pollution and the Arctic: polarities between principles and practice", in: Vidas (note 62), 175 et seq. (183 et seq.), with further references.

[101] Rothwell (note 79), 66.

[102] UNEP (OCA)/LBA/IG.2/7, 5 December 1995; reproduced in *Environmental Policy and Law* 26 (1996), 37.

[103] The assessment of this Programme of Action is not altogether positive; see van der Zwaag (note 100), 183.

[104] See above note 18.

[105] See above note 18.

The reduction of land-based pollution has also been attempted under the framework of the Convention on Long-Range Transboundary Air Pollution.[106] The 1998 Protocol to the Convention on Long-Range Transboundary Air Pollution addressing Persistent Organic Pollutants includes various provisions dealing with the prevention or minimization of emissions of persistent organic pollutants; twelve substances are targeted for elimination. The Protocol on Heavy Metals, 1998, equally tries to reduce emissions. Furthermore, the North American Sound Management of Chemicals Initiative of 1995, is also relevant in this context.[107]

Land-based pollution is a considerable problem for the Arctic area. It was identified as one of the major reasons for environmental degradation of Arctic marine spaces.[108] The AEPS has continuously given attention to the negative effects of land-based pollution in the Arctic area. At the 1998 Arctic Council Meeting an Arctic Council Action Plan to Eliminate Pollution of the Arctic was formally adopted. Its effects in practice, however, are still to be seen.

As far as Antarctica is concerned, only rudimentary rules exist for land-based pollution. According to article 5 of Annex III to the Protocol, it is possible to directly discharge sewage and domestic wastes into the sea. For larger stations maceration is required which does not account for heavy metal, bacteria or chemicals. This provision meets the standards of article 207, para. 4 UNCLOS, which does not provide for any objective environmental standards because, as already mentioned, it lacks substantive content.

To sum up, in this respect at least the regime for the Arctic is far more advanced than regime that is established by the Convention on the Law of the Sea. This is of no consequence with respect to conflicts between competing regimes, since a global, law-of-the-sea-based regime for the protection of the marine environment still must be developed. The respective rules concerning Antarctica are equally deficient. Van der Zwaag draws the attention to the fact that there is a proliferation of in-

---

[106] *ILM* 18 (1979), 1442 et seq.

[107] The relevant resolution and a description of the subsequent initiatives are available on the website of the North American Commission for Environmental Cooperation: <http://www.cec.org>, last visited 23 January 2002.

[108] Van der Zwaag (note 100), 177 et seq.

ternational environmental agreements for the Arctic, which threatens to overwhelm national, and local management capabilities.[109]

(e) Intervention and Other Matters

Another international agreement relevant in respect to the environmental regulation of polar marine regions by different treaties is the Convention Relating to Intervention on the High Seas in Cases of Oil Pollution Casualties, 1969.[110] This Convention mandates the coastal State concerned to take action on the high seas in cases of casualties in order to protect the marine environment within its national jurisdiction.

The practical application of this Convention in polar waters is limited. As in other contexts, in the Antarctic Area the question of sovereignty arises, making interventions on the basis of this Convention highly unlikely. Unfortunately, the Antarctic Treaty Consultative States have not yet developed a system of their own. Therefore, due to article IV Antarctic Treaty, a regulatory gap exists as far as environmental-oriented interventions are concerned. This is particularly problematic because, under the climate and ice conditions, Antarctic casualties are very likely to occur and have already occurred.[111] As the issue of sovereignty is irrelevant to Arctic waters, the situation is different for Arctic marine areas and the Convention is, in principle, applicable.

The Convention on Oil Pollution Preparedness Response and Cooperation, 1990,[112] complements the Convention Relating to Intervention on the High Seas in Cases of Oil Pollution Casualties. States Parties are under the obligation to take all appropriate measures in accordance with the Convention to prepare for and to respond to an oil pollution incident. Ships under the flag of one of the States Parties are obliged to have an oil pollution emergency plan as adopted by the IMO. The Convention also seeks to enhance national capacity to respond to oil pollution incidents. It requires the designation of national authorities responsible for: (1) oil pollution preparedness and response; and (2) the

---

[109] Ibid, 195 et seq.

[110] *ILM* 9 (1970), 25 et seq.

[111] See M. Barinaga/ D. Lindley, "Wrecked Ship Causes Damage to Antarctic Ecosystem", *Nature* 337 (1989), 495.

[112] *ILM* 30 (1991), 733 et seq.

reception of oil pollution reports. Finally, each State Party must establish a national contingency plan for preparedness and response.

This Convention, as it does not depend on national territorial sovereignty, can be applied in both marine polar regions. In regard to Antarctica it fills in part of a gap left by the Antarctic Treaty Consultative Parties, which, so far, have been unable to agree on relevant rules in spite of the fact that article 15 and 16 of the Protocol to the Antarctic Treaty obliges them to develop regulations.

(f) Protection and Conservation of Fauna and Flora

Annex II to the Environmental Protocol to the Antarctic Treaty reconfirms the obligation to conserve Antarctic fauna and flora. Basically, when negotiated, the States Parties did not do much more than update the Agreed Measures for the Conservation of Antarctic Fauna and Flora.[113] Annex II constitutes a broad regulatory framework which has no equivalent in the UN Convention on the Law of the Sea or any of the other international agreements under its umbrella. This is due to the fact that both systems follow, as already indicated, fundamentally different approaches. Whereas the regime on the law of the seas is generally utilitarian, the Antarctic regime strives for the protection of the ecosystem. Only in one aspect do the two regimes touch, namely with respect to the introduction of alien species. Whereas article 196 UNCLOS mandates that the States Parties *develop* rules, Annex II to the Protocol consists of *fully developed* rules. So far, under the regime of the law of the sea, the response to harmful aquatic organisms in ballast water and their transferal to other places is entirely regulated by Guidelines issued by the IMO. The respective resolution of the IMO[114] notes the objectives of the Convention on Biological Diversity and that the transfer and introduction of alien aquatic species with ballast water threatens the conservation and sustainable use of biological diversity. This is one of the rare examples where an attempt has been made to accommodate legal regimes, or at least their objectives developed elsewhere and with a different focus, by supplementing existing law. Arti-

---

[113] Reprinted in Handbook of the Antarctic Treaty System 8th ed. 1994, 2,048.

[114] A868(20).

cle 4 of Annex II goes even further since it categorically prohibits the introduction of alien species in Antarctica.[115]

Generally speaking the Antarctic regime concerning the protection of fauna and flora has no equal in international law covering the same subject as far as the intensity of the regulations is concerned. This also has a utilitarian aspect, since much of Antarctic scientific research focuses on the Antarctic fauna and flora. Hence, its protection is covered by the twin objectives of the Protocol to the Antarctic Treaty: (1) the comprehensive protection of the Antarctic environment, and (2) the designation of Antarctica as a reserve for science.

(g) Exploration and Exploitation of Marine Living Resources in Antarctica and under the Convention on the Law of the Sea

aa) Fishing

According to articles 61 and 119 UNCLOS, the basic provisions governing the exploitation of the living resources of the sea, exploitation of marine living resources has to be undertaken in a way to

> "maintain or restore populations of harvested species at levels which can produce the maximum sustainable yield."[116]

Apart from these provisions, Part XII must be taken into account when dealing with the regulations of the UN Convention on the Law of the Sea concerned with fishing. Furthermore, the 1995 Fish Stocks Agreement,[117] which introduced the precautionary principle, must be taken into consideration.

The Convention on the Conservation of Antarctic Marine Living Resources[118] follows an approach different from the approach taken by the UN Convention on the Law of the Sea. Its objective is "the conserva-

---

[115] The Convention on Biological Diversity is another example of a far-reaching approach with respect to alien species, since in its article 8, lit. (h) it obliges its States Parties to prevent the introduction of as well as provide for the eradication of alien species, where necessary to protect the diversity of ecosystems, habitats and species.

[116] Although the Convention on the Law of the Sea follows, in general, a utilitarian approach its article 61, para. 4 provides for some amelioration of that approach.

[117] See above note 36.

[118] Antarctic Treaty Handbook (note 113), 178.

tion of Antarctic marine living resources," the term "conservation" in this context includes rational use. The specific invocation of rational use is important as it establishes that the objective of the Convention is a balance between the use of the resources and their preservation free from fishing and other interference.[119] The principle of "conservation," in accordance with which any exploitation must be conducted, is set out in article 3, para. 3 of the Convention. This includes the obligation to prevent the reduction of the size of any harvested population to levels below those that ensure its stable recovery. In this respect, the provisions resemble those of the Convention on the Law of the Sea. To this utilitarian aspect, however, two ecosystem-based considerations are added. States Parties are under an obligation to maintain a balance with respect to harvested Antarctic marine living resources, including dependent and related populations. Additionally, States Parties are obligated to prevent changes in the marine ecosystem which are not potentially reversible over two or three decades. States Parties are even under an obligation to minimize the risk of such changes. In this context, ecological as well as changes in the population of living resources are relevant.

The Convention on the Conservation of Antarctic Marine Living Resources in contrast to the Convention on the Protection of Antarctic Seals does not contain operational conservation provisions. It seeks to achieve its purposes by stipulating an objective and certain principles and then establishing an institution, the Commission for the Conservation of Antarctic Marine Living Resources, which possesses the authority to give effect to the objective and those principles.[120] It thus creates a structure that represents nearly all the characteristics of an international institutional resource management regime. In this respect its approach also differs from the approach taken by the Convention on the Law of the Sea.

Although the approach followed by the Convention on the Conservation or Antarctic Marine Living Resources is significantly different from that of the UN Convention on the Law of the Sea they can easily be reconciled. According to article 118 UNCLOS, States Parties are called upon to cooperate in the conservation and management of the living resources of the high seas. No dissonance results if they decide to develop a regime which is less utilitarian than anticipated by article 119

[119] Watts (note 55), 218.

[120] Article IX.

UNCLOS and tends more towards an ecosystem-based approach. The UN Convention on the Law of the Sea, designed as a framework agreement, is quite flexible in this respect, as has also been discussed in regard to its relation to the Convention on Biological Diversity. It is, in principle, open to the development and implementation of a regime concerned with harvesting that is based on a different approach, as long as the resources harvested are not overexploited. Further, it permits the establishment of a regime devoid of operational provisions on conservation where the conservation measures are to be taken on an ad hoc basis. This model favors the conclusion that international environmental agreements are best pursued at two levels: (1) umbrella, universal agreements that enshrine minimum objectives and minimum standards, and (2) which are open for particular sub-regimes that apply higher standards.

bb) Whaling

The legal situation prevailing with respect to whaling is based on several international instruments adopted over a long period of time, during which the attitude towards whaling has changed significantly. The most important instruments of international law dealing with whaling are: (1) the UN Convention on the Law of the Sea; (2) the International Convention for the Regulation of Whaling, 1946 (ICRW);[121] (3) The Protocol to the Antarctic Treaty; and (4) the Convention on the Conservation of Antarctic Marine Living Resources. There are additional relevant instruments, all of which will be addressed, as appropriate. The ICRW is periodically updated by the International Whaling Commission through amendments to the Schedule, which forms part of the ICRW.

The interrelationship between these instruments is complex. The Convention on the Conservation of Antarctic Marine Living Resources gives priority to the International Convention for the Regulation of Whaling, although it theoretically also covers whales within its territorial scope. This does not mean, however, that the Convention on the Conservation on Antarctic Marine Living Resources is without relevance for whaling. The Protocol to the Antarctic Treaty excludes whaling from its scope of application; yet, here again the Antarctic Ma-

---

[121] *UNTS* 161, 74. The ICRW was amended by a Protocol in 1956, *UNTS* 338, 366.

rine Living Resources agreement remains relevant. The UN Convention on the Law of the Sea also covers whaling. However, there is little overlap in substance, a result of the fact that the existence of the International Convention for the Regulation of whaling was taken for granted.

The ICRW's objective is to conserve whales. Respective powers are vested in the International Whaling Commission in the furtherance of this objective. The Commission acts by revising and amending the Schedules to the ICRW, which are an integral part thereof. This permits flexible developments on a wide range of issues. However, the regime on whaling has certain deficiencies. In particular, the International Whaling Commission cannot fix national quotas or limit the number of fleets or land stations. In 1982, agreement was reached to set zero catch limits on all commercially exploited stocks, while three States, Japan, Norway and the USSR, maintained objections. In 1994, a Revised Management Procedure was adopted. Following the 1992 Rio Conference on Environment and Development. The Revised Management Scheme follows the precautionary principle. In 1994, the Commission established a Southern Ocean Sanctuary in which commercial whaling is prohibited irrespective of stock status, for a ten-year term. Japan lodged an objection to this, to the extent that it applies to Antarctic Mink whales.[122] The sanctuary regime merely consists of a prohibition on whaling; no consideration is given to the preservation of habitat.[123]

As already indicated, the Convention on the Conservation of Antarctic Marine Living Resources also covers whaling. Its article VI reads:

> "Nothing in this Convention shall derogate from the rights and obligations of Contracting Parties under the International Convention for the Regulation of Whaling..."

This clause establishes the priority of the ICRW. It does not, however, rule out the application of the Convention on the Conservation of Antarctic Marine Living Resources. This means that the Convention on the Conservation of Antarctic Marine Living Resources may apply to

---

[122] For further details see P. Birnie, "Whaling Regime", *EPIL* IV, 1469 et seq.; M.C. Maffei, "The Protection of Whales in Antarctica", in: F. Francioni/ T. Scovazzi (eds.), *International Law for Antarctica* (1996), 171 et seq.; H.S. Schiffman, "The Protection of Whales in International Law: A Perspective for the Next Century", *Brooklyn J. Int'l L.* 22 (1996), 303 et seq., all with further references.

[123] Maffei (note 122), 201 et seq. on the meaning of the sanctuary.

whales (cetaceans) in a way that is compatible with the rights and obligations under ICRW. In practice, then, the Convention on the Conservation of Antarctic Marine Living Resources becomes relevant when the ICRW does not operate because a particular species is not covered by the ICRW or because the Whaling Commission fails to come to an agreement regarding a specific matter.[124] Furthermore, the Convention on the Conservation of Antarctic Marine Living Resources has relevance for States that are not members of ICRW.

The ICRW and the Convention on the Conservation of Antarctic Marine Living Resources differ in several respects. The ICRW is the more comprehensive regime, particularly with respect to its territorial scope. For example, the Convention on the Conservation of Antarctic Marine Living Resources only provides protection as long as the whales stay in the area of application of the Convention. Apart from that, the approach of the Convention on the Conservation of Antarctic Marine Living Resources is more ecosystem-oriented. However, the Commission for the Convention on the Conservation of Antarctic Marine Resources cannot remedy the major deficiency of the ICRW because it also fails to set national quotas or limit the harvesting capabilities of the fishing fleets engaged in whaling.

The potential overlap between the two regimes has been recognized in the Convention on the Conservation of Antarctic Marine Living Resources, which provides for some cooperation between the respective bodies. Article XXIII, paragraphs 3 and 4 of the CCAMLR read:

> "3. The Commission and the Scientific Committee shall seek to develop cooperative working relationships, as appropriate, with intergovernmental and non-governmental organizations which could contribute to their work, including ... the International Whaling Commission.
>
> 4. The Commission may enter into agreements with the organizations referred to in this Article....".

Moreover, according to article IX, para. 5 of the CCAMLR, the Commission shall take full account of any relevant measures or regulations established or recommended by existing fisheries commissions, which also includes the Whaling Commission. The Whaling Commission has also expressed the desire to cooperate with the institutions under the Convention on the Conservation of Antarctic Marine Living Resources.

---

[124] Maffei, ibid at 187, argues into the same direction.

The relevance of the Protocol to the Antarctic Treaty is limited in this context. The Final Act of the Eleventh Antarctic Treaty Special Consultative Meeting, during which the Protocol was adopted, establishes, in articles 4 and 7 of its Annex II, the priority of the ICRW. As has been already noted with respect to the Convention on the Conservation of Antarctic Marine Living Resources, this does not mean that the Protocol cannot be invoked. Its main function may lie in providing protection for species not covered by ICRW and *vis-à-vis* States which are not parties to ICRW.

Another international agreement, which is instrumental for the protection of whales, is the Convention on International Trade in Endangered Species of Wild Fauna and Flora, 1973 (CITES).[125] This Convention contains specific provisions applicable to whales. All Antarctic whales have been entered into Appendix I with the result that trade in these or products thereof is prohibited. Traditional whaling States, such as Norway, have, however, entered reservations. The Conference of States Parties and the Whaling Commission have made efforts to enter into some cooperation on the issue of whaling.[126]

A further international agreement, which also covers whaling, is the Convention on the Conservation of Migratory Species of Wild Animals, 1979 (Bonn Convention - CMS).[127] The main feature of the Bonn Convention is its double nature: (1) animals listed in Annex I are protected, including habitat protection; whereas (2) species listed in Annex II are protected under special agreements to be separately concluded. The blue whale (*Baleanotera musculus*) and the humpback whale (*Megaptera novaeanglia*) are both protected under Appendix I. However, article XII, para. 2 of the Bonn Convention provides that its provisions do not affect the rights and obligations of States Parties under other international agreements. This means, in practice, that a State party of the ICRW could object to the protection of humpback whales and this would not be considered a violation of the Bonn Convention.

The UN Convention on the Law of the Sea adds little in substance.[128] It mandates that States Parties cooperate in the protection of whales and

---

[125] *ILM* 12 (1973), 1088 et seq.

[126] For details see Maffei (note 122), 196 et seq.

[127] *ILM* 19 (1980), 15 et seq.

[128] See articles 64, 65 and Annex I.

provides for the possibility of establishing a more restrictive regime.[129] The international instruments mentioned to this point can easily be reconciled with the UN Convention on the Law of the Sea in regard to whaling because the latter permits additional standard setting. Accordingly, the international instrument can be regarded as establishing such standards.

C. International Agreements Concerning Global Environmental Problems

I. Introduction

(Matz)

The last thirty years have seen a proliferation of instruments dealing with environmental problems which are understood to be of a global scope and, hence, global concern. The following are among those considered to be the most acute global environmental problems, including: (1) the deterioration of the composition of the atmosphere, particularly by ozone depletion, (2) the adverse effects of greenhouse gases on the global climate, (3) the dramatic loss of biological diversity, (4) the increasing deterioration of the soil by desertification with its socio-economic impacts, and (5) the problems caused by world-wide transport and disposal of hazardous wastes with the potentially dramatic implications for water, soil and air. The most important of global, international agreements address these issues, including: (1) the Framework Convention on Climate Change (FCCC)[130] and its Kyoto Protocol,[131] (2) the Vienna Convention on the Protection of the Ozone Layer[132] and

---

[129] The interpretation of these two provisions, in particular their relationship is unclear. It is unfortunate to have whales listed as highly migratory species thus making article 64 UNCLOS applicable. It is probably reasonable to consider article 64 UNCLOS as *lex specialis*. This would exempt whaling from the optimum sustainable yield principle and would open the possibility for a more species-oriented approach.

[130] See above note 7.

[131] See above note 7. The Protocol has not entered into force yet.

[132] *ILM* 26 (1987), 1516 et seq.

its Montreal Protocol,[133] (3) the Convention on Biological Diversity,[134] (4) the Convention to Combat Desertification,[135] and (5) the Basel Convention on the Transboundary Movement of Hazardous Wastes and their Disposal.[136]

The following section consists of three parts. First, it examines potential conflicts in regard to the relationship between different agreements aiming at the comprehensive or partial protection of biological diversity. Second, it analyses the potential conflicts in the relationship between the global conventions on climate change, biodiversity and desertification, all of which represent the most important global outcomes of the Rio Conference.[137] Third, it discusses conflicting international regime on the transport of wastes and rules based on the law of the sea.

II. The Relation between Agreements Concerning Nature Conservation and Biological Diversity

(Matz)

As already noted in the discussion dealing with the relationship between the Convention on the Law of the Sea and the Convention on Biological Diversity, the CBD may reflect different categories of links to and potential conflicts with respect to other international environmental agreements. Since the Convention on Biological Diversity is one of the major global environmental agreements, potential conflicts to other treaties are significant not only for the effectiveness of legal regulations in this field of environmental law but also for the development of different kinds of solutions to conflicts in general.

Besides links to and conflicts with agreements that completely or partially deal with environmental issues, the Convention on Biological Di-

---

[133] See above note 7.

[134] See above note 16.

[135] See above note 8.

[136] *ILM* 28 (1989) 657 et seq.

[137] Although the Convention to Combat Desertification was not, like the other two, laid out for signature during the Earth Summit, it is a true product of the conference; its negotiation and contents are a direct result of the UNCED and its documents, e.g. the Agenda 21.

versity can also conflict with agreements on global economic issues and particularly world trade issues. Some potential conflicts with agreements covering economic issues that are also affected by the Convention on Biological Diversity include: (1) treaties that establish barriers to free trade to pursue their aims, e.g. the Montreal Protocol on Substances that Deplete the Ozone Layer; and (2) the regulations arising out of the WTO treaty system which deal with the fair and equitable sharing of benefits, technology transfer, and particularly, intellectual property. Another link to a distinct field of law may result from the provisions on *in situ* conservation of biological diversity and indigenous peoples. Since article 8, lit. (j) CBD requires the fair and equitable sharing of benefits derived from indigenous knowledge, this can be regarded as a link to the protection of minorities and, consequently, to international human rights law. However, a discussion of these issues is outside the scope of this study, which concentrates on the neglected issue of conflicts in international environmental law, i.e. between international environmental agreements.

1. Introduction: the CBD and Nature Conservation Agreements

Two aspects can be distinguished with respect to overlap with and conflicts between the Convention on Biological Diversity and other agreements. One issue refers to the relationship between the Convention on Biological Diversity and international agreements dealing with the protection of other environmental components or against environmental phenomena such as climate change. Such issues are subject to detailed discussion in several sections of this study.[138] This section, rather, addresses the relationship between the Convention on Biological Diversity and traditional agreements concerned with nature conservation, i.e. agreements aiming at the protection of species, habitats, ecosystems and landscapes.

Overlap with and links to agreements concerned with nature conservation may result in a doubling of efforts. But because of their potentially diverging approaches and programs, there is also a risk of conflicts. This would be the case, for example, if one agreement promotes the absolute preservation of a species while another, overlapping treaty is based upon the sustainable use of the same species. However, since the objec-

[138] E.g. see above in relation to the Convention on the Law of the Sea Part I B. II. and below Part I C. III. in relation to climate change and desertification.

tives of the agreements, even if they differ in detail, are in principle comparable, it is more probable that the different agreements double their efforts than contradict one another. In this case there may be, depending upon the legal structure and respective cooperation measures, a good chance for streamlining and the mutual reinforcement of different agreements concerned with nature conservation, particularly if the Convention on Biological Diversity could be regarded a framework agreement.

While, strictly speaking, the Convention on Biological Diversity is also an agreement concerned with nature conservation, its scope goes much further and includes many issues (e.g. rights of indigenous peoples or rules concerning intellectual property rights) which distinguish the treaty from the traditional agreements concerned with nature conservation. The Convention on Biological Diversity is a particularly far-reaching result of international environmental negotiations. It was originally planned as an umbrella convention that should encompass all agreements concerned with nature conservation that existed at the time the CBD was being negotiated.[139] Among the agreements concerned with nature conservation that existed at that time were the following important global and regional treaties: (1) the Washington Convention on International Trade in Endangered Species of Wild Flora and Fauna, 1973;[140] (2) the Bonn Convention on the Conservation of Migratory Species of Wild Animals, 1979;[141] (3) the Bern Convention on the Conservation of European Wildlife and Natural Habitats, 1982;[142] (4) the Ramsar Convention on Wetlands of International Importance Especially as Waterfowl Habitat, 1971;[143] and (5) the UNESCO Convention for the Protection of the World Cultural and Natural Heritage, 1972.[144]

At the time of the drafting of the Convention on Biological Diversity the idea of combining and strengthening existing agreements concerned with nature conservation in order to establish a new international in-

---

[139] United Nations Environment Programme: Report of the Governing Council on the Work of Its Fourteenth Session, UN Doc. A/42/25 (1987).

[140] See above note 125.

[141] See above note 127.

[142] *UKTS* 56 (1982), Cmnd. 8738.

[143] *ILM* 11 (1972), 969 et seq.

[144] *ILM* 11 (1972), 1358 et seq.

strument had already been abandoned in favor of a new framework.[145] Due to political and legal doubts, the intergovernmental negotiations soon also abandoned the concept of a formal umbrella convention. Hence, the Convention on Biological Diversity does not replace agreements concerned with the protection of species and ecosystems, but rather aims at formulating general principles and obligations for the protection of biological diversity.[146] However, the convention is naturally very closely linked to all agreements concerned with nature conservation, if only thematically, and may, in this respect, provide a functional framework. The scope of these various agreements concerned with nature conservation can substantially overlap with the Convention on Biological Diversity and, while the opportunities for mutual reinforcement shall be stressed in this study, potential conflicts shall not be disregarded.

2. *Categories of Agreements Concerned with Nature Conservation and the Development of International Nature Conservation Law*

In contrast to the modern approach pursued by the Convention on Biological Diversity, earlier agreements concerned with nature conservation mainly focus on the protection of only certain components of biological diversity. Different categories of agreements can be distinguished according to their scope, the issue addressed and the degree of protection. In principle, international legal regulation for the protection of biological diversity has developed from the protection of species to the protection of habitats and ecosystems and the protection of genetic resources to a modern and comprehensive approach to conserve all biodiversity, although in some cases the line between these groups of agreements is not easy to draw.

---

[145] R. Wolfrum, "The Protection and Management of Biological Diversity", in: F.L. Morrison/ R. Wolfrum (eds.), *International, Regional and National Environmental Law* (2000), 355 et seq. (357 in note 7).

[146] S. De Klemm/ C. Shine, *Biological Diversity Conservation and the Law: Legal Mechanisms for Conserving Species and Ecosystems* (1993), 17.

(a) The Protection of Species

The protection of species is, by comparison, an older field of international environmental law.[147] A species is, according to the biological definition, an animal group in which the individual members can breed with one another but, due to genetic, physiologic or behavioral barriers, cannot breed with other members of other groups.[148] The genetic variability within a species, i.e. the sum of genetic characteristics within the gene pool of a species, had not been granted importance in the early approaches taken with respect to the protection of species. Instruments on the protection of species most often concern single species which are regarded as important or certain groups of species with certain attributes, e.g. migratory species.

This approach towards the protection of species given way to an approach focusing on the protection of habitats and ecosystems, and ultimately on biological diversity in general. The approach to the protection of species, including the justification for protection and the reasons certain species were selected, began to change as early as the period following World War II.[149] The approach represented by agreements from the early 20th century hardly have anything in common with the more modern approaches to the conservation of species which emerged after World War II, not to mention the current, comprehensive approach taken towards the conservation of biodiversity. For example, treaties like the Convention on the Protection of Birds Useful to Agriculture and the 1900 Convention Designed to Ensure the Conservation of Various Species of Wild Animals in Africa, Which Are Useful to Men or Inoffensive,[150] identified species meriting protection based on the distinction between species perceived to be harmful or useful to human

---

[147] First agreements had been concluded at the beginning of the last century, e.g. the Convention on the Protection of Birds Useful to Agriculture, 1902, *IPE* IV, 1615 et seq., or the Convention between the United States of America, the United Kingdom of Great Britain and Northern Ireland, and Russia, for the Preservation and Protection of Fur Seals, 1911, *IPE* VIII, 3682 et seq.

[148] See e.g. E. Mayr, *Das ist Biologie* (1998), 178 et seq.; E. Wilson, *Der Wert der Vielfalt* (1997), 54 et seq.

[149] On the development of concepts for species protection see also M.C. Maffei, "Evolving Trends in the International Protection of Species", *GYIL* 36 (1993), 131 et seq., R. Wolfrum, "International Environmental Law: Purposes, Principles and Means of Ensuring Compliance", in: Morrison/ Wolfrum (note 145), 41 et seq., Sands (note 18), 26 et seq. and 370 et seq.

[150] See above note 15.

activities. Those species considered harmful under the Convention on the Protection of Birds, e.g. grain eating birds that could interfere with agriculture, could be reduced. On the other hand, those birds considered neither harmful nor useful enjoyed no protection. These and comparable agreements were mainly anthropocentric and oriented towards exploitation in a manner no longer controlling in more recent treaties and, particularly, not by the modern agreements which focus on the sustainability of biodiversity.[151] More recent treaties, which were primarily concerned with the protection of specific species, provide for protection without explicitly distinguishing between those species' usefulness for human purposes.[152]

Another big step in the development of the protection of species in international law was the emergence of agreements that sought to protect species not only from capture or killing, but at the same time to protect their habitats. Agreements like the Bonn Convention started to include the protection of habitats and thereby build a bridge to a later-emerging type of agreement which is primarily oriented on habitat and ecosystem.

The instruments that address only certain species or habitats have in common the pursuit of a sectional approach that does not provide for comprehensive protection of biological diversity. Yet another form of sectional approach refers to all species, but seeks to regulate only certain behavior, e.g. trade, which is considered harmful. The most prominent example of this sectional approach is the Convention on International Trade in Endangered Species of Flora and Fauna (CITES). Although the agreement is considered a particularly successful instrument of international law, by its very approach, it only regulates a rather limited threat to biological diversity. However, due to the regulation of one specific activity, such an agreement might effectively fill in part of a

---

[151] Practically all modern environmental agreements are still anthropocentric, in that the value attached to environmental resources is often considered in accordance with categories of human amenity, e.g. for economic, cultural or aesthetic reasons. The concept of sustainable use is, however, considered an incentive for protection and has developed considerably from early exploitation agreements. While some new agreements also recognize an intrinsic value of environmental resources, the main reasons for protection remain anthropocentric and focus on human survival and well-being.

[152] E.g. the International Convention for the Protection of Birds, 1950, reprinted in Ph. Sands, *Principles of International Environmental Law* (1995), Vol. IIA, 732 et seq.

framework on the comprehensive protection of all biodiversity against different sorts of threats.

(b) The Issue of Genetic Resources

The protection of genetic resources, an approach that developed later than the conservation of species, takes into consideration the genetic variability within a species and, furthermore, all plant and animal genetic material into its definition. The scope of agreements aiming at the protection of genetic diversity or genetic resources is, therefore, broader than the approach taken by agreements which seek only to protect species.[153] Yet, in contrast to agreements regarding the conservation of habitat or ecosystem, instruments on the protection of genetic resources usually do not include the protection of specific areas and are therefore less far reaching. From the perspective of a comprehensive approach, the conservation of genetic resources and genetic diversity is an essential aspect of the protection of biodiversity. On its own, however, the approach does not seem to be more viable than the protection of species, particularly if instruments refer only to some genetic resources, e.g. plant genetic resources. In this case the approach is restricted to a rather limited section of the overall biological diversity.

(c) The Protection of Habitats and Ecosystems

The protection of the habitats of endangered species and of ecosystems has developed as yet another stage in the protection of species. The protection of the habitat of endangered species is crucial for their survival and a common practice in modern agreements aiming at the protection of species.[154] Yet, agreements concerned with protecting habitat do not protect the diversity of ecosystems as such, since the starting point for the protection is a specific species considered to be endangered. As a consequence, although the protection of habitat for the

---

[153] The instrument that replaced the 1983 FAO Undertaking on Plant Genetic Resources, the new FAO International Treaty on Plant Genetic Resources 2001, has explicitly been established with a view to fulfill its objectives in accordance with the Convention on Biological Diversity. The treaty was adopted at the 31st session of the FAO Conference on 3 November 2001 and can be accessed at <http://www.fao.org/ag/cgrfa/IU.htm>, last visited 23 January 2002.

[154] See e.g. the Bern Convention.

benefit of a certain species also has the result of providing protection to all the other components and features of the particular ecosystem, the choice of the areas to be protected is not based upon the diversity of ecosystems as such, but on the occurrence of a certain species in that area. This approach, consequently, is not as far reaching as an approach that considers the diversity of ecosystems as valuable, regardless of whether a specific species is a part of that ecosystem.

The protection of ecosystems, regardless of the existence of a certain species therein, is rare in international law. Examples of this approach to nature conservation include the UNESCO Convention on the Protection of the Cultural and Natural Heritage and, to some extent, the Ramsar Convention on Wetlands of International Importance.[155] Mainly, however, agreements focus on the habitats associated with specific species of fauna and flora, such as the Bern Convention or the European Community Directive on the Conservation of Natural Habitats and of Wild Flora and Fauna (FFH-Directive).[156] The greater the number of species and, consequently, habitats that a convention considers to be valuable, the greater the resulting diversity of the ecosystems it protects and the closer the agreement comes to a more comprehensive approach to the protection of biological diversity.

(d)The Next Stage

As the last stage in the development of agreements concerned with nature conservation, the comprehensive approach of the Convention on Biological Diversity combines the issues addressed by the different agreements on species and habitat protection or the protection of genetic resources. The Convention on Biological Diversity does not set a priority on specific species or ecosystems but on their diversity and variability in general. While endangered species and ecosystems shall specifically be protected as well, this is only one of the mechanisms and not the sole objective. The extent of the scope and approach of the Convention on Biological Diversity becomes apparent, if one further

---

[155] The later, however, in its full title and in some of its provisions refers to wetlands, particularly as waterfowl habitat, and is, as a result, closely linked to habitats as well. It does, however, oblige States Parties to provide for the protection and wise use of all wetlands.

[156] Council Directive 92/43/EEC, *OJ* (1992), L206/7.

categorizes the different agreements aiming at the protection of biological diversity or components thereof with a view to their scope.

Agreements concerned with nature conservation can be categorized in different ways, e.g. according to whether they are oriented towards exploitation, conservation or protection.[157] Concerning the scope of these agreements, however, three other groupings are possible: (1) treaties potentially applicable to the protection of all species and habitats worldwide; (2) agreements concerned with the protection of all species and habitats in a certain region; and (3) treaties limited to a certain kind of species of habitat by otherwise international application.[158] According to such categorization the Convention on Biological Diversity is the only treaty that fulfils the conditions of the first type.[159] Although some other treaties also pursue a relatively far reaching subject matter, e.g. the ASEAN Agreement on the Conservation of Nature and Natural Resources, 1985, they are limited in their geographical scope, thus making the Convention on Biological Diversity the only global comprehensive treaty on the conservation and sustainable use of all aspects of biodiversity.

Yet, it is not only the potential applicability to all species and habitats that distinguishes the Convention on Biological Diversity from other agreements concerned with nature conservation. More important are the substantive provisions on the conservation and use of components of biological diversity which, because of new approaches and means, go altogether much farther than traditional agreements concerned with nature conservation.

---

[157] Nature conservation agreements can, according to De Klemm/ Shine (note 146), 37, be categorized as either conservation or exploitation agreements. However, the distinction between both categories has become more diffuse in respect to the concept of sustainable use of components of biological diversity.

[158] Sands (note 18), 370 et seq.

[159] Sands, ibid at 371 also mentions CITES as a member of the first category, because of its potential applicability to all endangered species world-wide. But since the treaty does not include habitats in its scope it cannot fully comply with the requirements.

3. The Scope of the Convention on Biological Diversity in Contrast to Other Agreements Concerned with Nature Conservation

The Convention on Biological Diversity, according to its definition in article 2 CBD, understands biological diversity to include diversity of ecosystems and within species. The affirmation of the world's biodiversity as the common concern of humankind as well as the detailed system of access to and use of genetic resources are important new features that justify claims that the Convention on Biological Diversity is a milestone in the development of modern environmental agreements.[160] The integration of ecological, economic and social factors in a single instrument, aiming to ensure the conservation and regeneration of biological resources, is an equally important innovation with respect to the development of new and comprehensive approaches to the protection of the world's biodiversity.[161] Another issue that substantially differentiates the Convention on Biological Diversity from other agreements is the inclusion of the *ex situ* conservation of biological diversity in article 9 CBD. The provisions most substantively concerned with the *in situ* conservation of biological diversity are, however, found in article 8 CBD on.

In contrast to agreements like the Bonn Convention, the Convention on International Trade in Endangered Species of Fauna and Flora or the EC FFH-Directive, the Convention on Biological Diversity does not include lists of endangered species or ecosystems in its provisions on the *in situ* protection of biodiversity.[162] In a similar vein, article 8 is not limited to addressing only some dangerous activities. The agreement is applicable to all components of biological diversity within zones of na-

---

[160] F. Burhenne-Guilmin/ S. Casey-Lefkowitz, "The Convention on Biological Diversity: A Hard Won Global Achievement", *YIEL* 3 (1992), 43 et seq. (47).

[161] See for example paragraphs 13, 19 and 20 of the Preamble of the Convention on Biological Diversity and, inter alia, articles 11, 15, 16, 18 and 20 on the integration of socio-economic considerations.

[162] This issue was subject to controversial debates throughout the negotiations. France in particular insisted until the final draft on the inclusion of binding lists to provide for stricter protection of endangered ecosystems. Since the majority of these ecosystems would have been located within developing countries, the resistance of these States lead to failure of the French approach; on this issue see G. Henne, "Das Regime über die biologische Vielfalt von 1992", in: T. Gehring/ S. Oberthür (eds.), *Internationale Umweltregime, Umweltschutz durch Verhandlungen und Verträge* (1997), 185 et seq. (191).

tional sovereignty and to all activities that are potentially harmful to the conservation of biodiversity. As a background to this non-sectional and comprehensive approach, the convention considers biological diversity to be valuable for ethical and economic reasons and because of its significance for the survival of humankind.[163] Such a motivation makes necessary a far-reaching approach to protection which includes all aspects of biological diversity and goes farther than traditional agreements concerned with nature conservation. The breadth of this approach is demonstrated by the provisions in article 8 subparagraph (j) which includes, among the measures to be taken for the conservation of biodiversity, the knowledge of indigenous peoples.

Another important difference in regard to many traditional nature conservation agreements is the concept of sustainable development pursued by the Convention on Biological Diversity. The Convention aims to protect biological diversity with measures aimed at conservation (articles 8 and 9 CBD), and at the same time, measures aimed the sustainable use of its components (article 10 CBD). While the Convention does not define the term conservation, other than in the specific meanings of *in situ* or *ex situ* conservation, it gives a definition of sustainable use.[164] According to article 2 CBD:

> "'sustainable use' means the use of components of biological diversity in a way and at a rate that does not lead to the long-term decline of biological diversity, thereby maintaining its potential to meet the needs and aspirations of present and future generations."

Since the preparations for the UNCED and the subsequent proliferation of the concept of sustainable development, international environmental law has taken an approach that promotes the sustainable use of resources as a means of their protection. Earlier agreements concerned with nature conservation pursued protection by freeing the subjects of the agreements of human use.[165] The Convention on Biological Diversity, the Framework Convention on Climate Change and, as a consequence of the Earth Summit, the Convention to Combat Desertifica-

---

[163] On these three criteria see Burhenne-Guilmin/ Casey-Lefkowitz (note 160), 43.

[164] According to Burhenne-Guilmin/ Casey-Lefkowitz, ibid at 50, States deliberately refrained from defining the term conservation so that the Convention can use the term in a more strict or a broader meaning according to its specific purposes.

[165] Wolfrum (note 149), 41.

tion were the first, and at the same time, the most important international treaties to transform sustainable development into binding rights and duties.[166] The agreements that integrate sustainable use, while having hardly anything in common with the agreements from the beginning of the 20th century which had their basis in exploitation, are now gaining predominance even when compared with agreements which are based on a protection approach. In this respect the Convention on Biological Diversity also represents a shift of paradigms in the law of international nature conservation.[167] With the integration of conservation and sustainable use, the agreement opens the way for all potentially viable measures necessary to pursue its objectives.[168] However, such a shift of paradigms (and the respective objectives and means that give it form in the Convention on Biological Diversity) poses a serious risk of creating conflicts with those older treaties that promote protection without any use.

4. Conflicts or a Chance for Cooperative Supplementation?

Since the Convention on Biological Diversity is the agreement, which is widest in scope and which has been ratified by the large majority of States, it has the potential to functionally employ other international agreements concerned with nature conservation in order to fulfill parts of its objectives and obligations, although it is not formally considered an umbrella convention. The Convention on Biological Diversity pursues an approach that focuses on objectives and soft obligations and gives the States Parties freedom and flexibility concerning the means to achieve these objectives.

The fundamental principles and objectives are a framework to be specified by national measures and the implementation of and compliance with other international agreements concerned with nature conserva-

---

[166] See e.g. S.H. Bragdon, "The Evolution and Future of the Law of Sustainable Development: Lessons from the Convention on Biological Diversity", *Georgetown Int'l Env. L. R..* 8 (1996), 423 et seq. (429).

[167] Henne (note 162), 185; concerning this issue and a general change in international environmental law by the concept of sustainable development see Bragdon (note 166), 428 et seq.

[168] Burhenne-Guilmin/ Casey-Lefkowitz (note 160), 50.

tion.[169] By implementing agreements that regulate certain components of the conservation of biodiversity States could partially fulfill their obligation to provide for coherent legal strategies for biological diversity. An important question in this respect is whether the Convention on Biological Diversity can be seen as a framework convention that is open to being implemented in cooperation with other international treaties.

Whether the Convention is a true framework convention is subject to debate, because of the many rather precise provisions the agreement includes.[170] Some elements, however, support the view that the agreement is a framework convention. For example, besides the possibility of deciding upon protocols and annexes, the Convention focuses on creating the obligation to achieve certain results rather than mandating certain behavior.[171] In this way, the Convention leaves room for the accomplishment of certain objectives by way of the inclusion and implementation of other agreements concerned with nature conservation agreements; a mutual supplementation of agreements by the way of cooperation. A cooperative approach would be consistent with the original aim: to develop a treaty on the conservation of biological diversity that fills in gaps in the international regulation of nature conservation, while taking into consideration existing agreements.[172]

Still, despite the potential possibilities for a mutual supplementation, the identification and subsequent harmonization of potential conflicts between agreements concerned with nature conservation and the Convention on Biological Diversity is particularly important. As already mentioned, the most likely conflicts arise out of the different approaches to nature conservation and sustainable use pursued by older agreements and the approach taken by the more modern Convention on Biological Diversity. This risk is limited with respect to those older agreements that already incorporate the approach that focuses on the sustainable use of ecosystems, e.g. the Ramsar Convention.[173] Agree-

---

169 A. Hubbard, "The Convention On Biological Diversity's Fifth Anniversary: A General Overview Of The Convention – Where Has It Been And Where Is It Going?", *Tulane Env. L. J.* 10 (1997), 415 et seq. (419).

170 See Burhenne-Guilmin/ Casey-Lefkowitz (note 160), 56.

171 Ibid at 57.

172 Ibid at 58.

173 Article 3, para. 1 Ramsar Convention. The concept of "wise use" as promoted by the Ramsar Convention is, according to decisions by the Ramsar Bureau equivalent to the common understanding of sustainable use, see S.C. Sny-

ments like the Bonn or the Bern Convention, however, refer only to protection against certain activities and not to the (sustainable) use of species. In agreements like these, the use of species seems to be considered a threat to and not as an incentive for better protection. Conflict with these and similar agreements seem likely, considering the CBD's view that sustainable use of biodiversity should serve as an incentive for more viable protection. The two approaches contradict one another and must be brought into coherence, if protection agreements shall be employed to implement objectives of the Convention on Biological Diversity.

Generally, conflicts can also occur between regional agreements and globally applicable treaties. Yet, there is also a specific potential to use regional agreements to fill in a framework. In the case of the Convention on Biological Diversity there is great potential to profit from the employment of regional instruments for the protection of components of biodiversity.[174] Treaties that are adapted to regional particularities are generally well suited to fill in a framework and provide for effective protection of specific regional features. A good example in this respect is the Bern Convention that pursues an approach, which is both focused on specific species or groups of species and the regions in Europe where they occur. The Standing Committee of the Bern Convention is responsible for the Action Theme of the Pan-European Biological and Landscape Diversity Strategy of the Council of Europe concerning threatened species and ecosystems. In the realm of their respective activities, the organs of the Bern Convention take it that they are implementing the objectives of the Convention on Biological Diversity.[175] A Memorandum of Understanding between the organs of the two agreements further promotes this approach. A regional approach within an international framework of fundamental principles and guidance could respect the fact that components of biodiversity in a particular region might need specific criteria and standards for their conservation. However, to effectively take over such functions, a streamlining and har-

---

der/ Wm.C. Muffett, "International Protection of the Soil", in: Morrison/ Wolfrum (note 145), 373 et seq. (377 et seq.).

[174] On the implementation of the Convention on Biological Diversity by regional agreements see Ch. Wold, "The Futility, Utility, and Future of the Biodiversity Convention", *Colo. J. Int'l Env. L. & Policy* 8 (1998), 1 et seq. (31).

[175] On the activities under the Bern Convention and the Pan-European Biological and Landscape Diversity Strategy see e.g. N. Matz, "Report: the Council of Europe", *YIEL* 10 (1999), 653 et seq. (654 et seq.).

monization of the approaches and fundamental principles of regional agreements to conserve biodiversity and the Convention on Biological Diversity as well as institutional cooperation for a concerted implementation is necessary.

A general trend in the direction of resolving conflicts and providing for harmonization and cooperation between traditional agreements concerned with nature conservation and the Convention on Biological Diversity has already begun to emerge, as is reflected by some Memoranda of Understanding being exchanged by the institutions of the Convention on Biological Diversity with the organs established by other agreements for nature conservation. The Memoranda of Understanding concluded with other organs, e.g. in the case of the Ramsar Convention on Wetlands of International Importance and the Bern Convention on European Wildlife and Natural Habitats, reflect the opportunity to use the newer Convention on Biological Diversity in conjunction with older agreements for a mutual reinforcement and coherence with respect to nature conservation. At the same time, such cooperative efforts can provide the necessary streamlining and harmonization of conflicts, should conflicting approaches, objectives or obligations be surface.

5. Conclusions: an Approach to Mutual Reinforcement

Existing nature conservation agreements do not, in principle, run counter to the objectives of the Convention on Biological Diversity; their specific approaches to nature conservation, however, might differ. The Convention on Biological Diversity is an instrument which, by its fundamental approach and design, can realize its objectives through the implementation of other international agreements. This is the case even though, formally, the Convention is not a framework convention with legal priority over other nature conservation treaties. As a consequence, the agreements to conserve either specific species, groups of species, ecosystems and habitats or genetic resources can fill in the more comprehensive approach to conservation and sustainable use of all biological diversity promoted by the Convention. In this way, these targeted agreements can promote certain components of the far reaching objectives of the Convention on Biological Diversity if conflicts in the approaches to the protection of biodiversity are harmonized. Forms of institutional cooperation, which will be discussed and developed more fully later in this study, might be a more viable way for harmonization in this constellation than a solution based upon the law of treaties, since the question is not to establish which treaty enjoys superiority but rather how to combine agreements to build a coherent network of international regulations aiming to achieve the conservation of nature.

Furthermore, an approach to mutual reinforcement with a view to promoting conformity and effectiveness in international environmental law might also ask for changes in the long-term strategy of the Convention of Biological Diversity. The implementation of other agreements concerned with nature conservation in order to pursue the objectives of the Convention on Biological Diversity can prevent a doubling of efforts and lead to a viable mutual supplementation. However, the States Parties to the Convention on Biological Diversity must be willing to take those subjects off their busy agendas that are already sufficiently addressed by other agreements.[176] By doing so, there would be more room to feasibly address gaps in the international framework of nature conservation. A fist step, however, requiring institutional cooperation and concerted action would be to identify those subjects, which are already suitably addressed by a certain agreement and to shift the regulation of this subject and the responsibility for it to the agreement and its organs, all in agreement with the States Parties involved.[177]

While the Conference of the Parties to the Convention on Biological Diversity has already made several decisions concerning the relation to other treaties and concluded some Memoranda of Understanding, these actions are still far from establishing a systematic strategy to harmonization and concerted, active network of different agreements concerned with nature conservation. This challenge should be a focus of activities of the Conference of the Parties in the near future.

III. Conflicts between the Convention on Biological Diversity, the Kyoto Protocol and the Convention to Combat Desertification

(Matz)

In contrast to the relationship between the Convention on Biological Diversity and nature conservation agreements, links to and overlap

---

[176] Similarly Wold (note 174), 3.

[177] So far the decisions regarding relationships with other agreements have not led to a final clarification of the problem. A comprehensive study on overlap and gaps in nature conservation law seems indispensable, see Wold, ibid at 14 and 25.

with treaties concerned with environmental issues other than nature conservation are even more prone to conflict. This has already become apparent in the discussion concerning the relationship between the Convention on Biological Diversity and the Convention on the Law of the Sea. Particularly in respect to treaties that regulate environmental as well as economic and/or developmental issues, e.g. the Convention on the Law of the Sea or the Convention to Combat Desertification, tensions can arise because these agreements already combine distinct issues in their provisions and may reflect compromises that make the harmonization with other environmental treaties more difficult. The same applies in relation to treaties, which focus on economic mechanisms and other innovative means of implementation, e.g. the instruments to prevent climate change. While different approaches and objectives may be a primary source of conflict, particularly for agreements concerned with nature conservation, the means of implementation in different environmental agreements can also differ considerably and require specific safeguards to prevent and to solve conflicts with respect to implementation.

This section of the study again focuses upon the Convention on Biological Diversity in examining contradictions between international environmental treaties. In this respect, links, conflicts and overlap between the CBD and agreements on the prevention of climate change, especially the Kyoto Protocol and the Convention to Combat Desertification, will be discussed. Particular attention will be given to conflicts that occur in the implementation phase.

1. Conflicts between the Convention on Biological Diversity and the Kyoto Protocol to the Framework Convention on Climate Change

(a) Introduction: Links and Potential Conflicts

Generally, like most environmental processes, the phenomena of global warming and of loss of biodiversity are interrelated. A change of the global climate always has direct effects on biological diversity, regardless of whether climate change is caused by natural phenomena or induced by anthropogenic activities. Although detailed scientific predictions are difficult to undertake, some scientific studies generally describe the potential impacts of a significant global climate change[178] by a

[178] A rise of the global average temperature by no more than 2° to 3° C may, for the delicate environmental balances upon which biological, ecological, me-

rise of the sea level and the consequential threat to islands and coastal regions, a loss of forests and wetlands, the extinction of species and a decrease of freshwater resources.[179] These possible changes will invariably also result in a variety of negative consequences for humankind, e.g. in regard to food security, health and other living conditions.

Global warming and a change of regional weather, particularly concerning precipitation, modify the conditions in natural habitats of flora and fauna. While an increase in temperature is not necessarily negative for all components of biological diversity, the delicate balance in ecosystems will be disturbed and this can cause the extinction of species.[180] Furthermore, in the case of global warming, international and national strategies will have to reconsider existing protected areas and nature reserves with fixed boundaries because a shift of climate zones can lead to the permanent migration of species from the nature reserves to other areas where they find the former climatic conditions necessary for their survival.[181] A rise of temperature on earth can also lead to the extinction of those plants and animals that cannot adapt to the changed living conditions, particularly if, in the case of small islands for example, the migration of species to other regions is impossible.[182] Certain types of ecosystems may be lost altogether, since a shift to other regions where the original climatic conditions now exist is not always possible, especially in regard to ecosystems in need of cooler climate and in regard to mountain ecosystems.[183]

---

teorological, chemical, physical and geophysical processes are based, already be considered significant.

[179] See L. Boisson de Chazournes, "The United Nations Framework Convention on Climate Change: On the Road Towards Sustainable Development", in: R. Wolfrum (ed.), *Enforcing Environmental Standards: Economic Mechanisms as Viable Means?* (1996), 286 et seq. (286 et seq.) with further references to the different scientific studies of the IPCC, UNEP and the WMO.

[180] M. Bowman, "Global Warming and the International Legal Protection of Wildlife", in: R. Churchill/ D. Freestone, *International Law and Global Climate Change* (1992), 127 et seq. (128 et seq.). A rise in temperature can lead to an increase in the growth of certain plants in an ecosystem, which can in turn drive out other species.

[181] In the case of permanent climate change ecological communities might permanently migrate to other regions, Bowman, ibid at 128.

[182] Ibid at 129 et seq.

[183] On the impact of global warming on these and other ecosystems see Bowman, ibid at 130 et seq.

The potential consequences global warming could have on biological diversity are neither explicitly subject to the Convention on Biological Diversity nor the Framework Convention on Climate Change or its Kyoto Protocol. However, the 4th COP to the Convention on Biological Diversity, 1998, in its Decision IV/7, recognized for the first time a direct relationship between the Convention on Biological Diversity and the regime on the protection of the global climate as well as the Convention to Combat Desertification. In paragraph 9 of this decision the COP requested that the Executive Secretary cooperate with the organs of the Framework Convention on Climate Change and the Convention to Combat Desertification in order to achieve the objectives of the Convention on Biological Diversity.[184] Since then, the issue is regularly on the agendas of the meetings of the treaty's organs[185] and gains increasing attention in the studies of certain other institutions.[186] Still, while the need for cooperation is recognized by the treaties' organs, they have not yet discussed the extent to which the agreements may be in conflict with one another.

A conflict between the Convention on Biological diversity and the international instruments to prevent climate change results particularly from forestry activities that are allowed under the Kyoto Protocol but which have an adverse effect on the conservation of biological diversity in forest ecosystems. Forests are both important for a stabilization of the global climate as well as for the conservation of biological diversity. Forests and, particularly, some rain forests, are so-called "hot-spots" for biodiversity and are therefore considered especially valuable with respect to *in situ* conservation.[187] Tropical rain forests may also be the

---

[184] Decision IV/7, Doc. UNEP/CBD/COP/4/12.

[185] See e.g. Decision V/21 of the 5th COP to the Convention on Biological Diversity, Doc. UNEP/CBD/COP/5/23, 160 et seq.; SBSTTA Recommendation V/1, para. 4, lit. (d), Annex I to Doc. UNEP/CBD/COP/5/3, 35 et seq.

[186] See UN University/ Global Environment Information Centre, *Global Climate Governance – Inter-Linkages between the Kyoto Protocol and other Multilateral Regimes* (1999) and WBGU, Sondergutachten, *Die Anrechnung biologischer Quellen und Senken im Kyoto Protokoll: Fortschritt oder Rückschlag für den globalen Umweltschutz?* (1998).

[187] "Hot spots" are regions with a high number of endemic species whose continued existence is severely threatened. On the 18 "hot spots" for biodiversity that have been identified in the late 20th century and other rain forest "hot spots" see Wilson (note 148), 318-329.

most effective reservoirs for atmospheric CO_2[188] and, consequently, their protection should be of foremost importance within the context of the Convention on Biological Diversity and the Framework Convention on Climate Change and its Kyoto Protocol. However, the flexible mechanisms for the implementation of the Kyoto Protocol and the achievement of the binding targets for developed countries may conflict the objectives of preventing and mitigating climate change.

In particular, the Kyoto Protocol's lack of incentives aimed at encouraging States Parties to preserve their natural forests, e.g. primary rain forests, is considered a failure which is likely to give rise to conflicts with the Convention on Biological Diversity. Instead of providing for incentives to preserve forest CO_2-reservoirs, the Kyoto Protocol may even indirectly encourage the reduction of natural forests for plantations of fast growing trees through its flexible mechanisms and through the possibility of crediting sinks as a positive factor in the accounting of national emissions, in the context of reduction targets.[189] This potential effect of the climate change regime can significantly harm other environmental objectives like the conservation of biological diversity and the protection of the soil.

(b) Sinks and Flexible Mechanisms under the Kyoto Protocol

To fully understand a potential conflict between the agreements to prevent climate change and the Convention on Biological Diversity some explanation with respect to sinks and the flexible "Kyoto-mechanisms" is necessary. The Kyoto Protocol fills in parts of the framework of the Framework Convention on Climate Change with its more concrete provisions and, most importantly, by providing for binding reduction targets of greenhouse gas emissions for those industrialized States enlisted in Annex I of the Framework Convention on Climate Change. These Annex I countries are obliged to reduce emissions by 5 % based upon the emissions of 1990 (article 3, para. 1 Kyoto Protocol). There are no concrete emission-reduction targets for developing countries. Neither does the Protocol establish any other new obligations; article

[188] UN University/ Global Environment Information Centre (note 186), 62.

[189] Already in 1992 the Global Biodiversity Strategy, WRI/IUCN/UNEP, *Global Biodiversity Strategy: Guidelines for Action to Save, Study, and Use Earth's Biotic Wealth Sustainably and Equitably* (1992), warned of such an effect that is considered detrimental to the conservation of biological diversity.

10 only puts into more concrete form the general obligations taken from article 4, para. 1 FCCC.

The flexible mechanisms for the implementation of the Kyoto Protocol are some of its more important innovations. However, some of the flexible mechanisms aimed at achieving the reduction targets allowed under the Protocol are considered problematic from an environmental and political perspective.[190] The flexible Kyoto Mechanisms consist of the Joint Implementation (article 4 Kyoto Protocol), which is already laid down in the Framework Convention, the Clean Development Mechanism (CDM, article 12 Kyoto Protocol), and the possible trade with emission certificates (article 17 Kyoto Protocol).[191]

Under a Joint Implementation program two developed States can implement their obligations together as a bigger economic region. Because of economic considerations, like cost-effectiveness and the promotion of innovations, industrialized States can fulfill their reduction targets jointly and decide, on the basis of economic considerations, on the internal quotas for each participating State.[192] The Clean Development Mechanism of article 12 of the Protocol is based upon a similar economic approach. By making use of this mechanism, industrial States can sponsor climate change mitigation projects in and together with developing countries or countries with economies in transition to a market economy and may, under certain conditions, include the reductions achieved by these projects in their own national emissions accounting in order to achieve their reduction targets. With respect to an overall reduction of emissions, the Clean Development Mechanism is of questionable value. Pursuant to the terms of the Clean Development Mechanism and in full compliance with the Protocol, developing States Parties can reduce emissions in one CDM-project and increase their overall emissions because they are under no obligation to reduce emissions in the first place. Consequently, developing States could, if this mechanism is not strictly regulated by the States Parties, easily avoid

---

[190] Concerning the political controversies on the Joint Implementation of the objectives and targets of the climate change agreements see B. Baker Röben, "Protection of Global Atmospheric Components", in: Morrison/ Wolfrum (note 145), 201 et seq. (215).

[191] Clear guidance is lacking, since a system still has to be elaborated by the States Parties.

[192] See S. Schuppert, *Neue Steuerungsinstrumente im Umweltvölkerrecht am Beispiel des Montrealer Protokolls und des Klimarahmenschutzübereinkommens* (1998), 195.

having to reduce emissions in their home economies without contributing effectively to a reduction emissions on a global scale. In recent decisions, the Conference of the Parties has, however, clarified that the respective mechanisms are in addition to domestic emission reductions and that they do not create or bestow any right to emissions on the part of Annex I States.[193]

Generally, concerning a reduction of greenhouse gases in the atmosphere, two possibilities can be pursued: (1) states can either reduce the emission of greenhouse gases; or (2) states can provide for biological capacities that bind CO_2 (which, based on the quantity of CO_2 emissions, is one of the most important greenhouse gases) from the atmosphere. Both possibilities can be pursued together. To reduce emissions, States can develop different national strategies, *inter alia*: (1) the establishment of plans to reduce the production of energy by fossil fuels, (2) the promotion of alternative sources of energy and of new concepts for traffic, and (3) emission trading.[194] Subject to certain conditions, the Kyoto Protocol also allows the creation of new biological capacities for the absorption of greenhouse gases from the atmosphere, so called sinks, as a positive factor in the national climate accounting of Annex I countries. The enhancement of capacities to absorb CO_2 from the atmosphere by biological means can, to some extent, compensate emissions of gases. According to the definition in article 1, No. 8 FCCC a

> "'Sink' means any process, activity or mechanism which removes a greenhouse gas, an aerosol or a precursor of a greenhouse gas from the atmosphere."

The Kyoto Protocol is based upon this definition and regulates, in its article 3, para. 3, the possibility of making the creation of sinks creditable toward the achievement of national emissions-reduction targets. According to article 3, para. 3 Kyoto Protocol, creditable sinks consist of activities of afforestation or reforestation, whereas deforestation is

---

[193] This is part of the so called Bonn Agreements on the Implementation of the Buenos Aires Plan of Action, see the Annex to Decision 5/CP.6, FCCC/CP/2001/5, 41 et seq.

[194] Whether emission trading is a viable means to reduce emissions is not free from doubt and depends upon the respective concept. Besides questions of viability, ethical considerations can be taken into account in respect to emission trading. A market for pollution that does not sanction pollution but merely regards it as economic transaction to which a certain price is attached is questionable from the viewpoint of environmental ethics, see e.g. J. Alder/ D. Wilkinson, *Environmental Law and Ethics* (1999), 217.

considered a biological source of emissions. During the negotiations leading to the Kyoto Protocol some States showed great interest in including other activities like the use of agricultural land or forestry management as creditable sinks in the realm of article 3, para. 3 Kyoto Protocol.[195] While article 3, para. 4 Kyoto Protocol explicitly allows the broadening of the scope of article 3, para. 3 Kyoto Protocol in regard to other creditable activities, the States Parties had for a long time not considered this issue. During the conferences in 2000 and 2001, however, when it became clear that questions concerning forestry and land-use would be crucial for the future fate of the Kyoto Protocol, these issues became a center of attention. As part of the core elements of the Buenos Aires Plan of Action the COP agreed to also include "forest management," "cropland management," "grazing land management" and "revegetation" in the catalogue of eligible land-use, land-use changes and forestry activities under article 3, para. 4 Kyoto Protocol.[196] For activities under article 12 Kyoto Protocol, however, eligible activities are still limited to afforestation and reforestation.[197]

Credits and deductions for biological sinks and sources of emissions are limited not only by the restriction to certain activities but also in regard to a fixed timeframe. The Kyoto Protocol only takes into consideration those activities the effects of which can still be measured in the first commitment period from 2008 to 2012. Areas subject to deforestation, afforestation or reforestation since 1990 create the so-called "Kyoto Forest," which is the basis for any creditable changes in biological carbon stocks. Those activities, which are still quantifiable in the commitment period, are either credited or deducted as a measurable change in the CO_2-accounting of an industrial State with respect to the reduction targets of 5 %, based on the 1990 baselines.

Account must be taken of the fact that the quantifiable changes concerning biological sources and sinks active in the first commitment period can be of little relevance. The greatest emission of carbon dioxide from deforestation can be measured during the year immediately following the logging. Consequently, if the activity is performed early enough, that is, before the commitment period, only a fraction of the overall emissions from biological sources will be accountable during the commitment period. This means that the biggest part of these damaging

---

195 WBGU, Sondergutachten (note 186), para. 3.3.

196 Annex to Decision 5/CP.6, Doc. FCCC/CP/2001/5, 45.

197 Ibid at 46.

emissions (resulting from deforestation), if performed between 1990 and 2007, will not serve as a deduction in the Annex I State Party's climate accounting. The same applies, in reverse, to reforestation measures. The biggest value as a credit in a State Party's climate accounting can be gained if reforestation is undertaken shortly before the beginning of the commitment period, when the growth of the trees is biggest and they sequester a lot of carbon. There is, however, no incentive for earlier reforestation.

Another shortcoming under the Kyoto Protocol, again concerning the regulation of creditable sinks and sources of emissions resulting from human activities, is the lack of clear definitions of afforestation, reforestation or deforestation. A lack of definition or explanation generally leaves important questions unanswered and, as a result, they may be subject to national political interpretation and discretion of the member States. Some issues in this context that might have been clarified by regulations in the Kyoto Protocol are: (1) the transformation of primary forests into plantations, particularly, plantations of mono- or almost mono-cultures and/or of non-native species and a differentiation between reforestation; and (2) forestry management that involves regular logging and replanting of trees in an area.[198] These points also constitute potential conflicts between the Kyoto Protocol and the Convention on Biological Diversity because some forms of forestry management can have adverse effects on the conservation of biological diversity. This is especially true of plantations, particularly if they replace primary forests. The recent Bonn Agreements, however, contain the definitions of "forest," "afforestation," "reforestation" and "deforestation" upon which the Conference of the Parties settled.[199] The respective definitions are included in a decision by the 7th Conference of the Parties.[200]

---

[198] WBGU, Sondergutachten (note 186), para. 3.2.

[199] Annex to Decision 5/CP.6, Doc. FCCC/CP/2001/5, 45.

[200] At present only an advance unedited version of the report is available, not stating the numbers of the decisions. The definitions are contained in the Annex to the decision on land use, land-use change and forestry.

(c) The Creation of Sinks and Potential Adverse Effects on Biological Diversity

Certain practices of forestry management can contradict the *in situ* conservation of biological diversity by their capacity to destroy or damage forest ecosystems. The most obvious example of a destruction of biodiversity in this respect is the complete logging of wood in forests or the burning of forest areas. However, reforestation with mono-cultural plantations is also contrary to the protection and restoration of ecosystems according to article 8, lit. (f) CBD. Accordingly, the COP to the Convention on Biological Diversity refers to the extraordinary role of "some forests" in the conservation of biological diversity in order to make a distinction between natural forests and those reforested areas that may be less valuable from a biodiversity perspective.[201] Generally, the Convention on Biological Diversity should, in light of the approach upon which it is based and objectives it sets based on that approach, be focused on the conservation of primary forests and respective forest ecosystems that can perform full ecological functions. While this is not explicitly stated by the Convention on Biological Diversity, the Work Programme on Forest Biological Diversity, although it does not give detailed guidance, stresses holistic and inter-sectional approaches and emphasizes the ecosystem approach of the Convention on Biological Diversity.[202] Industrial forestry, which promotes monocultures consisting of fast-growing native or non-native species, is one factor that threatens biological diversity. Consequently, if the Kyoto Protocol would give an incentive to perform such activities by crediting certain forestry activities, the implementation of the Protocol could conflict with the objectives and obligations of the Convention on Biological Diversity.

In this respect, the creation of certain sinks in order to meet reduction targets could conflict with the aims of the Convention on Biological Diversity with respect to the conservation of ecosystems. This is particularly true if used in combination with instruments like the Clean Development Mechanism. In the absence of directives from the regime's organs, States Parties to the climate change regime could fulfill their obligations under the Kyoto Protocol by creating sinks which may

---

[201] Doc. UNEP/CBD/COP/3/L.8.

[202] Work Programme on Forest Biological Diversity Under The Convention on Biological Diversity, Annex to Decision IV/7, Doc. UNEP/CBD/COP/4/12.

consist of mono-cultural plantations of indigenous or alien trees. The new decisions by the COP, although providing welcome elaboration of the issue, are not quite clear in this respect. Monocultures of pine trees, for example, may not differ from mixed forest concerning their potential to absorb carbon.[203] As a result, the mixed forest and the plantation are, from a climate change perspective, both of equal value because of their ability to bind CO_2 from the atmosphere.[204] However, monoculture plantations are easier to establish than a mixed forest ecosystem and, most importantly, easier to reuse for economic purposes. Concerning the protection of biodiversity, however, the differences between monoculture plantations and natural forest are significant. In regard to their ecosystem function, plantations resemble fields of crops more than natural forests, and they cannot offer the same degree of ecological and environmental functions and services as can primary or even secondary natural forests.[205]

Even more disastrous, from the perspective of the protection of biological diversity, is the possibility that the Kyoto Protocol might still offer an incentive to log primary forest prior to the commitment period, when an accounting of sinks and emissions sources is to be made. For the time between 1990 and 2008, greenhouse gas emissions from biological sources (resulting from deforestation) and the reduction of emissions through the creation of sinks play nearly no role in the national climate accounting because only those measures that still have an effect in the time between 2008 and 2012 are evaluated. As a consequence, States Parties can deforest an area prior to 2008 and use it for different purposes without being fully liable for the release of greenhouse gas that results and then reforest the area shortly before 2008 in order to gain the maximum advantages from the creation of a sink. With this possibility, the Kyoto Protocol could actually serve to promote the logging or burning of trees and an intensive short-term use of former

---

[203] WBGU, Sondergutachten (note 186), para. 6.1.8; however, according to UN University/Global Environment Information Centre (note 186), 66, primary tropical rainforests sequester more carbon than plantations of monocultures.

[204] However, if the original forest is logged prior to the creation of a plantation, the alleged equality gets out of balance because one would have to take into consideration the evaporation of CO_2 from the forest soil that occurs after the deforestation and which cannot be immediately absorbed by the plantation trees.

[205] UN University/Global Environment Information Centre (note 186), 65.

forest areas, e.g. for agricultural purposes. Such a practice can severely and in many cases irreversibly harm biological diversity, particularly if the deforested area is reforested with plantations of monocultures. Again, it is questionable whether the new decisions adopted on this issue could prevent such a practice.[206]

The threat for natural rain forests and other tropical or subtropical forests, which are rich of biological diversity, origins from the possibility of cooperation between developed and developing counties under the Clean Development Mechanism. This flexible mechanism under the Kyoto Protocol bears the risk of further promoting practices that endanger biological diversity in biodiversity rich areas in developing countries. By making use of the Clean Development Mechanism industrialized States could obtain climate credits, despite the destruction of ecologically especially valuable tropical or subtropical forests. A developing country, by participating in a project under the Clean Development Mechanism, could, for example, gain economic profits from the deforestation and agricultural use of a former primary forest area between 1990 and 2008, before it reforests the area with plantations, funded by financial resources of an industrial State. The developed State Party could in turn obtain credits for this practice,[207] although the original tropical forests may even have sequestered more carbon than the later plantations.[208] The accountable reforestation would hence not even be suitable to compensate for the loss of the primary forest and the respective release of CO_2 into the atmosphere and would not have any beneficial effects on restoring CO_2 concentrations on levels below that of 1990.

Such a practice that may include economic short-term profits, however, would again be an incentive for the developing country to first deforest areas of natural forests. Developing States could sell the wood and use the area for other purposes before shortly before 2008 the developed State Party, who also gets the credits for the respective sink, pays for the reforestation. While such a scenario is not even favorable from the climate change perspective, since the overall balance is not improved, it is

---

[206] To some extent this uncertainty is based upon the fact that COP7 has asked for additional expert advice from the IPPC on the issue and particularly on the assessment of emissions by land use sources and removal by sinks.

[207] UN University/Global Environment Information Centre, ibid at 62.

[208] Ibid at 66.

most adverse to the conservation of biological diversity and the respective provisions on *in situ* conservation of biodiversity in article 8 CBD.

The potential advantages from the substitution of natural forests with plantations may even be increased, if a State Party or its partner in a Clean Development Mechanisms project plants plantations with particularly fast growing trees, which can produce a high amount of credits in the climate balance in a short period of time, but which are non-native in the respective region. Eucalyptus for example is an especially fast growing species.[209] If planted in areas to which it is not indigenous ecosystems can be destroyed as other native species of flora and fauna are expelled. These potential consequences also contradict the ecosystem approach promoted by the Convention on Biological Diversity and some of its other objectives concerning the conservation of biodiversity *in situ*. A further aggravating factor relates to the practice of using artificial fertilizers on plantations to promote growth. Fertilizers containing nitrogen lead to an increased emission of nitrous gases from the soil. These gases are considered greenhouse gases as well. The crediting of sinks created by such activities and practices are an incentive to increase emissions of greenhouse gases, worsen climate change, destroy biological diversity and generally mock international environmental objectives.

Besides the damage done to biological diversity by the destruction of forest ecosystems, which cannot be compensated by later reforestation, studies have lead to the result that the reforested areas can even be a source of CO_2-emissions, if the evaporation of gases from the soil is taken into account.[210] In this respect the positive consideration of such activities as sinks in the national climate balance is – again – not even favorable from a climate change perspective, let alone from the view of the conservation of biological diversity. If one further considers that developing countries can get financial aid to reforest the areas of former original forests, which they destroyed for short term profit, under the Clean Development Mechanisms and that developed countries get

[209] In contrast to the 15 years it takes other tree species to reach their maximum growth, eucalyptus plantations in Brazil can be harvested every 4 – 6 years, see UN University/ Global Environment Information Centre, ibid, with further references.

[210] WBGU, Sondergutachten (note 186), para. 7.1.2.

credits for such practice it becomes apparent that the protection of the climate, biodiversity and the soil could be reversed.[211]

Consequently, while the Kyoto Protocol does not explicitly promote such a practice, it still doesn't take clear enough safeguards to prevent it either and, hence, possible implementation practices under the Kyoto Protocol could conflict with the Convention on Biological Diversity. Although the 7th Conference of the Parties (serving as meeting of the Parties to the Kyoto Protocol) decided in its Decision on Land use, land-use change and forestry:[212]

> "1. (e) That the implementation of land use, land-use change and forestry activities contribute to the conservation of biodiversity and sustainable use of natural resources".

Nevertheless, since potential conflicts are not explicitly identified, it is questionable whether such a statement can prevent an implementation that contradicts the objectives of the Convention on Biological Diversity. Future decisions, preferably prepared by a joint committee of the two agreements, would be highly desirable. The Convention on Biological Diversity is not mentioned by the respective decisions on land use and forestry.

(d) Conclusions Concerning the Relation between the Convention on Biological Diversity and the Kyoto Protocol

The objectives and obligations of the Convention on Biological Diversity in regard to the protection of forest ecosystems can be in conflict with the indirect incentives offered by the Kyoto Protocol to consider sinks as a means to reduce CO_2 in the atmosphere, without safeguarding that forest ecosystems are conserved. The statement that biodiversity shall not be influenced by the implementation of the Kyoto Protocol is valuable as a first step, yet it is not necessarily sufficient to prevent conflicts. Like in respect to the relationship between the Convention on Biological Diversity and the Convention on the Law of the Sea the potential conflicts to the instruments to prevent climate change do not consist of incompatible obligations between the respective instru-

---

[211] Ibid. See also R.G. Tarasofsky/ S. Oberthür, *Forest-Related Multilateral Environmental Agreements: A Survey of Provisions and Interactions*, Paper for "Ecologic", April 2001, 14.

[212] At present only an advance unedited version of the report is available, not stating the numbers of the decisions.

ments. In this respect the contradictions are conflicts of implementation, since the Kyoto Protocol does not prescribe the destruction of primary forests to grow wood in plantations.

The main failure of the Kyoto Protocol in regard to conflicts with the Convention on Biological Diversity is the remaining lack of incentive to maintain primary forests and build sinks according to binding and explicit guidelines of sustainable forestry. The Kyoto Protocol does not yet provide for an effective strategy to include the aims of the Convention on Biological Diversity into its regulations as to avoid certain implementation measures that achieve emission reduction targets by damaging forest ecosystems.

The Kyoto Protocol in its article 3, para. 3 refers to obligations of the member States derived from other international agreements on the sustainable practice of forestry activities. Explicit and binding international rules that give guidance on sustainable forestry, however, are lacking in international law. While the Work Programme on Forest Biological Diversity elaborated by the Convention on Biological Diversity on the occasion of its 4th COP gives some – rather vague – guidelines on sustainable forestry management and the conservation of biological diversity, it does not contain any binding standards.[213] Neither do the non-binding Forest Principles concluded at the UNCED contain any specific criteria. Two more, equally non-binding programs on sustainable forestry result from the International Panel of Forests (IPF) Proposals for Action and the International Forum on Forests (IFF) Proposals for Action.[214] Still, as a result it is doubtful whether article 3, para. 3 Kyoto Protocol can contribute to the prevention of conflicts of implementation.

To a comparable degree, objectives of the Convention to Combat Desertification or the protection of wetlands under the Ramsar Convention are neglected by the Framework Convention on Climate Change and its Kyoto Protocol. As a consequence tensions between the climate change agreements and these treaties cannot be excluded either. The in-

---

[213] Annex to Decision IV/7, Doc. UNEP/CBD/COP/4/12. In their recommendation to the 4th COP the IUCN and the WWF have suggested to persuade the SBSTTA and the *Thematic Panel on Forest Biodiversity*, yet to be established, to collaborate with the International Forum on Forests (IFF) to establish guidelines on *inter alia* the restoration of diversity in plantations, the prevention of the introduction and the control of non-native species into forest ecosystems, IUCN/WWF, Recommendations May 1998, 3.

[214] See also Tarasofsky/ Oberthür (note 211), 43 et seq.

security that exists in regard to a consolidated implementation of the agreements makes the decision on priorities concerning the implementation a matter of political discretion and obstructs systematic synergies. Such synergies, however, are essential to prevent further conflicts of implementation and to streamline international regulations on the environment to eventually establish a coherent network of international environmental law. Even if the Kyoto Protocol and the Convention on Biological Diversity do not contradict one another in all aspects, the close interrelation of ecological processes calls for a formal recognition of their interrelation and the respective harmonization to enhance effectiveness of international environmental regulations. A consolidation of the treaties e.g. by a joint protocol on climate change and biodiversity,[215] but also by other legal or institutional means is necessary to provide for a viable, coordinated international framework in this respect.

2. *The Convention to Combat Desertification and the Convention on Biological Diversity*

(a) Introduction: Desertification and Links to Other Agreements

The Convention to Combat Desertification belongs to the group of the most important modern international environmental agreements, including: (1) the Convention on Biological Diversity; (2) the treaties on climate change, and ozone depletion; and (3) the Basel Convention on the Transport of Hazardous Wastes and their Disposal. Like the Convention on Biological Diversity, the Convention to Combat Desertification is also much more than a traditional agreement concerned with nature conservation. Both its scope, especially in light of the inclusion of socio-economic considerations and objectives, and the means it uses to achieve its goals go much farther than merely providing for the conservation of some specific areas. However, the Convention to Combat Desertification is not based on an ecosystem approach and, for this reason, it is considerably less effective when compared with many agreements concerned with nature conservation and must be distinguished from modern agreements in several ways.

The agreement refers to areas defined by certain criteria to address a phenomenon long neglected in international law. Desertification is a degree of land degradation caused by various, mainly anthropogenic, processes leading to the soil's loss of biological or economic productiv-

---

[215] Bowman (note 180), 144.

ity and complexity.[216] Draught, as opposed to desertification, is the natural failure of the usual precipitation in an area (article 1, lit. (c) CCD).

The most common human activities responsible for degradation of the soil's quality in dry land areas include: (1) agricultural overuse, (2) the overuse of pastures for cattle, (3) deforestation and (4) incorrect irrigation methods.[217] The Convention to Combat Desertification, in its article 1, lit. (f), I)-iii), lists some processes that, either based upon anthropogenic mismanagement or (natural) climatic change, cause further degradation of the soil. These processes, which are directly responsible for desertification, are the erosion of the soil by wind and/or water, the deterioration of the physical, chemical, biological or economic characteristics of the soil and the permanent loss of natural vegetation. These single aspects can also reinforce one another.

If the reasons for and consequences of desertification are examined, links to the issues regulated by other international agreements become apparent. Desertification is closely linked to climate change and the loss of biological diversity and, consequently, the links between the regulations in the international agreements concerned with their issues are manifest. Climate change and desertification can influence each other to some extent. The deforestation of land in dry-land regions (also involving a destruction of biological diversity) could cause a change in the local climate leading to an increase in the rate and degree of desertification. However, while the actual influence desertification has on climate change may be minor,[218] global warming and the resulting possibility of unusual weather phenomena can have a negative impact on the ongoing desertification of dry-lands. Particularly adverse effects can result, when the interaction of these factors leads to their mutual reinforcement, e.g. when a region affected by erosion as a consequence of

---

[216] In this context one has to distinguish between the spread of true deserts and the issue addressed by the Convention to Combat Desertification, i.e. the degradation of land in dry land areas. The encroachment of deserts is less significant, if compared with the degree of desertification caused by degradation of dry lands, see Snyder/ Muffet (note 173), 383.

[217] W.C. Burns, "The International Convention to Combat Desertification: Drawing a Line in the Sand?", *Michigan J. Int'l L.* 16 (1995), 831 et seq. (836); K.W. Danish, "International Environmental Law and the 'Bottom-Up' Approach: A Review of the Desertification Convention", *Indiana J. Global Legal Studies* 3 (1995), 133 et seq. (139).

[218] Danish (note 217), 139.

unsustainable use and deforestation, is subject to heavy rainfalls and tempests, which in turn have been caused by global climate change and which strip away the remaining fertile soil in the affected region.

The Convention to Combat Desertification and the Convention on Biological Diversity are also closely linked. Arid, semi-arid or dry sub-humid areas are generally fragile ecosystems due to the little precipitation they receive.[219] Any degradation of the land invariably causes a loss of bio-diversity in these regions. In this respect, the loss of ecosystems and the species living therein as well as the loss of genetic resources is at issue. Many important, nutritious plants, including wheat, barley and sorghum, have their origin in arid or semi-arid areas. The same applies to fodder plants and plants native to dry lands that are of medicinal use.[220] Consequently, the genetic diversity of these plants, which must be considered of special importance and value for humankind, may be severely threatened if the original ecosystems of these plants are destroyed by desertification.

The destruction of sensitive ecosystems in dry-lands, e.g. the cutting of trees and bushes for firewood, can also initiate and promote desertification by causing the loss of the soil's capacity to store water and by creating a greater threat of erosion after the loss of the vegetation cover. As a result, the damage done to biological diversity in areas threatened by desertification can trigger a continuing process at the end of which biological diversity in an area is severely deteriorated and the soil has lost its ecological and economic functions.

As a consequence of the links between the problems of the loss of biodiversity, climate change and desertification, solutions to these problems may also be inter-connected, if the approaches as well as potential implementation measures are harmonized. Only after potential conflicts have been eliminated and agreements have been streamlined can a potential for mutual reinforcement based upon the interrelations between the agreements been realized. The Convention to Combat Desertification mentions the Framework Convention on Climate Change and the Convention on Biological Diversity in its Preamble and in article 8, para. 1 CCD. The Convention to Combat Desertification even emphasizes a potential mutual reinforcement of the treaties by stating that the efforts undertaken to combat desertification can also promote the achievement of the goals of the other two agreements. However,

---

[219] Ibid at 135.

[220] Burns (note 217), 848.

this provision has not yet led to any concrete efforts to harmonize the treaties.

(b) Potential Conflicts between the Convention on Biological Diversity and the Convention to Combat Desertification

One might suppose that conflicts between the Convention on Biological Diversity and the Convention to Combat Desertification might be similar to those contradictions discussed in the relation to the Convention on Biological Diversity and the Kyoto Protocol. It is also reasonable to assume that, because the Convention to Combat Desertification is sometimes considered an agreement concerned with nature conservation, that there is a greater potential for synergies and harmonization. Although the latter thesis does not rule out the existence of conflicts between the treaties, it presupposes a relationship less prone to conflicts and more amenable to mutual reinforcement, particularly as far as the conservation and restoration of ecosystems affected by desertification or draught are concerned. However, the relationship between the Convention to Combat Desertification and the Convention on Biological Diversity differs considerably from the relationship between the CBD and agreements concerned with nature conservation. Such agreements, despite potential conflicts, are concerned with certain issues that can contribute to the implementation of the Convention on Biological Diversity and hence fill in part of the framework of the CBD. The Convention to Combat Desertification is not as closely linked with the Convention on Biological Diversity are not that closely linked. Furthermore, due to the approach taken by and its scope, the Convention to Combat Desertification can not be counted among the traditional agreements concerned with nature conservation because it addresses only certain areas of land.

aa) Conflicting Approaches

Potential conflicts between the agreements can arise out of the fact that the Convention to Combat Desertification is more strongly based upon socio-economic criteria than the Convention on Biological Diversity. This is especially true regarding certain priorities in the realm of the conservation and restoration of degraded ecosystems. In particular, the ecosystem approach pursued by the Convention on Biological Diversity can collide with economic considerations under the Convention to

Combat Desertification. In this respect the potential conflicts between the two conventions largely represent a conflict of approaches.

Since the Convention to Combat Desertification is strongly based upon the needs of people living in areas threatened by desertification (first preambular paragraph of the CCD), the conservation of the soil serves as a means to achieve food security for these people. Although the agreement considers ecological functions of the soil, it is not ecosystem orientated in its approach. Ecosystems and their functions are mentioned neither in the realm of measures to prevent desertification nor concerning restoration of degraded land. This fact gains significance in a possible constellation concerning reforestation or restoration of degraded land.

In fact, a conflict in this respect resembles the situation discussed with respect to the conflicts between the Convention on Biological Diversity and the Kyoto Protocol, since a mechanism to combat desertification might be seen in the reforestation with plantations and/or the restoration of the vegetation cover by non-native species. The objective to prevent or stop erosion of the topsoil and the establishment of a vegetation cover to store water in the upper layers of the soil may be achieved by species that had not been part of the original ecosystems or by plantations. In both cases such a practice would contradict the obligation under the Convention on Biological Diversity to restore degraded ecosystems.

Both agreements require the restoration of degraded areas and therefore, at least partially, correspond in respect to one of their objectives. While the Convention to Combat Desertification, in contrast to the Kyoto Protocol, does not give an incentive to damage ecosystems, neither does is provide for any incentives to actually protect or restore the degraded ecosystems with a view to the performance of their full functions. The priority is solely the ecological and economic function of the soil and other aspects of functioning ecosystems are neglected. Again, although the main basis for this conflict may be seen in the failure of the Convention to Combat Desertification to incorporate an ecosystem approach into its regulations, the problem is also a matter of implementation, the means to prevent the degradation of land could, in principle, be performed in accordance with the objectives and obligations under the Convention on Biological Diversity, despite the fact that incentives for such a behavior are lacking in the provisions of the Convention to Combat Desertification.

bb) Conflicts Arising out of Implementation

The Convention to Combat Desertification does not suggest concrete measures to prevent or combat desertification. Neither the Convention's main part nor the annexes establish obligations regarding which specific activities to combat desertification must be included in the national, regional and sub-regional plans-of-action to be established by the affected States Parties. In this respect, the regime is open for the inclusion of an ecosystem management approach consistent with the Convention on Biological Diversity. This view is similar to that which was discussed with respect to the relationship between the Convention on Biological Diversity and the Convention on the Law of the Sea. The earlier discussion regarding the CBD and UNCLOS also emphasized that the management criteria established for natural resources under national jurisdiction could be based upon the stricter standards of the Convention on Biological Diversity. States Parties, although not obliged to do so by the CCD, can adopt measures to combat desertification that are consistent with their obligations under the Convention on Biological Diversity. The question is whether they lack the political motivation to take this course, for economic or other reasons.

Only Annex III to the Convention to Combat Desertification explicitly requires the inclusion of rules consistent with the CBD in national action plans (article 4, lit. (f) Annex III to the CCD). However, not even this provision ensures that implementation measures in affected communities comply with the regulation on the restoration of ecosystems when performing specific activities to prevent or combat desertification, e.g. forestry measures. The other annexes only mention biological diversity as one factor to be taken into account when establishing action plans. Neither the Convention nor the annexes provide for any explicit guidance as to the criteria to be respected when implementing the framework provisions and action plans. The statement of a potential mutual reinforcement of the Convention to Combat Desertification and the Convention on Biological Diversity appears rather formal and has no substantial influence on the harmonization of conflicts between the treaties' approaches and implementation measures.

3. Conclusions

The tensions and conflicts between the Convention on Biological Diversity and both the Kyoto Protocol and the Convention to Combat Desertification reflect the incoherence of international environmental law in a most significant way; these treaties are in conflict even though they are the result of modern negotiations and, to a certain extent, follow the same underlying considerations, e.g. sustainable development. Approaches to harmonization and the creation of synergies, between these contemporaneously negotiated agreements not to mention, the prevention of future conflicts, remain underdeveloped. The decisions taken by the treaties organs regarding the necessity of cooperation with other agreements have not, so far, lead to systematic and coherent strategies on the harmonization of environmental agreements but only to some singular Memoranda of Understanding of questionable viability.

While the potential conflicts between agreements concerned with nature conservation may be easier to coordinate because they may all eventually form part of the same regime (a regime on international conservation of biological diversity), agreements that concern different environmental issues are more difficult to harmonize. This applies to the Convention on Biological Diversity in regard to the law of the sea as well as to the subjects addressed by the treaties discussed in this section. Their coordination is a question of specific forms of institutional cooperation as well as, to some extent, the law of treaties.

IV. Conflicts Related to the Regime on Transport and Disposal of Wastes

(Wolfrum)

1. Introduction

The issue of the transport and disposal of hazardous wastes was for a long time discussed controversially in international politics. Whereas Western industrial States were generally in favor of limiting the production of waste and encouraged recycling, they nevertheless considered the disposal of waste elsewhere, i.e. in a different place than where it was generated, as a reasonable option. African States particularly to this tradition objected because they felt they were being treated like an inexpensive disposal ground for wastes generated by industrialized States and were therefore being forced to suffer the consequences of inexpertly performed disposal of hazardous wastes. The result of these two different approaches were two international agreements: (1) the Convention on the Control of Transboundary Movements of Hazardous Wastes and Their Disposal, 1989 (Basel Convention)[221] and (2) the Convention on the Ban of the Import into Africa and the Control of Transboundary Movement and Management of Hazardous Wastes Within Africa (Bamako Convention).[222]

2. *The Basel Convention and the Bamako Convention*

The Basel Convention prohibits the export of hazardous wastes and other wastes without the prior approval of the importing State. The exporting State is under an obligation to prohibit such export to States that have banned the import of such wastes unless consent obtained by the importing State is first obtained.[223] The Basel convention covers substances that are disposed of or are intended for disposal or are required to be disposed of by national law.[224] This definition seems quite broad, although, in fact, the Convention only covers the management of hazardous wastes. Waste is considered to be hazardous only if listed in the Annexes to the Basel Convention or if qualified as such by national legislation of the Party of export, import or transit and notified to the Secretariat of the Convention. In that respect, Bamako Convention has a broader scope. The Basel Convention does not cover radioactive wastes because other international instruments provide for their regulation. As a result priority is given to the specialized instruments and conflicts resulting from an overlap of regulations are avoided.[225]

---

[221] *ILM* 28 (1989), 657 et seq.

[222] *ILM* 30 (1991), 775 et seq.

[223] Article 4, para. 1, and article 6 of the Basel Convention.

[224] As to the legislative history of the Basel Convention see Kummer (note 91), 38 et seq.

[225] Article 1 reads: Scope of the Convention

"1. The following wastes that are subject of transboundary movement shall be "hazardous wastes" for the purpose of this Convention:

(a) Wastes that belong to any category contained in Annex I, unless they do not possess any of the characteristics contained in Annex III; and

(b) Wastes that are not covered under paragraph (a) but are defined as, or are considered to be, hazardous wastes by the domestic legislation of the Party of export, import or transit.

2. Wastes that belong to any category contained in Annex II that are subject to transboundary movement shall be "other wastes" for the purpose of this Convention.

The disposal of wastes is also defined in rather broad terms. It includes landfill, release into watercourses, the sea, or the sea-bed, incineration, permanent storage, or recycling.[226] Accordingly, there is some overlap with the law of the sea regime concerned with dumping and the regimes on dumping for polar areas.[227]

The primary obligation imposed by the Basel Convention is to manage the transboundary movement of wastes in an environmentally sound manner. This obligation applies to exporting, transit, and importing States alike.[228] It also applies to trade with non-parties which may only be conducted under an agreement providing for management no less environmentally sound than is required under the Basel Convention. What is meant by "environmentally sound management" is defined in the Convention only in general terms:

> "taking all practicable steps to ensure that hazardous waste or other wastes are managed in a manner which will protect human health and the environment against the adverse effects which may result from such wastes".[229]

---

3. Wastes which, as a result of being radioactive, are subject to other international control systems, including international instruments, applying specifically to radioactive materials, are excluded from the scope of this Convention.

4. Wastes which derive from the normal operations of a ship, the discharge of which is covered by another international instrument, are excluded from the scope of this Convention."

Annex I lists a number of substances, including waste oils/water, hydrocarbous/Water mixtures and surface treatment of metals. Annex III lists hazardous characteristics, including explosive substances, flammable liquids and solids, and poisonous and infections substances. The Conference of Parties have by Decision IV/9 added two Annexes, Annex VIII and IX, containing, respectively, wastes characterized as hazardous and not hazardous under article 1 (1) (a).

[226] See Annex IV; referring both to operations which do not lead to the possibility of resource recovery and recycling (A) and operations which may lead to recovery and recycling (B).

[227] See in particular the clause in article 4, para.6 on the Antarctic region and para. 12 on the marine zones under the sovereignty or jurisdiction of coastal States of the Basel Convention.

[228] Article 4 Basel Convention.

[229] Article 2, para. 8 Basel Convention, equally the Bamako Convention article 1, para. 10.

This opens the possibility for further specifications through guidelines, such as the Cairo Guidelines and Principles of Environmentally Sound Management of Hazardous Wastes, 1985.[230] Although these Guidelines are not obligatory, their adoption by UNEP attaches persuasive force to them as a basic standard for States to meet in fulfilling their obligations under the Basel Convention.

The means of controlling the movement of hazardous waste is the mechanism of prior informed consent. The export of wastes into a State other than the state from which the wastes originated requires the prior, informed, written consent by the importing State and by the State of transit. This requirement can be seen as an expression of territorial sovereignty if transit is required over land territory or coastal waters or if the disposal of wastes in such areas is pursued. As far as transit through territorial waters is concerned, the rules of the UN Convention on the Law of the Sea on the freedom of navigation have to be taken into account. This means that coastal States may restrict the passage of ships carrying hazardous wastes by referring them to particular sea-lanes or requiring that they take particular safety measures. They may not, however, exclude the passage altogether.[231]

The obligations under the Bamako Convention reach farther. They ban the import of all hazardous wastes into Africa from non-Contracting Parties, whatever the reason. This gap between the two agreements has, to a certain extent, been closed. The Conference of Parties to the Basel Convention, by Resolution II/12, has limited transboundary movements from OECD States to non-OECD States of wastes destined for final disposal, and has established a phasing out of wastes meant for recycling or recovery operations. The Conference of Parties has also adopted the prohibition on the transboundary movement from OECD States to non-OECD States in Decision III/1, as an amendment to the Basel Convention.[232] This amendment has to be ratified by three-

[230] UNEP/WG.22/3, approved UNEP/GC.14/30 (1987).

[231] See article 21 and 22, para. 2 UNCLOS and the particular regulations of MARPOL 73/78 (note 74) on oil, noxious liquids and chemicals in bulk.

[232] Its paragraph 1 refers to operations which do not lead to recovery and recycling whereas paragraph 2 refers to operations aimed at recovery and recycling.

fourths of the Parties present at the time of the adoption of the amendment, which currently leads to the requirement of 62 ratifications.[233]

The Conference of Parties, by providing for an amendment of the Basel Convention, made it quite plain that Decision II/12, although formulated in mandatory terms, cannot be considered binding. At the most it might provide for a provisional application of the amendment. In particular, the reference to a date concerning the phasing out of recycling, at which point the amendment could not have entered into force, points in that direction.

Another difference between the two Conventions is the wider scope of the Bamako Convention, which includes both hazardous and household wastes. This difference, however, is not as significant as it may seem, particularly if one considers the practical relevance. The Bamako Convention has not been as widely ratified as the Basel Convention and, in particular, only few States Parties have issued the required legislation on the implementation of this Convention.

---

[233] As of 26 October 2001 27 States, including the European Community has ratified the Amendment. It reads in its relevant parts:

"Insert new preambular paragraph 7 bis:

Recognising that transboundary movements of hazardous wastes, especially to developing countries, have a high risk of not constituting an environmentally sound management of hazardous wastes as required by this Convention;

Insert new article 4A:

1. Each Party listed in Annex VII shall prohibit all transboundary movements of hazardous wastes which are destined for operations according to Annex IV A, to States not listed in Annex VII.
2. Each Party listed in Annex VII shall phase out by 31 December 1997, and prohibit as of that date, all transboundary movements of hazardous wastes under article 1 (i) (a) of the Convention which are destined for operations according to Annex IV B to States not listed in Annex VII. Such transboundary movement shall not be prohibited unless the wastes in question are characterised as hazardous under the Convention.

Annex VII

Parties and other States which are members of OECD, EC, Liechtenstein."

3. The Basel Convention and the Bamako Convention and Their Relationship with International Instruments Concerning Land-based Pollution and Dumping

As already indicated both the Basel and the Bamako Convention have some clauses referring directly or indirectly to the respective instruments against dumping or the pollution of the sea from land-based sources. The Bamako Convention is more explicit in this respect. The Basel Convention refers to the sovereignty States have over their territorial sea, the authority they can exercise in their exclusive economic zones and concerning their continental shelves. The convention stresses, however, that the freedom of navigation is to be respected. The Bamako Convention addresses the dumping at sea directly. The respective provision reads:

> "Parties in conformity with related international conventions and instruments shall, in the exercise of their jurisdiction within their territorial waters, waterways, territorial seas, exclusive economic zones and continental shelf, adopt legal, administrative and other appropriate measures to control all carriers from non-Parties, and prohibit the dumping at sea of hazardous wastes, including their incineration at sea and their disposal in the sea-bed and sub-seabed.
>
> Any dumping of hazardous wastes at sea, including incineration at sea as well as seabed and sub-seabed disposal, by Contracting Parties, whether in internal waters, waterways, territorial seas, exclusive economic zones or high seas shall be deemed to be illegal."

This provision clearly covers the same subject matter as the relevant Conventions against dumping. However, since these Conventions do not exclude the more strict standards upon which the Bamako Convention is based, no conflicts arise in respect of international instruments concerning the dumping of wastes at sea.

The situation is different in respect to the Basel Convention. The necessity to provide for some coordination between the Basel Convention and the regulation under MARPOL 73/78 was recognized as early as the Final Act of the Basel Conference,[234] although the full extent of potential overlap had not been fully anticipated.

The most sensitive issue is the transport of hazardous wastes. Article 4, para. 12 of the Basel Convention seems to leave unaffected the naviga-

---

[234] Resolution 5 invites UNEP and IMO to review the existing rules on transport of hazardous wastes.

tional rights in the exclusive economic zone, which in this respect is treated as the high sea. Maritime States have interpreted this to mean that prior notice or consent for passage of vessels carrying hazardous substances is not required, but not all coastal States seem to accept this view.[235] The Bamako Convention is somewhat clearer in this respect. It explicitly recognizes

> "the exercise by ships and aircraft of all States of navigation rights and freedoms as provided for in international law and as reflected in relevant international instruments."

International standards for the carriage of dangerous goods also govern some aspects of the transport of hazardous waste. The most important instrument on the carriage of dangerous goods is the MARPOL 73/78.[236] Some differences between the rules of MARPOL and the instruments concerning the transport of wastes exist. First, whereas Annexes II and III of MARPOL 73/78 are legally binding, the Cairo Guidelines are not. The regime under the Basel Convention goes further than the rules on dangerous goods by requiring that packaging, labeling and transport should conform to generally accepted rules and standards and take account of internationally recognized practices, whether or not these are otherwise obligatory.[237]

Concerning a relationship between the rules on dumping and waste management, there is considerable overlap between the respective rules. To a certain extent, the Basel Convention and the Bamako Convention cover the same ground as the London Convention. The same is true for some regional instruments. Generally, the overlapping scope of the respective agreements can result in reinforcement or conflict. As previously noted, the London Convention originally aimed for the restriction and control of dumping at sea while acknowledging that dumping had come to be considered one of the freedoms of the high seas. In recent years, the tendency toward phasing out dumping and incineration at sea prevailed.[238] The difference between the Basel Convention and the London Convention lies in the following point. The Basel Conven-

---

[235] See reservation of the United Kingdom to the Basel Convention, *Int'l & Comp. L. Q.* 39 (1990), 944 but see also the Note Verbale of Haiti of 18 February 1988, *LOSB* 11 (1988), 13.

[236] Annexes II and III; for reference see note 74.

[237] Article 4, para. 7, lit. (b); equally the Bamako Convention in article 4, para. 3.

[238] See above Part I B. III. 3. (c).

tion covers, and the same is true for the Bamako Convention, the transport of wastes from the State where it had been generated to another State. The London Convention, however, deals with wastes generated in the territory of a State party that are transported to and disposed of in the high seas. Accordingly, the two regimes are designed to supplement each other, although in practice this design suffers from noticeable gaps. After the adoption of the Basel Convention in 1989 the issue of the relationship between the Basel Convention and the London Convention was discussed intensively by the Consultative Meeting of the Contracting Parties to the London Convention and by the Ad Hoc Group of Legal Experts of IMO on Dumping.[239] Efforts were undertaken to coordinate the two regimes.

Although this is a prime example of institutionally initiated efforts aiming for coordination between the two regimes, divergences persist. The range of wastes covered by the Basel Convention and by the London Convention do not match completely. The Basel Convention deals only with hazardous wastes, while the London Convention embraces the dumping of wastes as such. Furthermore, a comparison of Annex I and II of the London Convention with Annex VIII of the Basel Convention reveals that they do not cover the same substances. However, due to the different activities addressed by the two conventions and their diverging objectives, a complete overlap of the covered substances could not be expected and may even be unnecessary.

The scope of activities covered by the Basel Convention also differs from that of the London Convention.[240] The Basel Convention attempts to limit the transboundary movement of wastes but it does not regulate the disposal of wastes directly. The London Convention, however, deals with the disposal and, although not directly, transport of the wastes. Overlap only results when wastes are transported by ship and accidentally dumped. [241]

---

[239] See Kummer (note 91), 183 with further details.

[240] See in particular Kummer, ibid at 184 et seq. Her assessment, however, is no longer correct due to the changes to the London Convention.

[241] Account has to be taken in this respect of the IMO regime on the transport of dangerous goods by sea. For a detailed introduction in this respect see C.E. Henry, *The Carriage of Dangerous Goods by Sea* (1985). The development of the International Maritime Dangerous Goods Code started in 1960 with the view to supplement the International Convention for the Safety of Life at Sea. Since its final adoption in 1965 the Code has undergone many changes. In 2000 the Maritime Safety Committee of IMO adopted a revised and reformatted In-

A further area of conflict exists. As mentioned before, both the Basel Convention and the London Convention deal with dumping or incineration at sea in the Antarctic region. The Basel Convention as well as the Bamako Convention and most of the other regional conventions previously discussed, prohibit any movement of hazardous wastes to Antarctica for the purpose of any form of disposal whether or not these wastes are subject to transboundary movement as defined by the Convention. The same is true under the Antarctic regime, since any transportation of wastes into the Antarctic treaty area is to be considered a violation of the Protocol to the Antarctic Treaty on Environmental Protection. Therefore, although various treaty regimes cover the same subject matter they come to the same result. The conflict among the regimes is, in this respect, more theoretical than real.

There is finally some overlap between the regime under the Basel Convention and the regime on the control of land-based pollution of the sea. Article 207 UNCLOS sets out a number of general obligations with respect to land-based pollution of the sea.[242] They include the obligation on the part of States to endeavor to establish global and regional rules, standards and recommended practices and procedures. The existing treaties in this field are all regional, including: (1) the Athens Protocol for the Protection of the Mediterranean Sea against Pollution from Land-Based Sources, 1980;[243] (2) the Quito Protocol for the Protection of the South-East Pacific Against Pollution from Land-Based Sources, 1983;[244] (3) the Kuwait Protocol Concerning Pollution from Land-based Sources, 1990;[245] (4) the Helsinki Convention, 1992;[246] (5) the Bucharest Protocol on Protection of the Black Sea Marine Environment against Land-Based Pollution, 1992;[247] (6) the OSPAR Con-

---

ternational Maritime Dangerous Goods Code. Further, it was decided to make sections of the Code mandatory aiming at an entry into force date of 1 January 2004.

[242] See above Part I C. III. 4.

[243] *ILM* 19 (1980), 869 et seq.

[244] Text reproduced in: *International Environmental Law: Multilateral Treaties* (W. Burhenne (ed.)), 983: 54.

[245] Treaty text accessible at <http://www.sedac.ciesin.org/pidb/texts/pollution.land-based.south-east.pacific.1983.html>; last visited 23 January 2002.

[246] See above note 18.

[247] Treaty text accessible at <http://www.sedac.ciesin.org/pidb/texts//acrc/BlackSeaLBP.txt.html>; last visited 23 January 2002.

vention, 1992;[248] and (7) the Mediterranean Hazardous Wastes Protocol.[249]

Overlap and potential conflicts between the Basel Convention and the OSPAR Convention may exist. The OSPAR Convention deals with pollution from land, including transboundary pollution.

It does not, strictly speaking, prohibit transboundary pollution. This is in line with article 2, paragraph 1 (a) of the OSPAR-Convention, according to which Contracting Parties are obliged to "... take all possible steps to prevent and eliminate pollution ..." This obligation is reiterated in article 3 of the OSPAR-Convention. Art. 21 OSPAR-Convention does not strengthen the obligation under article 2, 3 and 5, but rather establishes procedural rights for neighboring countries in the case of transboundary pollution.

Annex I to the OSPAR-Convention gives further details as to how the prohibition of pollution of the sea from land based sources is to be implemented. For example, States Parties are required to use the best available techniques for point sources and the best environmental practices for diffuse sources. Apart from that, Annex I requires States Parties to establish an authorization system for point sources.

Technically, there is the possibility for overlap with the Basel Convention. However, it is minimal. It is very doubtful that the pollution of the sea from land-based sources can be considered a "transfrontier movement of hazardous wastes" in the meaning of article 2 of the Basel Convention. This notion implies some measure of intent which cannot be considered to be inherent to the pollution generally resulting from land-based sources. Such interpretation is based upon article 4 of the Basel Convention, which speaks of export and import of wastes.

Annex II of the OSPAR Convention deals with dumping. Here again, the possibility for conflict with the Basel Convention exists. It is, however, not particularly relevant, because the scope of activities covered by the respective instruments differs.

Finally, account has to be taken of article 4, paragraph 12 of the Basel Convention, which may be read as to give priority to international treaty law tailored to provide for regulations concerning maritime activities.

---

[248] See above note 18.

[249] See T. Scovazzi/ W.R. Sheate, "The Mediterranean Hazardous Wastes Protocol", *Euro. Env. L. R.* 6 (1997), 244 et seq.

The main reason why possible overlap and conflicts between the Basel Convention and international agreements concerning the prohibition of land based pollution are of little relevance rests in the different approaches upon which the two regimes are based. The treaty regimes on pollution from land-based sources do not address the transport of wastes to the site of disposal whereas the Basel Convention focuses thereon. The Basel Convention, instead, is rather unspecific with respect to the disposal of wastes after they have reached their final destination. The rule that the disposal should be carried out in an environmentally sound manner merely formulates a principle rather than a rule meant for direct application. Accordingly, the regimes on pollution from land-based sources and the Basel Convention should be considered complementary since they focus on different aspects of the same activity.

4. Conclusions

An assessment of the various regimes concerned with the management of wastes, including their transport, reveals that there is a distinct proliferation of international instruments. These instruments may be separated into two groups, one dealing with the transport of wastes the other with their disposal, including incineration. There is some overlap within each of these groups and among these groups. This overlap is of a limited relevance in practice. All the respective instruments are designed as framework agreements. In that respect they are comparable with the Convention on the Law of the Sea. Further specification through other international agreements, protocols and, as an innovation, non-binding guidelines, is possible. Given the generality of many frameworks, such specification is necessary. This provides for a flexible system that can easily be adapted to technical innovations or new insights or requirements, including the coordination with other instruments. Furthermore, the instruments to which reference has been made do not differ significantly as far as their objective is concerned. They all strive for the minimization of the disposal of wastes even by restricting their transport. Finally, the attempts by the institutions charged with administering certain instruments to address overlaps or conflicts should be noted. This practice, however, needs broadening and strengthening.

V. Disposal of Disused Offshore Installations

1. Introduction

Occasionally it is reported that disused offshore installations or other structures have been dumped in the sea to improve the living or spawning conditions for fish or the growth of corals. Despite these intentions, the dumping of such installations or structures runs counter the overall tendency to curtail or abolish dumping. Therefore another interesting, albeit limited, area exists in which different treaty-based objectives related to the marine environment may collide. The disposal of offshore installations in the sea to improve certain aspects of the marine environment is neither envisaged by article 60 UNCLOS nor is it fully reflected in the offshore Installation Guidelines of the Assembly of the IMO.[250] The respective Decision of the Ministerial Meeting of the OSPAR-Commission[251] and the specific Guidelines for Assessment of Platforms or Other Man-Made Structures at Sea of the 19th Consultative Meeting of the Contracting Parties to the London Convention[252] are more balanced in this respect. They may, however, raise a different problem.

2. The Approach Taken by the IMO, under OSPAR and under the London Convention

According to article 60 UNCLOS, installations which are abandoned or no longer in use shall be removed to ensure safety of navigation. The IMO is called upon in this article to develop relevant standards. Such removals shall have due regard for fishing and the protection of the marine environment. The Guidelines of the IMO give further substance to these principles, proceeding from the premise that abandoned or offshore installations are to be removed to and disposed of on land. At sea leaving the installations or only partially removing them is the exception which, accordingly, requires a specific justification. The IMO Guidelines do not provide for the dumping of installations or structures

---

[250] Resolution A. 672 (16), 19 October 1989.

[251] Summary Record OSPAR 98/14/1-E, Annex 33.It has to be noted that in 1999 OSPAR has developed Guidelines on Artificial Reefs in Relation to Marine Living Resources. They have to be taken into account, too.

[252] Adopted in 1997.

for the benefit of marine life. This is due to the mandate of the IMO, which is limited to the safety of ships and of navigation.

The OSPAR Decision is somewhat different although it also prohibits the dumping as well as the abandonment of unused offshore installations or parts thereof.[253] It opens the possibility, however, of dumping such installations if it is permitted and accordingly controlled by the competent national authority. This exception only applies to structures having the particular design described in Annex I and it is available only after the positive and the negative aspects of the various forms of decommissioning have been properly assessed.[254] The OSPAR Decision is based upon the application of the principles of proportionality and it also invokes the precautionary principle. The application of the latter results in a preference being given to the options of reuse, recycling or finally disposed of offshore structures on land.

The Guidelines under the London Dumping Convention are more flexible in that respect, although they emphasize the policy of Annex 2 of the 1996 Protocol of the London Convention, which seeks to progressively reduce the need to use the sea for the dumping of wastes. This instrument has also invoked the precautionary approach. However, these Guidelines allow consideration of the positive aspects dumping may have.[255] Thus, in particular circumstances, the overall policy to reduce dumping may yield to environmental considerations concerning marine habitat improvement.

Under the OSPAR-Convention as well as under the London Dumping Convention, the placement of decommissioned platforms and installation is possible as long as such placement serves a purpose other than mere dumping.[256] The main difference between the two instruments is that placement under the OSPAR Convention requires authorization whereas the London Convention does not.

---

[253] Summary Record (note 251), para. 2.

[254] See Annex II.

[255] Para. 7.6.

[256] Article 1, lit. (g) (ii) OSPAR-Convention; article II, para. 1, lit. (b) (ii) London Convention. Both Conventions do not consider activities as dumping, if the placements are done "for a purpose other than the mere disposal." The same applies to the Protocol of 1996 to the London Convention (article 1, para. 4 (2)).

3. Conclusions

This limited example demonstrates that conflicts concerning various environmental objectives may exist or develop. A settlement has, however, been achieved within the institutional framework of the said instruments. This was made possible by the fact that the Meeting of States Parties to the Convention on Biological Diversity was not called upon to formulate a position on this issue. Had it been required to do so, it might have more forcefully advocated the position that dumping enhances the conditions for marine life. The overlap or even conflict between these instruments can only be solved by invoking the *lex specialis* rule. The Contracting Parties of the OSPAR Convention are bound by the rules of the convention and those rules developed under its mandate. However, this does not absolve them from implementing the IMO-Guidelines.

VI. The Recycling of Ships

1. Introduction

The life span of ships is limited raising questions about the disposal of unused ships. At least theoretically several options for the disposal or recycling of ships exist: (1) Laying up; (2) conversion to floating off-shore storage and/or production units; (3) disposal in ships-graveyards; (4) use as jetties, breakwaters or artificial reefs (similar to decommissioned off-shore installations); and (5) some means of recycling. Of these different options, in practice only the last (recycling) is realistic.

Ships which no longer meet the respective safety standards or standards for an environmentally safe operation constitute a permanent risk to the marine environment. Accordingly, the decommissioning of substandard ships should be promoted. As a consequence, regulations concerning the decommissioning of ships should be assessed from this point of view. This applies, even if it means choosing between two potentially environmentally harmful options: the decommissioning of ships on the one hand, which can involve environmental hazards from the dismantling and (partial) disposal of ships, and the continuing operation of a substandard ship on the other hand. If a regulation restricts the decommissioning of substandard ships because of the alleged negative environmental impacts resulting from its being decommissioned, this may result in keeping substandard ships in use. In this case the negative impact on the marine environment from accidents may be much worse than the environmental risk from decommissioning. In any case there is, from the point of view of sound environmental policy, a strong interest in the decommissioning of ships in an environmentally friendly manner. Technical guidelines on this issue are a necessity.[257]

The decommissioning of ships must conform to international environmental standards as well as to national ones. Non-conformity with international standards is particularly relevant in regard to: (1) the use of decommissioned ships as temporary jetties, breakwaters or artificial reefs; and (2) their deposit in ships-graveyards is intended. Such an approach may not be in conformity with international environmental law, since such a disposal and use of shipwrecks is most likely to create permanent environmental hazards. This applies in particular if hazardous substances and materials are still contained in the wrecks. The potentially beneficial influence that man-made structures, used as artificial reefs, may have on the marine environment, e.g. as spawning grounds, can also be discussed in this context. In this respect, a discussion would follow the lines of the debate over the problem of dumping of installations which was discussed above and which favors a tendency to avoid any kind of dumping of installations or other wastes.

The question regarding which international environmental rules govern the decommissioning of ships, strictly speaking, does not fit into the frame of this study. This is not a question of conflicts between different international environmental regulations but rather the problem whether and to what extent international environmental law covers this aspect of shipping.

2. *Does the Basel Convention Cover the Recycling of Ships?*

It has been argued that the Basel Convention on the Transboundary Movement of Hazardous Wastes and their Disposal contains regulations which are of relevance for the recycling of ships, or, more accu-

---

[257] The Technical Working Group of the Basel Convention (TWG) has recently been working on the elaboration of such guidelines, see, e.g. the presession documents to the meeting in January, 2002, in which a draft of revised Technical Guidelines on Environmentally Sound Management for Full and Partial Dismantling of Ships, Doc. UNEP/CHW/TWG/19/7, was approved and shall be sent to the next Conference of the Parties to the Basel Convention in December, 2002. Furthermore, a Code of Industry Practice on Ship Recycling was agreed upon in August, 2001. This code of practice is reprinted in Doc. UNEP/CHW/TWG/19/INF/4.

rately, for the sailing of ships to harbors for recycling.[258] As has been indicated above, the notion of "wastes" as used in the Basel Convention is quite broad and would not generally preclude the interpretation that ships could themselves be "waste" under certain circumstances. The Basel Convention also covers the export of material for recycling. Nevertheless, it is clear that the deliberations of the Basel Convention originally did not actually consider ships themselves as wastes and, what is more important, that the Basel Convention itself has so far not appropriately addressed problems of disposal and recycling of abandoned ships.

The latest developments, however, demonstrate at least a strong interest on the part of the Technical Working Group as well as the Legal Working Group of the Basel Convention to engage in the creation of regulations for the environmentally-sound management of the partial or full dismantling of ships.[259] In the following section the findings of the Legal Working Group are considered relevant for the evaluation of potential conflicts between the Basel Convention and other treaties concerned with the dismantling of ships, although the views expressed are not necessarily shared by the authors of this study. The technical guidelines of the TWG are less important for the legal evaluation of the issue.[260] In a legal assessment of the issue it is particularly important to examine the findings of the Legal Working Group when confronting the task of determining whether the vessel can be considered "waste." This is also true with respect to determining whether the sailing of a ship constitutes the "transboundary movement" or "transfrontier shipment" of wastes and which State is the "State of export" with respect to vessels destined for dismantling.

[258] As has been pointed out earlier, the Basel Convention regulates the export of wastes. The Conference of Parties has prohibited the export of wastes from OECD-countries to non-OECD countries. It has further decided on a respective amendment to the Basel Convention albeit with a slightly different scope of application.

[259] See the documents mentioned above in note 257 as well as Doc. UNEP/CHW/LWG/4/4 on the legal aspects of the dismantling of ships and Doc. UNEP/TWG/LWG/1/INF/3 issued on the occasion of the first joint meeting of the Technical and the Legal Working Group to the Basel Convention.

[260] The Legal Working Group in Doc. UNPE/CHW/LWG/4/4 relies upon a paper written by G. Ulfstein, presented by Norway in 1999, which is now contained in the annex to the decision.

(a) The Consideration of Vessels as Wastes

The definition of wastes as established by the Basel Convention does not quite fit when applied in relation to ships. The definition clearly was not meant to cover disused vessels and vessels sailing to a destination where they shall be dismantled. Because of the complex nature of a ship one has to distinguish whether the ship as such is abandoned and therefore to be completely disposed of, or whether only parts of the ship shall be dismantled and potentially reused, e.g. fuel oils or metal parts, while the rest of the vessel is intended for repairs and continued sailing. In the latter case clearly only the dismantled parts and not the vessel as such must be considered wastes.

The main problem with the definition of wastes is the subjective intent to dispose of an object. According to the respective definition, this intention is necessary. It is possible to argue that, as long as a ship is engaged in transport, fishing or other legal activity under the Convention on the Law of the Sea, there is no reasonable basis for any claimed intent to dispose of the ship. As a consequence, it would not be considered waste under the Basel Convention.[261] Since the intention to dispose of a ship is difficult to discover, particularly, if the vessel still engages in the transportation of cargo, it might be better to favor the view that a ship constitutes waste only if it is sent to another State for the sale purpose of being dismantled there. However, even in this case, account must be taken of the fact that such sailing vessels, are still ships entitled to, enjoy the right of freedom of navigation. Therefore, considering such ships to be wastes, the export of which can be significantly restricted under the rules of the Basel Convention, would not be in conformity with article 90 UNCLOS since this provision refers to the movement of ships under the "freedom of navigation" without specifying the purposes for which movement may or may not be pursued. Here, account has to be taken of article 4, para. 12 of the Basel Convention which ensures that the Basel Convention does not infringe upon the jurisdictional rights of coastal States in respect to the exclusive

[261] Ulfstein in the Annex to Doc. UNPE/CHW/LWG/4/4 argues a bit differently. He states that, despite the fact that a ship is still engaged in transport of cargo on its way to the port where the dismantling shall take place, it must already be considered waste, because at that point in time its disposal is intended. If the decision has, however, only been taken to dismantle in some distant future and meanwhile the vessel engages in transport activities, it cannot yet be considered waste.

economic zones, the continental shelves and the sovereign rights concerning coastal waters and the rights and duties concerning navigation.

(b) The Responsibilities of the State of Export

Another problem arises from the question, which State shall be considered the State of export according to the Basel Convention. This question also has implications with regard to article 90 UNCLOS. The freedom of navigation is formulated as the right of the State whose flag the respective ship is entitled to fly. Therefore, in general and with exceptions, e.g. concerning a lack of seaworthiness and hazards of pollution of the marine environment, only the flag State may limit the freedom of navigation of its vessels. However, the flag State cannot necessarily be considered as the exporting State as referred to in the Basel Convention.[262] As a consequence, if a port State wishes to restrict the sailing of a vessel destined for dismantling, e.g. because it is sailing to a non-OECD country, it does not have jurisdiction to do so under the UN Convention on the Law of the Sea. It cannot be argued that flag States that are States parties to the Basel Convention have, by agreeing to the Basel Convention, also agreed to permit interference with its vessels by port States. This conclusion follows from article 4, para. 12 Basel Convention which states that there shall not be interference with the exercise of navigational rights and freedoms.

In general, the port State from which the vessel departs for the destination where it shall be dismantled must be considered the State of export. This State, and not the flag State, would be responsible for obtaining the necessary consent from the State of destination and potential transit States. At the same time, as explained above, this State cannot hinder a ship flying under the flag of another State to leave its ports in order to sail to another State for its dismantling. It follows that, for a ship proceeding from the State A and being under the flag of State B, the State of export would be State A. But State A does not have, according to the

[262] See article 1, paragraph 10: "State of export" means a Party from which a transboundary movement of hazardous wastes or other wastes is planned to be initiated or is initiated: "This means that the State of export is the State from which the transboundary movement; i.e. the physical action of moving the waste starts or is planned to start. Otherwise the obligation that the waste must be taken back does not make sense.

Convention on the Law of the Sea, any possibility to stop that ship from leaving its ports, provided it is seaworthy.[263]

This problem can either be overcome by amending the Convention on the Law of the Sea to modify the powers of the port States or by amending the Basel Convention to redefine the concept of "State of export" so as to also include the flag State. However, port States have little information about foreign vessels and also little incentive to regulate their activities.[264] At present, only those port States which are at the same time the respective flag State of a ship could prevent it from sailing to another State's ports for recycling. This example may suffice to demonstrate that the Basel Convention is not yet fully designed to deal with ships on their voyage to recycling. A further possibility to deal with the issue might be to introduce more objective criteria into the Basel Convention regarding when and under what circumstances a vessel may be considered waste.

3. Conclusions

It has been argued that ships ready for decommissioning or recycling may be considered waste. Accordingly, their sailing to the shipyard for dismantling should in the absence of specific rules that more viably address the issue be considered an export of waste restricted if not prohibited under the Basel Convention. It has been stated, however, that the recycling of ships has its merits, especially from the perspective of the protection of the marine environment. This is particularly true if the principle of sustainable development is taken into account. In contrast thereto, some parts of either the ship itself or substances resulting from the operation of the ship, e.g. residual oil, acid from batteries and asbestos, must be considered hazardous wastes posing potentially serious environmental problems when the ship is dismantled.[265] The question

---

[263] Otherwise article 219 UNCLOS would apply. It is not possible to base the respective powers of the port State upon article 211 UNCLOS. This provision deals with pollution of the sea from vessels. This means, taking into consideration the drafting history of that provision, pollution from the ship's routine. This would not cover pollution from the prospected dismantling of a ship.

[264] Doc. UNEP/CHW/LWG/4/4.

[265] Oil residues from the normal operation of ships do not come under the Basel Convention, they are excluded by virtue of article 1, paragraph 4, of the Basel Convention from its scope of application, because they are covered by the MARROL Convention.

whether some parts of ships must be considered hazardous wastes must, however, be separated from the question when and under what circumstances a ship must itself be considered waste and, particularly, which legal rules apply in this context.

The use of the Basel Convention for restricting ships to sail for recycling yards has been discussed. Even if it is assumed that ships themselves, in contrast to only some material contained in the vessels, constituted wastes, once the intention for their disposal is demonstrated, the application of the Basel Convention would not necessarily contribute to any amelioration of the environmental risks resulting from the dismantling of ships. It would only cover ships if they sailed from an OECD country under the flag of an OECD country to a shipyard of a non-OECD country and if such ships were not carrying any cargo. Otherwise, the current rules of the UN Convention on the Law of the Sea on the freedom of navigation and the respective authority of flag States cannot be overcome.

It seems to be more promising to design new rules and regulations concerning the recycling of ships which clarify the relation between the UN Convention on the Law of the Sea and the Basel Convention. In particular, new regulations must also take into consideration the health of workers engaged in dismantling ships, along with the marine and terrestrial environment of the State where such dismantling takes place. However, the whole issue should not only be seen from the point of view of the dismantling process. It would be preferential if these considerations would lead to a reconsideration of the construction and outfitting of ships. The construction and outfitting of ships should ensure that materials are avoided that pose environmental risks if and when the respective ship will be dismantled. This issue comes under the mandate of the IMO.

Part II

Approaches to the Coordination of International Environmental Agreements

A. Introduction to the Coordination of International Agreements

(Matz)

Two different approaches to the coordination of environmental agreements can generally be distinguished: (1) the employment of the mechanisms of the law of treaties; and (2) mechanisms based upon structures of environmental governance, i.e. mainly mechanisms of institutional cooperation. The approaches do not necessarily exclude one another. The two approaches might actually supplement each other, depending upon their scope and their ability to address the problems discussed in Part I. The scope and viability of these approaches, as well as their respective mechanisms, are the focus of the second Part of this study.

Structures of institutional cooperation to coordinate international environmental law have lately received increasing attention from the institutions involved, e.g. by UNEP, but also from scholars and practitioners. An important feature in this regard is the creation of organs by international environmental agreements. The formation of organs and subsidiary bodies by international environmental agreements causes modern environmental treaties to resemble international organizations; it also facilitates cooperation with States, other treaties and international organizations. Many new or emerging structures and mechanisms of institutional cooperation involve treaty organs such as Secretariats, Conferences of the Parties or subsidiary bodies.

In general, mechanisms of environmental governance are political rather than legal tools. Nevertheless, governance clearly has legal implications, concerning, e.g. the law of cooperation or the law of international organizations. Governance mechanisms for the coordination of international agreements that are based upon institutional cooperation differ fundamentally from those provided for by the law of treaties. Distinctions between the mechanisms concern their respective functions as well as their ability to address the issue. Some of the regulations of the law of treaties address conflicts between and the priority to be given to parallel treaty regulations. For this reason the law of treaties seems capable of contributing to the coordination of colliding international agreements. An in-depth analysis, however, reveals significant functional shortcomings.

B. Conflict Clauses in International Environmental Agreements

(Wolfrum/Matz)

I. The Purpose of Conflict Clauses: an Introduction

The starting point for a discussion of the reliance upon the law of treaties as a solution to treaty conflicts is the principle that there is no hierarchy of treaties in international law. In contrast to the different forms of national legislation, e.g. Executive orders, Parliamentary acts and the constitution, all treaties exist as self-contained entities, generally enjoying equal validity in international law.[266] However, the States Parties to an agreement can regulate the relation between one particular treaty and other international agreements. In fact, most modern agreements contain a provision, a so-called conflict clause, that regulates the agreement's relationship with other international conventions. Since the conflict clause only regulates which obligations of a State party prevail in regard to another State, such a practice does not establish a general

[266] The only potential exception to this rule is the UN Charter. However, whether the Charter actually is a higher-ranking agreement due to its Article 103 or its constitutional character (or both factors), is subject to controversial discussion. The issue is of little relevance concerning the discussion of international environmental agreements. As to the effects of Article 103 UN-Charter see e.g. K. Ipsen/ W. Heintschel von Heinegg, *Völkerrecht* (1999), chapter 3, § 12, para. 18, S. Kadelbach, *Zwingendes Völkerrecht* (1992), 28; T. Meron, "On a Hierarchy of International Human Rights", *AJIL* 80 (1986), 1 et seq. (13); G.E. do Nascimento e Silva, "Le Facteur Temps et les Traités", *RdC* 54 (1977, I), 242; Jenks (note 10), 401 et seq.

hierarchy of treaties, in which a treaty is ranked according to its nature or content. These clauses may serve different purposes. Generally they are meant to avoid that treaties covering similar or at least partially overlapping subject matters contradict each other. Therefore their primary objective is the safeguarding of a general coherence of international law.

However, such clauses may equally serve more particular purposes. If an agreement is considered comprehensive such conflict clauses are designed to ensure that the overriding principles of the comprehensive treaty will prevail or – in other words – not be derogated by more specific international agreements. Conflict clauses are common if an agreement refers to a previous one. In this case such clause may be in protection of grand father rights. A different objective is pursued if a comprehensive treaty refers to later, more specify ones. In this case it is the objective of the respective clause to leave room for future legal developments. This is particularly the case for treaties designed as an umbrella or framework agreement where subsequent agreements are meant to fill in this framework. While the implementing agreement formally remains a self contained entity, its content is closely tied to the framework to which it contributes. The UN Convention on the Law of the Sea is a particularly good example of a framework convention that employs implementing agreements to specify its content and regulate certain issues more comprehensively. For example, article 211, paragraph 1 UNCLOS calls upon States to establish international rules and standards to prevent, reduce and control pollution of the marine environment. Such rules necessarily supplement the UN Convention on the Law of the Sea and must conform to the latter. This relationship is clarified by clauses contained in the implementing agreements.[267]

---

[267] See e.g. article 4 of the 1995 Fish Stocks Agreement, see above note 36, which reads: "Nothing in this Agreement shall prejudice the rights, jurisdiction and duties of States under the Convention [on the Law of the Sea]. This Agreement shall be interpreted and applied in the context of and in a manner consistent with the Convention [on the Law of the Sea]." In contrast to such a potential hierarchy between the Convention on the Law of the Sea and implementing agreements, other agreements lacking a framework character explicitly state that a hierarchy between those treaties considered mutually supportive and the referring agreement shall not be established. An example of such an explicit denial of a hierarchy can be found in the preamble of the Rotterdam Convention on the Prior Informed Consent Procedure for Certain Hazardous Chemicals and Pesticides in International Trade, *ILM* 38 (1999), 1 et seq.

While conflict clauses in international agreements have in common the fact that they were negotiated to clarify the relationship between the respective treaty and other instruments of international law, their wording and scope can differ significantly. Conflict clauses in international environmental agreements are the first means to be invoked in order to establish which treaty prevails in respect to which State. Only if the interpretation and application of conflict clauses does not clarify the relationship between two colliding agreements, are the provisions of the Vienna Convention on the Law of Treaties[268] invoked in an attempt to settle conflicts between treaties.

II. The Formulation of Conflict Clauses in Environmental Agreements

Different categories concerning the content and scope of conflict clauses must be distinguished. Generally, six different options concerning the regulation of the relationship of a treaty with other treaties are possible: (1) no provision in the agreement;[269] (2) preambular language; (3) clauses providing for the suppression of the referring agreement in the body of the treaty; (4) specific savings clauses that provide for the prevalence of existing treaties in the body of the agreement; (5) general savings clauses in the body of the agreement; and (6) qualified savings clauses.

Conflict clauses, so called savings or without-prejudice clauses, might provide that the existing rights and obligations of States arising out of other international agreements take priority. This is the most common kind of conflict clause. If contained in the preambular paragraphs a common formulation of such clauses provides that existing rules and the referring treaty shall be mutually supportive.[270] It is more difficult

---

[268] See above note 5.

[269] This is, for example, the case concerning the Framework Convention on Climate Change and its Kyoto Protocol. In this case the next step would be to invoke he rules of the Vienna Convention on the Law of Treaties in an attempt to settle conflicts.

[270] The latter formulation has, for example, been used in the preamble of the Cartagena Protocol on Biosafety to the CBD, *ILM* 39 (2000), 1027 et seq., in regard to trade and environment agreements and in the preamble of the Stockholm Convention on Persistent Organic Pollutants, *ILM* 40 (2001), 532 et seq.

to assess the scope of suppression clauses, which not only establish the priority of the new agreement over existing but also over future agreements. The greatest difficulty with such clauses is that they attempt to restrict States' sovereignty in their treaty-making capacity in future negotiations.

1. Clauses that Provide for the Preference of Existing Treaties

Depending upon their exact wording clauses that provide for the priority of "existing" or "previous" treaties are sometimes difficult to apply. They do not always clearly distinguish the varying scope of the respective international agreements. Consequently, they cannot necessarily help to prevent or solve conflicts between provisions of different treaties.

(a) Differences Concerning the Scope of Clauses

Usually the regulation that establishes the priority of existing rights and obligations is rather general. Examples of a specific reference in one international agreement to another, providing that the rules of the latter shall prevail, are rare. Article 22, para. 1 CBD, for example, refers to existing rights and obligations of the contracting Parties, without referring to any particular treaties. A bit more specific is the example of the Environmental Protocol to the Antarctic Treaty. According to the Final Act of the Eleventh Antarctic Treaty Special Consultative Meeting nothing in the Protocol on Environmental Protection shall derogate from the rights and obligations of Parties under the Convention on the Conservation of Antarctic Marine Living Resources, the Convention for the Conservation of Antarctic Seals and the International Convention for the regulation of Whaling. This clause is meant to establish that the rights and obligations of States Parties under these Conventions are not prejudiced. Although this clause seems to achieve some form of coordination amongst the respective treaties, its meaning is far from clear.

Certainly, particular rights such as the right to hunt whales or to engage in fishing are not curtailed by the Protocol on Environmental Protection. However, it is questionable whether the Protocol embraces activities that go beyond those permitted by these Conventions, e.g. fishing out of season. Would this be a violation not only of the Convention on the Conservation of Antarctic Marine Living Resources but also of the Protocol? The answer must be negative. This clause aims to establish areas of competence. Fishing, whether legal or illegal under the Convention for the Conservation of Antarctic Marine Living Resources, is to be dealt with under this Convention and not under the Protocol.

A similar specific, without-prejudice clause can be found in article 1, para. 4 of the Basel Convention.[271] It provides that wastes which derive from the normal operation of ships are not covered by the Basel Convention. This clause is meant to separate the scope of the Basel Convention from the one of MARPOL 73/78. It is the disadvantage of this type of clauses that they can disrupt a substantive unity. Violations of the Convention for the Conservation of Antarctic Marine Living Resources as well as violations of the Protocol on Environmental Protection, to make use of the international agreements to which reference has been made, equally constitute violations of the Antarctic marine ecosystem and should be treated under the same regime.

Another example of a clause that states that rights and obligations in previous international agreements prevail is article 3 of Annex IV of the Environmental Protocol to the Antarctic Treaty.[272] This is an example of a specific reference to another agreement. Article 3 of Annex II provides that any discharges of oil into the sea shall be prohibited except in cases permitted under Annex I of MARPOL 73/78. In fact, this provision ensures that, as far as exemptions are concerned, there will be no discrepancy between Annex IV (of Environmental Protocol to the Antarctic Treaty) and MARPOL 73/78.[273] The possibility of a legal conflict is excluded. However, there is a price for that harmonization. If the Antarctic Treaty Consultative Parties were of the view that the respective rule of MARPOL 73/78 were inappropriate, and given the climate conditions in the Antarctic that is not a totally unrealistic scenario, they would have to change Annex IV.

Sometimes general savings clauses which on first sight, provide for the priority of existing treaties, contain a qualification that can in fact reverse the result of the application of the clause. Such qualifications can make the application of conflict clauses and their capacity to clarify fields of competence even more obscure. Article 22, para. 1 CBD[274] is an example because it establishes the priority of existing rights and obligations only in so far as their exercise does not pose the risk of serious

---

[271] See above note 136.

[272] See above note 17.

[273] See above note 74.

[274] See above note 16.

damage or threat to biological diversity. In other words this clause provides that all instruments, the exercise of which poses a risk of a serious threat to biological diversity, shall be inferior to the exercise of the Convention on Biological Diversity. Only those that do not seriously harm biological diversity shall prevail. The interpretation of this clause furthermore faces difficulties, since there are no criteria as to when the exercise of rights and obligations poses a serious threat to biological diversity. It is doubtful that this clause can prevent or solve conflicts.

Another difficulty with respect to article 22 CBD is its second paragraph, which contains a specific savings clause. The provision establishes the superiority of the rights and obligations based in the law of the sea, i.e. mainly (though not exclusively) the UN Convention on the Law of the Sea. However, establishing the superiority of "rights and obligations" necessarily neglects more general elements of the UN Convention on the Law of the Sea and the broader law of the sea, including those provisions that do not constitute rights and obligations but reflect approaches, principles and organizational matters. A broad interpretation of the provision i.e. one that would establish prejudice of the law of the sea in general over the Convention on Biological Diversity, does not take into account that a more clearly worded phrase could have easily been chosen to reach this objective and that the regime on biological resources under the law of the sea could then not be supplemented and reinforced by the Convention on Biological Diversity. This difficulty demonstrates the necessity of precisely formulating clauses that do not leave room for interpretation. Otherwise the objective of conflict clauses, to establish competences and prevent conflicts, cannot be met.

As a consequence of the unclear wording of article 22, para. 2 CBD the relationship between the two agreements is far from being settled. This also becomes apparent, when considering article 311 UNCLOS. This is a particularly far-reaching example of a conflict clause. The conclusions that must be drawn from the application of article 311 UNCLOS, the conflict clause of the UN Convention on the Law of the Sea in its relation to the Convention on Biological Diversity, is that the two clauses are not fully compatible.[275] Consequently, the relation between the two conventions cannot be solved by merely referring to the respective conflict provisions in the agreements.

---

[275] Wolfrum/ Matz (note 22), 477.

(b) When Does an Instrument Exist?

The main difficulty concerning general clauses is to establish which rights and obligations of States stem from "existing" instruments. When does an obligation that is rooted in an international treaty come into existence?[276] To establish the existence of international treaties or the existence of obligations for a specific State, it is possible to rely upon the time of the adoption of an instrument, the time of the signature of the respective State, or the time of the ratification or the entry into force of the treaty. While the adoption of an instrument does not establish any rights and obligations for later States parties, the signature does in so far as States may no longer engage in activities that run counter the object and purpose of a treaty (article 18 VCLT). However, this duty differs from the specific rights and obligations owed by the States parties once an instrument that they have ratified enters into force or once they accede to an agreement that had previously entered into force. Specific rights and obligations, which may be in conflict with one another, are only fully applicable after an instrument enters into force. The date of the entry into force or, if States accede the date of accession, specifies the time at which rights and obligations for a State exist.

The timing of the entry into force of an agreement depends, however, to some extent on coincidence, particularly if agreements are negotiated within the same timeframe. In the case of the Convention on Biological Diversity and the Framework Convention on Climate Change, the coincidental nature of the date of the entry into force of the conventions becomes apparent. Both were opened for signature on the same date, however, the Convention on Biological Diversity entered into force on 29 December 1993 and the Framework Convention on Climate Change on 21 March 1994. As this example shows, the inclusion of a conflict clause that provides for the priority of existing treaties is not necessarily based upon considerations of how different treaties can best be brought into harmony. As a consequence the application of conflict clauses, even if they are simple "without-prejudice" clauses, leads to difficulties. Maybe in future treaty negotiations reference to existing instruments should be specified, e.g. by referring to treaties that are in force at the time of the entry into force of the referring agreement. In any case special attention must be given to the difficulties of interpretation raised in this context.

---

[276] This question is similar to that raised in regard to a *lex posterior* rule, because in this context, again, one has to establish when an agreement came into existence, i.e. which one is the older and which is the later agreement.

2. *Clauses that Provide for an Agreement's Priority over Existing and Future Agreements*

Treaties that provide for their priority over existing treaties and, particularly, over future agreements, are even more problematic. It is an expression of the progressive development of law if a clause establishes the priority of a newly negotiated treaty over conflicting prior treaties. This process permits particularly in international environmental law, environmental protection to evolve and develop along with scientific insights as well as the paradigms on how and to what extent environmental protection should be pursued develop. In this regard, a clause that provides for the priority of the latest agreement in time clarifies the relationship between colliding new and older treaties on related issues. An example of such a suppression clause is contained in article 11 of the International Convention on Civil Liability for Bunker Oil Pollution Damage, 2001, and article 42 of the International Convention on Liability and Compensation for Damage in Connection with the Carriage of Hazardous and Noxious Substances by Sea.[277]

Some extended suppression clauses, however, attempt to limit the discretionary power of future negotiators by establishing the treaty's priority over existing treaties as well as future conventions. Most typical in this respect is article 311, para. 3 UNCLOS. According to this provision States Parties may conclude agreements modifying or suspending the operation of the UN Convention among them. However, they may only do so provided that the agreements do not relate to provisions the derogation from which is incompatible with the effective execution of the object and purpose of the UN Convention on the Law of the Sea. Through this clause the application of the common heritage principle is ensured and it has assumed a character similar to that of a peremptory norm of international law.

Article 311, para. 3 UNCLOS as far as the prospected effects are concerned, is a useful clause because it preserves the predominance of a particular instrument or rather of central provisions thereof. Such an undertaking can provide for clarity and stability and therefore serve as a mechanism for preventing or limiting future derogation. However, such

---

[277] The respective articles read: "This Convention shall supersede any Con vention in force or open for signature, ratification or accession at the date on which this Convention is opened for signature, but only to the extent that such Convention would be in conflict with it; however, nothing in this article shall affect the obligations of States Parties to States not party to this Convention arising under such Convention."

clauses considerably limit the sovereign treaty-making powers of States and will not be accepted lightly.

Whether such provisions actually have the legal capacity to prevent States from derogating is questionable. Even if States agree to the priority of an agreement over future, derogating treaties, they can still adopt such instruments in the future. The adoption of future treaties with derogating content certainly involves a breach of the treaty which prohibits such instruments, e.g. the UN Convention on the Law of the Sea because of its article 311. It does not mean, however, that the derogating, future instrument is null and void. In this respect, the legal force of conflict clauses that prohibit the future derogation from a treaty is limited.

III. Conclusions

Many international agreements concerning the protection of the environment contain clauses that attempt to coordinate the scope of the various agreements by establishing the priority of one over the others. These clauses are guided by the belief that some coordination efforts are necessary. Besides the problems of interpretation discussed above, another difficulty in regard to such clauses is that they are static rather than dynamic. As a result they may exclude certain activities from regulations which are based on new insights and are probably more effective. For example, it would have been much more effective to apply the ecosystem approach of the Protocol for Environmental Protection of the Antarctic Treaty to whales, as opposed to exempting whaling in its totality from the applicability of this Protocol.

Such clauses are, despite all their shortcomings, mechanisms to overcome contradictions between various international instruments on the protection of the environment. The identification of overlap between treaties and regimes must be given particular importance in treaty negotiations and the conflict clauses must be formulated accordingly, i.e. in a manner that respects a capacity for a mutual supplementation of regimes. Conflict clauses in international law will be necessary as long as the development of international environmental law is based upon a sector approach. In practice, special attention must be given to clarity, i.e. unambiguous wording of conflict clauses, in order to prevent later difficulties of interpretation. In this regard conflict clauses that contain qualifications that need further definition such as "serious harm" should in general be avoided. If conflict clauses are missing, if they contradict one another or if they are unclear, recourse is necessary to the rules under the Vienna Convention on the Law of Treaties.

C. The Law of Treaties and its Capacity to Solve Conflicts

(Matz)

The law of treaties consists of rules of customary international law and the Vienna Convention on the Law of Treaties. To a significant extent, but not exclusively, this "treaty on treaties" codifies the relevant customary law of treaties. It is regarded as the most important instrument of reference regarding questions on the law of treaties.[278] Despite being the relevant codification of the law of treaties, the Vienna Convention is by no means so comprehensive as to provide for regulations for all problems and questions arising in the realm of the law of treaties. The issue of conflicts between treaties is one of these less-developed areas. With a view to article 30 VCLT, the issue of conflicts has been described as a particularly "obscure" aspect of the law of treaties.[279] However, gaps in the regulation of conflicts between agreements might not be the only difficulty when trying to coordinate and harmonize agreements according to the rules of the law of treaties. The objectives and the function of the law of treaties in general raise doubts as to whether the law of treaties can serve as a viable mechanism of coordination.

I. Some Aspects Concerning the Law of Treaties: an Introduction

1. The Function of the Law of Treaties

The law of treaties does not, by its nature and function, strive to provide for a harmonization or coordination of the contents of different international treaties. The law of treaties, with very few exceptions,[280] is not concerned with the content of treaties but rather with technical

---

[278] Even before its entry into force and also for non-parties the Vienna Convention is a widely accepted instrument of reference.

[279] Sinclair (note 6), 93.

[280] The rules on *ius cogens* being one of them.

questions concerning their creation, entry into force and termination.[281] The law of treaties provides for a catalogue of regulations that establish the general basis for each international agreement. In this function, the law of treaties, without being of an absolute character, strives to standardize the regulation of certain questions relevant to all international treaties and thereby provide for reliability and the settlement of potential disagreements between States before they arise. At least this is the case if those States negotiating an agreement do not decide to depart from the law of treaties by including specific, contradictory regulations in the new agreement.

In contrast thereto, the rules of the law of treaties do not contemplate the achievement of a coherent international legal system by a harmonization of different agreements. To the degree that the law of treaties regulates questions of conflicts between agreements, it tries to establish which treaty is applicable or enjoys priority for a State party in regard to another State. This consideration can be further illustrated by sketching out the situation that establishes the kind of conflict with which the law of treaties is concerned: State A has concluded a first treaty with State B and a second treaty with State C. State A's obligations arising out of the first and the second treaty collide and as a result State A must either breach its treaty with State B or with State C. Such a scenario and the corresponding rules are based upon a bilateral and contractual understanding of treaties. Furthermore, even if one (or both) of the treaties concluded by State A is multilateral, the approach to solving the conflict is by its nature, a bilateral one because it concerns the clarification of the duties a State must perform with regard to another State. The focus is not upon bringing the agreements into conformity for all participating States but on the relations between one State and, on a bilateral basis, the other States with which it has entered into contracts.

In this respect, the solution of conflicts in the framework of the law of treaties has a slightly different notion than the harmonization of agreements at issue in this study, because the latter aims at the coherence of the contents of the agreements and, preferably, results that are binding upon all States parties. As a consequence of its function to regulate the applicability of treaties in regard to specific States the law of treaties can

---

281 See C. Tietje, "The Changing Legal Structure of International Treaties as an Aspect of an Emerging Global Governance Architecture", *GYIL* 42 (1999), 26 et seq. (27).

only have a limited role in the broader of coordination and harmonization of international environmental law.

2. The Distinction between Law-making and Contractual Treaties and its Relevance

Another aspect that reduces the relevance of the law of treaties with regard to the solution of conflicts between modern agreements refers to the distinction between contractual and law-making treaties.[282] So-called law-making treaties concern the agreement on substantial norms by which the States parties to the treaty pursue a common objective. In contrast thereto, contractual treaties concern specific obligations that depend the States Parties' compliance with the principle of *do ut des.*[283] By their nature contractual treaties are generally bilateral treaties; law-making treaties, on the other hand are multilateral because they pursue the objective of establishing material norms for the accomplishment of a common goal. However, such a categorization is by no means absolute.

The law of treaties, in many aspects, concerns bilateral contractual treaties rather than multilateral law-making agreements. As a consequence, it does not really provide suitable tools for the solution of conflicts between different multilateral agreements that promote the coherence of an international treaty system. This is also true with respect to the Vienna Convention on the Law of Treaties. Although the Vienna Convention does not explicitly distinguish between contractual and law-making agreements, its rules, if examined closely, reflect this distinction

---

[282] A distinction between so-called contractual treaties and law-making treaties has been the subject of a discussion for decades. Particularly, but not exclusively, the older literature favors a distinction that also results in different rules concerning the two categories; see e.g. A.D. McNair, "The Functions and Differing Legal Character of Treaties", *BYIL* 11 (1930), 100 et seq.; Jenks (note 10), 401 et seq.; K. Doehring, *Völkerrecht* (1999), para. 329. While many modern scholars reject a distinction, see e.g. Ipsen/ Heintschel von Heinegg (note 266), chapter 3, § 9, para. 7; A. Verdross/ B. Simma, *Universelles Völkerrecht* (1984), para. 537, the discussion of applicable rules and objectives of the law of treaties on conflicts between agreements show that there are in fact significant differences between treaties that are contracts and treaties that try to establish universal legal rules.

[283] See S. Rosenne, *Developments in the Law of Treaties 1945 – 1986* (1989); Ipsen/ Heintschel von Heinegg (note 266), chapter 3, § 9, para. 7.

and favor the contractual model.[284] In total they are much more concerned with bilateral[285] and contractual[286] treaties than on multilateral law-making agreements.

Modern treaties, e.g. in the fields of humanitarian international law, human rights, environmental law and the law of the sea, set up material rules for the behavior of their member States aiming at collaboration and community and not at the exchange of performances. They try to establish obligations, preferably with a universal character. This objective is also closely linked to the nature of the issues addressed by modern agreements. While older treaties often settled issues such as the borders between two States, modern agreements address topics that require the diligence of a great number of, and preferably all, States in order to achieve their objectives. International environmental agreements are viable examples of this development because objectives, like the protection of the ozone layer or of resources in the high seas, can only be achieved if a significant number of States are legally bound by and willing to comply with international regulations.

Agreements that aim to establish legally binding principles, rules and obligations for as many States as possible are, as a consequence, multilateral law-making agreements. They have hardly anything in common with bilateral contractual treaties in regard to their objectives, functions and institutional settings. Those treaties that regulate the management and use of global resources, i.e. the environmental agreements subject to this study, belong to this category of law-making treaties. This is so because the obligations established by these agreements do not depend upon the reciprocity of specific performances, but reflect instead the pursuit of a common objective.[287] Although such agreements can also establish a framework of interdependent obligations, e.g. concerning the dependence of obligations of developing countries on the fulfillment of developed States' financial obligations, this element does not

---

[284] Doehring (note 282), para. 329 in footnote 3, gives several examples for an implicit distinction between contractual and law-making treaties in different regulations of the Vienna Convention.

[285] S. Verosta, "Die Vertragsrechtskonferenz der Vereinten Nationen 1968/69 und die Wiener Konvention über das Recht der Verträge", *ZaöRV* 29 (1969), 654 et seq. (678).

[286] On the orientation of the law of treaties towards contractual agreements see R. Wolfrum, "Globale Ressourcen gemeinsam verwalten – Neue Entwicklungen im Umweltvölkerrecht", *MPG-Jahrbuch* (1997), 73 et seq. (77).

[287] Ibid, 75.

characterize the agreement as such. This link reflects new principles which aim for the achievement of the objectives of the treaty. This higher, common objective remains the characteristic feature of those multilateral environmental agreements which establish a link between substantial and financial obligations.

II. Treaty Interpretation as a Means of Harmonization

The question posed in the introduction to this section, regarding which of two colliding agreements should enjoy legal priority or validity can be settled by two approaches. First, a solution can be achieved through the application of rules on conflicts that give priority to one agreement over the other. Second, means can be invoked that try to uphold as much of the content of the legal regulations of both treaties, hence harmonizing them without abolishing either of them completely. The law of treaties primarily pursues the first approach, e.g. in its rules on conflicts according to article 30 VCLT or in rules on *lex posterior* or *lex specialis*. Only in some circumstances does the law of treaties strive to uphold two diverging agreements by modifying their regulations. This is, to some extent, the case when a harmonizing approach to treaty interpretation is applied to conflicting treaty regulations. Characterizing treaty interpretation as a "harmonization approach" does not refer to any special form of interpretation but merely to the aim and direction of interpretation that is otherwise performed in accordance with the general rules of treaty interpretation. A harmonizing approach to the interpretation of two colliding treaties follows a relatively soft approach in order to coordinate agreements, since it is not concerned with the abolition of the regulations of either of the treaties. If two treaties can be brought into harmony by an interpretation that coordinates their contents, those mechanisms that establish the priority of one of the treaties, e.g. the *lex posterior* rule, do not have to be invoked. The rules on interpretation as codified by the Vienna Convention form the basis of the harmonizing approach to the interpretation of international agreements.

The use of interpretation as a means to avoid conflicts between or settle conflicting norms is a familiar part of domestic law. Interpretation is also a common mechanism for the settlement of conflicts between European Community law and the national law of the member States. In German national law all laws must be interpreted in a way that conforms to the German Basic Law, Germany's constitution. The same applies to the European Community law, which, at least concerning its application if not its validity, enjoys superiority with respect to the national law of the member States. As a consequence, national law must be interpreted in such a way that it does not collide with European Community law. In both cases, in contrast to the relationship between different international treaties, there exists a hierarchy of norms and the inferior norm is interpreted so as not to collide with the superior. The general lack of such a hierarchy among international treaties makes it more difficult to undertake a harmonizing approach to interpretation.

1. The Basic Rules on the Interpretation of Treaties

Articles 31-33 VCLT lay down the rules regarding the interpretation of international agreements as codified by the Vienna Convention. According to article 31, para. 1 VCLT, the text of a treaty has to be interpreted in good faith

> "in accordance with the ordinary meaning to be given to the terms of the treaty in their context and in the light of its object and purpose".

This basic rule of treaty interpretation contains four relevant elements: (1) the obligation to undertake the interpretation in good faith; (2) the importance of the ordinary meaning rule; (3) the relevance of the object and purpose of a treaty;[288] and (4) the relevance of the treaty's context.[289] The requirement to interpret a treaty in good faith, although actually not being a specific rule of interpretation,[290] is a direct result of the rule of *pacta sunt servanda*, laid down in article 26 VCLT. Since the interpretation of a treaty is an integral part of its application, the examination and assessment of materials relevant to the interpretation must be performed in good faith.[291]

---

[288] The term "object and purpose of a treaty" is an integral part of the terminology concerning international treaties, see H.F. Köck, "Zur Interpretation völkerrechtlicher Verträge", *ZÖR* 53 (1998), 217 et seq. in footnote 7.

[289] Ibid, 218 et seq.

[290] An interpretation in good faith alone cannot give any indications as to the meaning of a certain treaty term. The requirement to interpret a treaty in good faith only draws the attention to the limits of interpretation that lie in arbitrariness and over-subtlety, ibid, 218 in footnote 5.

[291] A. Aust, *Modern Treaty Law and Practice* (2000), 187.

(a) The Ordinary Meaning Rule of Interpretation

The approach to treaty interpretation taken by the Vienna Convention focuses on the objective meaning of the text to be clarified. The underlying assumption, upon which the rule in article 31, para. 1 VCLT is based, is that the text of the treaty is the authentic expression of the intentions of the parties. In this respect, the ICJ has stated that the purpose of treaty interpretation was not to revise treaties or to read into the text of treaties issues that they do not explicitly address or that cannot be drawn out of a reasonable understanding of the text.[292] However, the ordinary meaning shall be determined after consideration of the specific context in which the terms are used. In this respect, article 31, para. 2 VCLT is relevant because it helps identify the elements that can be considered a part of the context in which a term has been employed and which factors, other than the context, can be considered when clarifying a text. Other indications of the will of the parties at the time the treaty was negotiated are only considered as a subsidiary source, e.g. in the *travaux préparatoires*. This rather subjective means of interpretation (consideration of the intent of the negotiating parties) only applies if the meaning of the relevant text cannot be established from the ordinary meaning of the language used, in light of the context in which the language is used, and in consideration of the object and purpose of the treaty.

(b) The Object and Purpose of a Treaty

Article 31, para. 1 VCLT requires that a treaty be interpreted in accordance with its object and purpose. This rule contains a teleological element. Despite the focus of the basic rule of treaty interpretation on the objective, textual approach, the consideration of teleological elements as well as some subjective aspects shows the synthesis of different methods of interpretation enshrined in the VCLT. The teleological aspect of interpretation may help to harmonize different agreements because different agreements in the same field, e.g. international environmental

[292] Interpretation of Peace Treaties with Bulgaria, Hungary and Romania, *ICJ Reports* (1950), 229; Case Concerning Rights of Nationals of the United States of America in Morocco, *ICJ Reports* (1952), 196; Certain Expenses of the United Nations Case, *ICJ Reports* (1962), 159; South West Africa Cases (Second Phase), *ICJ Reports* (1966), 48; see also R. Jennings/ A. Watts, *Oppenheim's International Law* (1992), vol. I, parts 2-4, § 632.

law, may be said to share the same object and purpose in accordance with which they must be interpreted.

Different considerations are possible when undertaking an assessment of the object and purpose of a treaty in the treaty-interpretation context. The object and purpose of a treaty as such may differ from the object and purpose of one of its unclear and potentially conflicting provisions.[293] While the consideration of partial objectives as expressed in specific treaty provisions can increase discrepancies between agreements, the overriding object and purpose of a treaty, e.g. the conservation of natural resources or the sustainable use of resources, could be a clearer guideline for a harmonizing interpretation of different agreements. In this regard, the consideration of the object and purpose of an agreement in the interpretation process presents particular potential for a harmonization of treaties.

In addition to various questions regarding the determination of the object and purpose of a treaty,[294] it is particularly problematic to establish what is covered by the term "object and purpose" of a treaty. Particularly, it is difficult to determine whether the object and purpose of a treaty permits a distinction between the partial objectives outlined by or contained in one or several treaty clauses, or whether the object and purpose refers exclusively to purpose of the treaty as such or to its overarching objectives. The Vienna Convention does not distinguish between the different kinds of objects and purposes that can be traced back to a treaty. This fact, as well as the lack of any hint as to a distinction in the documentation of the *travaux préparatoires*, speak against drawing a meaningful distinction between the overarching object and purpose and more specific objects and purposes arising out of individual treaty provisions.[295] Furthermore, the interpretation of treaty provisions in accordance with the object and purpose of specific provisions can result in a lack of coherence within a single regulation. This would, consequently, diminish the viability of the treaty itself. Such a practice would not only obstruct the harmonization of a treaty with other trea-

---

[293] Köck (note 288), 225.

[294] See J. Klabbers, "Some Problems Regarding the Object and Purpose of Treaties", *Finnish YB Int'l L.* 8 (1997), 138 et seq. (139).

[295] See ibid, 152.

ties, but it would also hinder the more general clarifying function of treaty interpretation.[296]

Concerning the harmonization of treaties, some attention must be given to the overarching object and purpose of the treaties because there is a better chance of creating conformity between treaties that have a common object and purpose. However, very general objectives like the protection of the environment or sustainable development, are unlikely to be considered the relevant object and purpose of a treaty. Sustainable development is a concept that could gain importance as a guideline for interpretation in this context, if it could be said to be the object and purpose of several, if not most, modern environmental treaties. The concepts of sustainable development and sustainable use of resources guide all agreements that were concluded during or after the Earth Summit in Rio de Janeiro in 1992. Consequently, the concept of sustainable development could be regarded as a common and overriding motive of the different agreements. But, can such a common element also constitute the common object and purpose of a treaty and thereby contribute to a harmonizing interpretation? Reliance upon overriding concepts, such as environmental protection or sustainable development, could promote the harmonization of treaties but they do not necessarily help clarify certain unclear terms because general objectives (the protection of the environment) lack definition. Furthermore, one must assume that overarching objectives have, during the negotiation of treaties, already had their influence on specific provisions of the treaties and still failed to produce greater clarity and coordination. As a consequence, the consideration of objectives, which are essential but overarching, cannot necessarily provide a better approach to harmonization.

It follows that the interpretation of a treaty must consider the specific object and purpose of a treaty as such. This excludes the consideration of partial objectives drawn from specific provisions of the treaty. This also excludes the exclusive reliance upon more general objectives such as the environmental character of a treaty. The object and purpose of a treaty lies somewhere between these points. While there are no clear guidelines as to how to determine the object and purpose of a treaty, the

---

[296] A similar line of argumentation is employed in order not to distinguish between the object and the purpose of a treaty, but to understand the term "object and purpose" as a single concept. If the object of a treaty was something broader or overarching in contrast to the purpose, most treaties would promote the same object, the promotion of human welfare, and the notion of the object of a treaty as a tool of interpretation would become obsolete. Ibid, 148.

determination of these elements can, in most cases, be determined by having a look at the agreement's title and any specific treaty provisions that articulate the treaty's objectives. Unless two treaties share an object and purpose this element of interpretation does not generally provide for better harmonization in the interpretation process of treaties.

2. *Article 31, para. 2 VCLT: the Context*

In addition to the wording of a treaty provision, including the preamble and the annexes to a treaty, interpretation can also take other agreements between the parties into consideration. These materials are reflective of the treaty's context and they include agreements entered into on the occasion of the conclusion of the treaty (out which the uncertain terms arise) as well as documents adopted and accepted by the parties as treaty-related documents that help define the context of a treaty (article 31, para. 2). Because of the difficulty of reaching acceptable compromises during treaty negotiations, such agreements and documents play a special role in the negotiation and adoption of treaties. Some potential treaty provisions that could not be explicitly expressed in the treaty because of political considerations, may be contained in these contextual materials and may take on particular relevance in the consideration of the treaty's context in the interpretive process.[297]

For the harmonization of agreements after the conclusion of a treaty, declarations and documents issued or produced at time the treaty was adopted play only a limited role. Only in the rare case that such contextual materials make reference to potential conflicts, the resolution of which could not be hammered out in the negotiations of the treaty itself, do these materials, from the time an agreement was negotiated, gain relevance. Often, States Parties cannot anticipate conflicts at the time of the negotiation of an agreement because conflicts only emerge with respect to agreements concluded at a later time. Anticipating conflicts at the time of negotiation is also difficult because they often arise only with respect to the unforeseeable consequences and associations of implementation. For these reasons, subsequent agreements as opposed to contemporaneous declarations of context are of greater relevance to the interpretation (with a view towards harmonization) of international treaties.

---

[297] Aust (note 291), 190.

In this case, as in the others described above, the interpretation of a treaty is not a traditional tool for the coordination of conflicting agreements. The interpretation of treaties serves to clarify unclear terms but not to change or amend an agreement. This significantly limits the role treaty interpretation can play in harmonizing conflicting treaty regulations. Still, the clarification of the wording and thus the meaning of a treaty need not remain a static process. The interpretation of treaties has evolved to allow, again within certain limits, a dynamic element to be introduced on top of the provisions in article 31, para. 3, lit. (a) – (c) VCLT.

3. The Provisions of Article 31, para. 3 VCLT

If the application of the basic rule of interpretation does not lead to clarity concerning the meaning of a provision, further tools of interpretation must be invoked. This is particularly to be expected in the process of harmonizing agreements by way of treaty interpretation. This is the case because the coordination of treaties involves difficulties that can often be settled by reference to circumstances outside the respective agreement instead of referring solely to text and context. The circumstances that can be considered as aides to the interpretation of a treaty, according to the respective provisions in the Vienna Convention, are by no means inferior to the ordinary meaning rule and the consideration of the context. All these means of interpretation are to be employed on an equal footing.[298]

Article 31, para. 3, lit. (a) – (c) contains the rules relevant to the adaptation of a treaty based on changed circumstances and might, therefore, offer a way to harmonize agreements. According to the respective provisions, the interpretation of an agreement can take into account:

> "(a) any subsequent agreement between the parties regarding the interpretation of the treaty or the application of its provisions;
>
> (b) any subsequent practice in the application of the treaty which establishes the agreement of the parties regarding its interpretation;
>
> (c) any relevant rules of international law applicable in the relations between the parties."

---

[298] Jennings/ Watts (note 292), § 632 in footnote 17.

(a) Subsequent Agreements and "Authentic" Interpretation

According to article 31, para. 3, lit. (a) VCLT, agreements concluded by the parties after the adoption of the treaty text can be taken into account to interpret the agreement. This means of interpretation is particularly relevant if States parties notice a lack of clarity or if they become aware of ambiguities in the treaty text and want to provide for a clarification of the text without formally modifying or amending the treaty. The subsequent agreement does not have to take the form of an international treaty but may also be a declaration of the parties or a resolution of the treaty's organs concerning the meaning of the unclear provision.[299] The literature often discusses the mutual agreement of States Parties on the meaning of a treaty provision as the "authentic interpretation" of a treaty.

In particular, such an "authentic interpretation," i.e. the subsequent consensus of the States Parties regarding the interpretation of the treaty, could serve as a tool for the harmonization of diverging treaties. This means of interpretation is similar to an amendment of a treaty. The extent to which a term changes its meaning based on a subsequently declared authentic interpretation of the States Parties is central to determining whether the act constitutes an interpretation, amendment or modification.[300] Particularly if the amendment of the treaty would involve a formal and lengthy amendment procedure, authentic interpretation could be considered a means to achieve the same results in a less formal proceeding.[301] Upon its conclusion, an authentic interpretation is retrospectively binding upon all parties. The entry into force of a treaty amendment, however, usually depends upon the ratification by a certain number of parties and only relates to those parties that have ratified the amendment.

Still, an authentic interpretation requires consensus among the States Parties and this is the main obstacle on a practical level. Furthermore, with respect to legal issues, an authentic interpretation faces the same limitations that exist, in the context of the harmonization of conflicting treaties, with respect to the use of any other form of interpretation. In-

---

[299] For examples concerning such a proceeding e.g. concerning the Ramsar Convention on Wetlands of International Importance, see Aust (note 291), 192 et seq.

[300] See M.K. Yasseen, "Interprétation des Traités d'après la Convention de Vienne sur le Droit des Traités", *RdC* 151 (1976 III), 9 et seq. (45).

[301] See S. Sur, *L'Interprétation en Droit International Public* (1974), 200.

terpretation generally aims to clarify an unclear text and should not be confused with an easy option to change a treaty, without observing the respective amendment procedure. As a consequence, a harmonizing, authentic interpretation must be restricted to unclear provisions of agreements. It should not be systematically invoked to harmonize conflicts, where their solution would in fact require the amendment of the treaty. This error is especially likely to occur because many solutions to problems arising out of the application of a treaty can be settled with greater clarity by a formal modification or amendment.[302] In many cases, however, the harmonizing interpretation of international environmental agreements would cross the line between a permissible interpretation of a treaty and the amendment of a treaty, without the observation of the formal treaty amendment procedure.

The following example, taken from the proceedings of the Basel Convention, illustrates the necessity of proceeding with caution when trying to change a treaty by way of a modification of its interpretation. After the Conference of the Parties to the Basel Convention substantially amended article 4 of the Convention by Decision II/12, without following the formal amendment procedure of article 17, the non-governmental organization "Greenpeace" claimed that this decision only constituted an extensive interpretation of the agreement, not an amendment requiring the observation of the formal treaty amendment procedures.[303] However, the Conference of the Parties finally decided upon an amendment of the treaty to achieve the aims of Decision II/12, thereby underscoring the limits of interpretation as opposed to a revision by amendment.[304] In addition, while the advantages of the authentic interpretation are a higher degree of flexibility, the likelihood of achieving the required consensus significantly limits the availability of this device.

An authentic interpretation is perceived to be a direct expression of the principle of consensus. Consequently, an authentic interpretation announced by a subsequent agreement is not an independent and innovative tool of interpretation but rather reflects the fact that all parties to a treaty have agreed to a specific meaning of a treaty provision. Such a consensual agreement might be particularly difficult to achieve if overlap or conflicts with other international agreements are concerned. This

---

302 Aust (note 291), 193.

303 Further references see U. Beyerlin, *Umweltvölkerrecht* (2000), para. 100.

304 Decision III/1: Amendment to the Basel Convention, UNEP/CHW.3/35.

is particularly the case if some Parties to one agreement are not also States Parties to the other agreement. The possible result of such a situation is that the interests at stake might diverge, making a consensus significantly more difficult and unlikely.[305] The practical relevance of an authentic interpretation as an independent means of harmonizing conflicting agreements is, therefore, somewhat diminished.[306] A possible change, that would make this method of treaty interpretation a more viable tool for the resolution of conflicts between treaties, would be the establishment of decision-making procedures that allow binding majority decisions on such issues by the treaty organs. Such a proceeding would, however, not be in conformity with the principle of consensus, the observation of which is presently necessary for the propagation of an authentic interpretation.

Most modern environmental agreements allow as an *ultima ratio*, i.e. if all efforts to reach consensus have failed, majority-voting procedures.[307] In those cases in which the Conference of the Parties is empowered to interpret certain provisions, one can assume that the decisions regarding the interpretation shall be binding upon all States parties.[308] This is so even if the decision has been made by a majority vote in accordance with the rules of the treaty. Only if the Conference of the Parties can decide upon a binding interpretation by majority vote, would its competence reach farther than an authentic interpretation produced pursuant to the consensus of all the States Parties. One cannot automatically

---

[305] Yasseen (note 300), 44, perceives the negotiations on a subsequent agreement on the interpretation of a treaty as generally *délicates*.

[306] This could change, however, if there was an international forum that would decide upon the substantial harmonization of diverging agreements and leave the implementation of the results to the relevant Conferences of the Parties. Such a proceeding would combine environmental governance mechanisms with the implementation of decisions by the tools of the Vienna Convention on the Law of Treaties. But again, in many cases the formal amendment or modification of a treaty might be the correct way of implementation.

[307] E.g. article 29, para. 3 CBD.

[308] R. Churchill/ G. Ulfstein, "Autonomous Institutional Arrangements in Multilateral Environmental Agreements: A Little-notices Phenomenon in International Law", *AJIL* 94 (2000), 623 et seq. (641); this is for example the case in regard to article 10, para. 1 Montreal Protocol, on the basis of which the Conference of the Parties decided upon a list in Doc. UNEP/OzL.Pro.4/15, Annex III, which serves as an indications for the interpretation of the term "incremental costs".

assume the binding force, upon all member States, of a decision regarding the meaning of a treaty provision if a subsidiary clause regarding competence is the basis of the decision or if the Conference of the Parties relied upon implied powers. At least this is so if consensus could not be reached and the organ decides by majority vote, because the considerable weight assigned to State sovereignty speaks against an implicit transfer of sovereignty to such an extent. States are very likely to fear and reject the further loss of sovereignty they would suffer if an extensive interpretation could be made binding without their explicit consent.[309]

(b) State Practice

Another means of interpretation mentioned in article 31, para. 3, lit. (b) VCLT is to draw the meaning of uncertain treaty provisions from a consideration of the tacit practice of States Parties. An interpretation based on State practice resembles an interpretation achieved by way of subsequent agreement, one being tacit the other being explicit. Consequently, both means of interpretation can be considered forms of authentic interpretation.[310] At times authors use the term "quasi-authentic" interpretation when referring to the tacit (authentic) interpretation that depends on State practice.[311]

Provided that State practice regarding an interpretation of a treaty is consistent and commonly recognized and accepted, it is a valuable source of how the States parties generally understand the treaty.[312] However, in respect to the harmonization of different treaties the main problem is to actually reach tacit agreement about the interpretation. This is particularly so, because the tacit agreement must also be documented by equally tacit concerted action in regard to the implementation of the agreement.

---

309 In contrast thereto Churchill/ Ulfstein, ibid at 649, are of the opinion that States agreed to such a loss of sovereignty with the creation of quasi-autonomous treaty organs, although States have not fully grasped this aspect when creating the respective institutionalized treaties. Such an understanding promotes the progressive development of international environmental law and could promote the harmonization of international environmental agreements.

310 Yasseen (note 300), 52.

311 Sur (note 301), 361.

312 Aust (note 291), 194.

In principle, the problems with this method of treaty interpretation are similar to those associated with an explicit authentic interpretation: in regard to different environmental treaties, to which many but not all States are parties, any consensus on the interpretation and, accordingly, the implementation of the agreements is difficult if not unlikely. The problems, approaches to and interests at stake when trying to harmonize different treaties are very complex and generally hinder a consensual State practice in regard to the avoidance of overlap and to the resolution of conflicts. Furthermore, as mentioned before, not all States are Parties to all conflicting agreements, although modern environmental treaties are often called "global" or "quasi universal" agreements. Consequently, for some States, conflicts between agreements do not materialize because they are not Parties to one of the respective agreements. That may lead to a lack of necessity but also a lack of interest or diligence on the part of particular States regarding the specific interpretation of a treaty. While such States may nevertheless agree to a subsequent document regarding interpretation, it seems less likely that they would tacitly adopt the same practice as States which happen to be parties each of the relevant, conflicting agreements. It is, after all, only these latter States that suffer form the difficulties with implementation or compliance. It follows that the tacit State practice, in relation to the interpretation of treaties, is of little relevance as far as a process of a coordination of treaties is concerned.

(c) Rules of International Law

The regulation in article 31, para. 3, lit. (c) VCLT provides that States may take into account the relevant rules of international law as applicable between the parties in interpreting a treaty. This rule might gain particular weight concerning the coordination of different treaties. This is particularly so, if the consideration of relevant rules of international law is discussed within the realm of a dynamic form of interpretation.

According to a draft of the commission, article 31, para. 3, lit. (c) VCLT was originally meant to ensure that the text of a treaty was to be interpreted and the ordinary meaning of the treaty text determined in the light of the international law applicable at the time of the adoption of the treaty.[313] A proceeding pursuant to this original vision of article 31, para. 3, lit. (c) VCLT would have been in deference to the general prin-

---

[313] For further references see Sinclair (note 6), 138.

ciple that a legal element must always be considered in the light of the legal rules applicable at the time of its existence.[314] In respect to treaty interpretation, such an approach results in an interpretation *ex tunc* (in the light of the rules applicable at the time of the treaty's adoption) and not *ex nunc* (in the light of the rules applicable at the time of the interpretation). By interpreting a treaty *ex tunc*, the development of new rules of international law, e.g. in more modern treaties, cannot be taken into account. The evolution of international law, however, is particularly relevant concerning international environmental rules, because the last decades have seen the development and change of concepts, approaches and principles by new scientific insights and the change of political paradigms.

The ICJ has provided for an option to adapt treaties to changed circumstances in the form of the so-called "dynamic" interpretation. The ICJ has held that, under certain conditions, a treaty can be interpreted *ex nunc* and need not only be interpreted, as had been the rule, *ex tunc*. In the ICJ report on Namibia the Court held that, in contrast to the traditional understanding of treaty interpretation, an instrument has to be interpreted and implemented with regard being had of all the legal rules applicable at the time of its interpretation.[315] This "dynamic" interpretation of a treaty allows the treaty to change over time and in accordance with new relevant rules of international law. Such an approach can lead to the harmonization of environmental treaties by adapting them to new approaches and principles providing for the enhanced conformity of the international legal system.

A more dynamic approach to interpretation takes account of the fact that the meaning and common understanding of certain terms might change over time and that such a change may be documented by new, related rules of international law. The ordinary meaning of a term at the time of the interpretation might therefore be different to the interpretation it would have been given at the time the treaty in which it appears was negotiated. Treaties, particularly if they have been negotiated a long time ago, might be more viable if an interpretation of their terms is not static but adaptable and expressive of the understanding of terms at the time of their interpretation. To serve this purpose, treaty interpretation can and should consider new international rules as expressed by modern, subsequently enacted treaties, on similar issues.

---

314 Ibid at 138.

315 *ICJ Reports* (1971), 31et seq., see also *ICJ Reports* (1978), 34 f.

Yet, the opportunity the dynamic interpretation of treaties (by way of consideration of subsequently enacted or subsequently emerging international law) is subject to the limitation that not all terms can be interpreted in the light of *ex nunc* understanding. The Court has held that only those terms which, by their nature, are open for change can be interpreted *ex nunc*. Only those terms, which by their vagueness already imply a development in accordance with a changed understanding of States are eligible for dynamic interpretation. An example in international law is the phrase "good order."[316] Otherwise, the maxim that the ordinary meaning of a treaty provision may not be revised by later interpretation applies. Where the requirements of the ICJ are not met, States parties would have to invoke a formal amendment procedure to adapt the treaty to changed objectives.

4. Conclusion

The harmonization of multilateral agreements by way of treaty interpretation faces some difficulties which diminish its potential to be widely and systematically employed. The primary reason for this is that treaty interpretation, as a means for harmonizing conflicts among treaties, is dependent upon the identification of uncertain or unclear treaty terms as the source of the conflict. When a text is clear, according to its wording and context, interpretation cannot be the relevant means for the resolution of conflict. The limits of this method of harmonization are particularly clear in those cases, rare as they may be, in which States Parties deliberately establish a conflict with a prior-existing agreement and employ the clearest of language in the new agreement. The dynamic interpretation of treaties requires a treaty term that is by its nature open for development and change. Dynamic interpretation also requires the expression of the changed understanding of this term in other rules of international law. These double preconditions make the systematic application of this form of interpretation an unlikely means for harmonizing treaties. Furthermore, even where an open term could be interpreted in a dynamic way, the dynamic interpretation of that term leading to a harmonization of conflicting agreements would depend upon the chance that: (1) the conflict hinged on this particular term; and (2) that the conflict could be solved by giving the term its modern meaning.

---

[316] Ipsen/ Heintschel von Heinegg (note 266), 21.

However, despite these obstacles and limitations, the vague language of environmental treaties and the granting of discretion to member States concerning the implementation of treaties leave considerable room for States parties to avoid conflicts during the implementation phase. This discretion should be wisely used to promote a coordinated implementation of treaties even in the absence of a formal binding decision on the interpretation of a treaty text, e.g. by the treaty organs. In any event, the interpretation of treaties, despite its shortcomings, aims at the harmonization of the contents of treaties. In this sense, treaty interpretation strives for clarity, and perhaps harmony between conflicting agreements, without allowing the existence of a conflict to call the continued existence and application of one of the conflicting agreements, as such, into question.

III. The Regulation of Conflicts by the Vienna Convention on the Law of Treaties

1. Introduction

The Vienna Convention on the Law of Treaties represents the international community's provision of some general, codified rules on treaty making. The following paragraphs aim to explore the capacity and the limits of the rules of the Vienna Convention on the Law of Treaties with respect to conflicts between international environmental agreements, in particular its article 30.

According to the rule of *pacta sunt servanda*, expressed by the law of treaties, a State is obliged not to breach any agreement into which it has entered. Under some circumstances, however, this general rule is sacrificed in favor of more specific regulations. If two agreements conflict and the simultaneous application of the agreements raises complications, article 30 VCLT provides rules for determining which agreement enjoys applicability as against which States Parties. While conflicts between bilateral agreements are relatively easy to solve, conflicts between multilateral agreements, like the environmental treaties at issue in this study, are substantially more difficult to resolve.

2. The Scope of Article 30 VCLT

Article 30 VCLT addresses the terms under which a subsequent treaty, treating the same subject matter as an earlier agreement, enjoys priority. Its five paragraphs establish a relatively detailed outline of the issue.[317] Despite the specificity of its provisions, article 30 VCLT suffers from a substantial shortcoming which reduces its viability as a means of resolving conflicts between international law agreements: the application of article 30 VCLT is limited to a conflict created by a subsequent agreements that address the same subject matter. The article's applicability as a mechanism for resolving conflict is restricted to conflicts between treaties that fulfill these criteria.

The determination of what is meant by "subsequent" treaties and by the condition that they must address the "same subject matter" is crucial to an understanding of the scope of article 30 VCLT and its practical relevance to conflicts between international environmental treaties. Significantly, the Vienna Convention does not provide a regulatory scheme for the resolution of conflicts between agreements that do *not* address the same subject matter. Consequently, conflicts like those that arise between the regulations on dumping and the Basel Convention on Hazardous Wastes are only subject to article 30 VCLT if the treaties deal with the same subject matter.

The criteria that should be employed in establishing whether two treaties are dealing with the same subject matter have not yet been settled. Some authors' favor a restrictive interpretation;[318] others take a broader approach.[319] During the negotiations of the Convention on Biological

---

[317] Although the approach of article 30 VCLT is guided by accepted principles of the international law of treaties such as the *pacta sunt servanda* rule and the *lex posterior* rule, the article is not seen as a codification of customary international law; see E. Sciso, "On Article 103 of the Charter of the United Nations in the Light of the Vienna Convention on the Law of Treaties", *ÖZöRV* 28 (1987), 161 et seq. (165).

[318] Lukitsch Hicks (note 3), 1660; Aust (note 291), 183.

[319] See e.g. L. Guruswamy/ B.R. Hendricks, *International Environmental Law* (1997): "For example, does the Basel Convention deal with the same subject matter as the GATT/WTO? If not, will the rule in Vienna Convention article 30 (4) (b) apply? Can it be argued that the Basel Convention deals with a specialized area and must obtain precedence over a more general treaty dealing with trade in the round? What if an environmental treaty were to say that its provisions will take priority over other treaties covering the same subject mat-

Diversity States flirted with the issue, discussing the question whether earlier treaties, particularly if not dealing with nature conservation issues, could be said to deal with the same subject matter. The discussion did not, however, reach any conclusive results.[320]

Generally, in order to establish that two agreements address the same subject matter, more is required than a demonstration that some provisions of the two agreements are in conflict. Making the existence of a conflict sufficient would render article 30's limiting clause (making the provision applicable only to this restrictive class of agreements) irrelevant. Unfortunately, neither the wording of article 30 VCLT nor the context (even when supplemented by a consideration of the *travaux préparatoires*) shed much light on the matter.

A restrictive interpretation of the criteria in article 30 VCLT seems favorable if one considers the potential consequences of a broad interpretation. A broad interpretation could lead to the conclusion that all international treaties dealing with the conservation of the environment qualify as treaties dealing with the same subject matter. As a consequence, article 30, para. 3 and para. 4 VCLT would provide that the most recently promulgated treaty would override all preceding, diverging environmental agreements with respect to States that are parties to both treaties. Particularly in the light of the parallel negotiations of the modern environmental agreements, there is no reason to conclude that the will of the States Parties to derogate from earlier agreements is necessarily expressed by the promulgation of a diverging, subsequent treaty.

The meaning of "the same subject matter" requirement of article 30 VCLT can be approached from two perspectives: (1) one can either refer to the subject of the treaty as such; or (2) one can refer to the subject of the single treaty provision in question. By following the first approach, one is led to the conclusion that the subject matter of the GATT (the establishment of rules to promote free world trade) and CITES (the protection of species by regulation of their international trade) agreements differ considerably, one being a treaty of international economic law and the other being an environmental agreement. The two agreements, according to this analysis, would not be considered treaties dealing with the same subject matter and article 30 VCLT

---

ter? Although one might be tempted to answer these questions in favor of the Basel Convention, there are as yet no conclusive answers to such problems."

[320] See Chandler (note 23), 149.

would not apply. If, however, one examines the subject matter of single provisions of the two treaties it is possible to find areas of application for article 30 VCLT, especially with regard to those provisions dealing international trade in goods. By this analysis, and if a conflict between the two was established in accordance with the rules of article 30 VCLT, the new GATT 1995, would have priority over CITES.[321]

A similar situation, i.e. that the general subject matter differs while the subject of specific, conflicting provisions are sufficiently similar, could also be discussed with respect to the UN Convention on the Law of the Sea and the Convention on Biological Diversity. Having regard to the fundamental scope and the objectives of the Convention on the Law of the Sea and the Convention on Biological Diversity, it is difficult to conclude that they represent treaties that address the same subject matter in the sense intended by article 30 VCLT.[322] Still, specific provisions from the two treaties can be applied in certain contexts, e.g. concerning protected areas, which lead to conflicts over similar subjects.[323]

Applying a broader basis of analysis to the question of "similar subject matter" can, however, be quite problematic. International environmental agreements concern a variety of different aspects of the environment and of environmental protection. Should it be sufficient, to trigger the applicability of article 30 VCLT, that they are all concerned with the protection of the environment? This would require the conclusion that States, by adopting a subsequent agreement on the protection of the global climate, express their will to override a treaty on the transport of wastes. Taken to its extreme, this view of the analysis required by the "same subject matter" requirement of article 30 VCLT, leads to the universal application of article 30 because all international treaties deal with human welfare in a broad sense. This broad basis of analysis would be unreasonable, rendering the qualifying preconditions of article 30 VCLT pointless.

Between these two choices, it seems better to apply the restrictive interpretation of the requirements of article 30 VCLT. Yet, exactly how re-

---

[321] Such a conflict between the two agreements exists in regard to the regulations for the trade of species, see Matz (note 14), 175.

[322] Wolfrum/ Matz (note 22), 473 et seq.

[323] Since the UN Convention on the Law of the Sea does not explicitly deal with protected areas not even the potentially conflicting provisions (the freedom of navigation and marine biodiversity reserves) can be said to address the same subject matter.

strictive the interpretation should be, cannot be easily settled. A general guideline might be to resolve to proceed from the assumption that treaties deal with dissimilar subject matters, in the context of article 30 VCLT, if the similarity of the subject matter addressed by provisions of the treaties is not plainly evident.[324]

Applying the restrictive approach, neither of the following treaty pairs would qualify for the application of article 30 VCLT because they do not adequately address the "same subject matter": (1) the Convention on Biological Diversity and the Framework Convention on Climate Change, or (2) the treaties on Antarctica and the UN Convention on the Law of the Sea. The fact that there is some overlap between these agreements that is reflected by conflicts does not change this conclusion. As a consequence, article 30 VCLT cannot generally be employed to address and solve the conflicts between the respective multilateral environmental treaties.

IV. Article 60 VCLT

Article 60 VCLT is another option that could be employed if conflicts between agreements arise. In the case of a substantial breach of the treaty by one of the parties, States can suspend or terminate the treaty with respect to the breaching Party. In the context of conflicts between agreements this means that a State, in breach of an agreement because it heeded its obligations arising out of a conflicting instrument, can face the suspension or termination of the breached treaty. This approach shows the originally bilateral concept of treaties especially reflected in the Vienna Convention on the Law of Treaties because, although article 60, para. 2 VCLT provides for specific rules for multilateral agreements, the regulation does not seem to provide appropriate terms for conflicts between quasi-universal treaties.

---

[324] There are only some cases in which the identity of the subject matters seems evident. One of the cases is the relationship between the UN Convention on the Law of the Sea and the Geneva Conventions on the law of the sea from 1958. The result that would have been reached by the application of the rules of article 30 VCLT also would have arise out of the application of article 311 UNCLOS, which explicitly provides for the superiority of the UN Convention on the Law of the Sea over the Geneva Conventions.

If two multilateral treaties are in conflict and if this conflict forms the basis for a substantial breach of one of the agreements, the suspension or termination of the agreement in regard to specific parties is not suitable for resolving the conflict between the treaties. Article 60 VCLT, by the sanction of suspension or termination of the treaty, aims to force a State party to treaty conform to the terms of the treaty. However, if the reason for a breach of treaties is a conflict with another multilateral agreement, a significant number of States are likely to face the same situation. Consequently, a solution to the conflict must be designed to involve all States parties and not sanction the behavior of one or more specific States.

In addition to the shortcomings of article 60 VCLT with respect to the harmonization of different treaties, the practicability of the suspension of a treaty as a sanction is questionable, at least as far as environmental agreements are concerned. In most cases sanctions lack viability in international environmental law.[325] Modern international environmental law frequently provides for incentives to comply with treaties in order to promote and maintain broad participation and to prevent pollution havens and free riders. In particular, developing countries are offered financial and technical assistance as an incentive to implement and comply with international environmental agreements. As a result, article 60 VCLT reflects an approach that is mainly considered outdated in international environmental law. The provision is not a suitable mechanism for the harmonization of international environmental law.

V. Lex posterior and lex specialis

Article 30 VCLT has, subject to several conditions, codified some special cases of the *lex posterior* rule. Due to the fact that the article itself applies only to treaties dealing with the same subject matter, the codification is of little use to the question on how to solve conflicts between multilateral environmental instruments. The applicability of a *lex posterior* rule and a *lex specialis* rule based upon customary international is the subject of the following discussion. Two aspects have to be distinguished in this context: (1) the consequences of the application of the rules to the validity of the agreement as such, e.g. whether it is termi-

---

[325] For a extensive discussion on the shift of paradigms from confrontational to non-confrontational mechanisms see Wolfrum (note 1), 7 et seq.

nated; and (2) the consequences of the application of the rules for specific States only, e.g. whether a State can free itself from an agreement that otherwise remains valid for the rest of the States Parties.

1. Lex posterior *as a General Rule of International Law*

As a rule of derogation the application of the *lex posterior* rule cannot provide for the coordination or harmonization of agreements covering identical or overlapping subjects but concluded at different times between the same parties. Under certain circumstances it could help to clarify the relation between different treaties by providing for a rule of preference that gives priority to one of the conflicting agreements. The distinction between bilateral and multilateral treaties is, however, important in the *lex posterior* context. In the case of several bilateral treaties between the same two States the later in time claims priority.[326] The same applies, as codified in the Vienna Convention, if the parties to multilateral agreements are identical. However, for those multilateral treaties not having identical[327] States Parties or for those referring to distinct functional objectives, it might be inappropriate to refer to a general *lex posterior* rule.[328]

A notion of a general *lex posterior* rule that could lead to the termination of the older agreement is based upon the will of the parties to derogate from their original legal rules by creating new and diverging rules. As a result the parties to both sets of rules must be identical[329] in

---

[326] According to B. Simma/ R. Bernhardt, *Charta der Vereinten Nationen – Kommentar* (1991), Artikel 103, para. 2, this rule does not only apply if the prior treaty is *lex specialis* to the later one.

[327] If, however, there is not at least one State that is a party to both multilateral treaties in question i.e. if the States parties are completely distinct, there is no conflict for the States parties involved in the respective treaties. As a consequence, the question which of the two treaties to apply is of no concern for these States. Accordingly, the *lex posterior* rule is of no practical relevance in this context.

[328] Jenks (note 10), 405, argues against any general rules based upon a time factor. By referring to a *lex priori* rule, he states that it is inappropriate and too simple a principle to always grant priority to the prior treaty in relation to a later one.

[329] There must be no absolute congruence of parties but at least all parties to the original agreement must also be party to the new treaty.

order that the assumption of willful derogation can be upheld. As we have seen, although the modern environmental agreements aim at universality, their parties are not absolutely identical. Consequently the rule of *lex posterior* cannot be invoked as a general means to settle conflicts between different environmental agreements by clarifying the priority the agreements enjoy against one another. It is not appropriate to solve conflicts in international law by subjugating one of the agreements to the other (and thereby the will of the States Parties to the subjugated agreement) in case the States Parties to the two agreements are not identical.

Quite similar considerations apply in regard to the question whether a single State can free itself from older obligations by referring to a subsequently concluded agreement. Often, the potential for conflicts with other agreements has not been identified when an agreement is negotiated, particularly with respect to the implementation phase. Consequently, it would be inappropriate to maintain that a State has freed itself from older obligations negotiated in a different context. However, the question to what extent a State is liable for the breach of a treaty it tries to justify by referring to a *lex posterior* rule has not been settled. In light of the doubts and shortcomings involved when applying a customary *lex posterior* rule it is necessary to conclude that the application of this rule, as a general means for resolving conflicts, leads to inappropriate results in international law.

Another important matter concerning rules that address the derogation from either the preceding or the subsequent agreement is how to fix the "age" of a treaty. The question is practically the same as in regard to conflict clauses that provide for either the prevalence over or the preference of "existing" agreements.[330] Since the treaty making procedure is a lengthy and at times cumbersome process, different stages in the process could qualify for the relevant date. Uncertainty in regard to the relevant date is particularly relevant if treaties have been negotiated within the same time span or if several years lie between the adoption and the treaty's entry into force. Comparing two agreements, one could refer to either the date of adoption, the opening for signature (if different from the date of adoption) or the entry into force of the agreement. Furthermore, if one considers the obligations of a specific State, as is the traditional approach in the law of treaties, it would be possible to refer to either the date of the adoption of the treaty, the date of signa-

---

[330] See above Part II, B. II. 1. (b).

ture, the date of ratification, the entry into force of the agreement or, if different, the entry into force for the State, e.g. by later accession.

The question of the "age" of conflicting treaties is, as has already been mentioned, also relevant with respect to conflict clauses, many of which provide for the priority of "existing" treaties. The issue of determining the chronological order of the treaties, also in this context, has not yet been fully settled. While the reference to the entry into force seems appropriate from the point of view that, before the entry into force specific obligations for the States parties do not arise,[331] the reference to the date of adoption seems appropriate when considering a subsequent development or change of law. This is particularly so if there are several years between the date of the adoption and the entry into force. In such cases a treaty more truly reflects the standards and the views of the States Parties at the time of its adoption rather than at the time of its entry into force. Consequently, agreements negotiated after the adoption of the prior treaty might better express the contemporary views of many Parties even if the earlier-adopted treaty enters into force at a date subsequent to the more contemporary treaty. However, especially with respect to those multilateral environmental conventions that have been agreed upon in parallel negotiations (e.g. the Convention on Biological Diversity and the Framework Convention on Climate Change) any reference to a *lex posterior* rule based upon the date of adoption or entry into force seems inappropriate.

2. Lex specialis *as a General Rule of International Law*

As part of the discussion of conflicts between international environmental agreements in Part I of this study, reference was made to the rule regarding the priority to be given to more specific agreements as against more general, parallel treaties. In principle, general agreements and more specific treaties addressing the same issue can exist alongside one another without necessarily calling the validity or applicability of either of the treaties into question. Where there is a conflict between two treaties, however, the more specific of the two would claim superiority according to the *lex specialis* rule.

---

[331] I.e. other than the duty to refrain from acts which would defeat the object and purpose of a treaty; see article 18 VCLT.

In regard to the rule of *lex specialis*, the main problem is to establish in which cases an agreement can be said to be more specific than another. This is relatively easy to resolve in the case of a framework agreement found to be in conflict with a more detailed agreement. In principle, the application of this rule could lead to the assignment of priority to the protocols to a framework convention over the framework convention itself. A protocol is an international treaty in itself with, usually, its own organs and institutional structures. Yet, it is most closely connected to the framework agreement it was established to supplement.

The fact that participation in protocols is in many cases open only for States that are Parties to the framework agreement reflects this close interdependence. Whether participation in a protocol is restricted to States and regional economic integration organizations that are also Parties to the framework convention results from the respective provisions of the protocol.[332] The underlying reason why protocols are often restricted to those States that are also Parties to the framework convention is that protocols build upon general principles and obligations laid out in the framework. The system established by the framework as the basic understanding of a preferably large group of States remains intact, even if not all States parties later also ratify the more specific protocols. As opposed to this States that only subscribe to some specific obligations set by protocols are not bound by the general objectives and principles and enjoy greater freedom that can contradict the establishment of a comprehensive regulative system on an issue.

The objective to comprehensively regulate a certain issue, although not in one act but by adopting several subsequent instruments, nevertheless requires by its approach that States have agreed to the underlying principles, aims and basic obligations in the framework. If States were free to just choose some specific protocols without agreeing to the overall objectives this would reflect the traditional piecemeal approach and in many cases contradict the creation of comprehensive regimes. Even if the framework is too abstract to give practical value to its regulations, it performs the essential function to tie States to the procedural framework of activity for a group of States parties i.e. a community of States

[332] See e.g. article 24, para. 1 Kyoto Protocol: "This Protocol shall be open for signature and subject to ratification, acceptance or approval by States and regional economic integration organizations which are Parties to the Convention. [...]"; see also article 9, para. 1 Protocol to the 1979 Convention on Long-range Transboundary Air Pollution on the Reduction of Sulphur Emissions or their Transboundary Fluxes by at least 30 Per Cent, 1985.

obliging themselves to act along the same lines concerning a specific issue.[333]

Because of these deliberations most framework conventions consider it vital to include States into the group of member States first, before they can also oblige themselves to more activities and duties that specify the basic principles and objectives. Consequently, they render the status as a States party to the framework convention a condition for the signature and ratification of or accession to the later protocols. Despite them being more specific, the application of the *lex specialis* rule in the case of potential contradictions between framework convention and the protocol is, as already mentioned, explicitly excluded by the respective protocols by referring to the superiority of the framework to fulfill the function of the framework-protocol approach.

As a consequence, conflicts between a protocol, which is specifically established to complete a framework convention, and the respective framework itself can be considered particularly rare. Furthermore, clauses in the texts of protocols make sure that the framework is not considered inferior to a protocol, in the event that a rare conflict emerges. A similar relationship exists with respect to a convention and its implementing agreements.[334] Protocols and implementing agreements alike, according to their nature, set out more specific rules regarding an issue regulated by the framework agreement. Unlike most protocols, however, participation in implementing agreements is not limited to States Parties to the substantive convention.[335]

It is much more difficult to use the *lex specialis* rule to resolve the conflict between two agreements that results if they address the same issue in equally specific terms, albeit from different angles. Many of the cases discussed in this context, in which two framework agreements conflict, can probably not been settled by the *lex specialis* rule. The same is true where treaties have equally specific, conflicting objectives that seek to address different problems. For a settlement of the conflict between the Convention on Biological Diversity and the Kyoto Protocol, for example, the *lex specialis* would not be of any relevance. It is not only diffi-

---

[333] See Beyerlin (note 303), para. 89.

[334] See e.g. article 4 of the 1995 Fish Stocks Agreement.

[335] That gave, e.g. the United States, the possibility to become a member to the Fish Stocks Agreement without having to be a States Party to the United Nations Convention on the Law of the Sea. The Fish Stock Agreement entered into force in December 2001.

cult to establish which of the agreements is more special. Even if the Kyoto Protocol were considered to be more specific because of the framework character of the Convention on Biological Diversity, giving the Kyoto Protocol priority pursuant to the *lex specialis* rule seems inappropriate because the two agreements deal with completely distinct objectives and only meet (and in fact, conflict) with respect to a very limited issue. In contrast thereto, an overlap between the regime on the environmental protection of Antarctica and the Convention on the Law of the Sea might, as indicated in Part I of this study, be settled in favor of the more specific rules applicable to the polar regions.

The *lex specialis* rule is applicable, and contributes to the resolution of conflicting international agreements: (1) with respect to an overlap of issues that would lead to a doubling of efforts, (2) for framework agreements, and (3) in favor of more specific treaties. For conflicting agreements which deal with equally specific issues or which are of a similar nature (either equally more vague, like framework agreements, or equally more specific) the rule is less useful. Again, in contrast to a coordination of agreements as such, the derogation from the more general rule in accordance with the more specific agreement is only applicable *inter se*, i.e. between those States Parties participating in both the more general and the more specific regime. The rule of *lex specialis* is of rather limited relevance with respect to the resolution of conflicts between agreements, though it has some utility in this context.

VI. Conclusions

A discussion of treaty interpretation, article 30 and 60 VCLT and the *lex posterior* and *lex specialis* rules, reveals that the law of treaties can only partially be employed as a tool to solve conflicts between treaties. The harmonization of the content of treaties calls for a forum for a common decision-making process. If the coordination of treaties has been agreed upon in such a context, the law of treaties, in a second step, can be employed to implement the decision, e.g. by an authentic interpretation, modification or amendment of a treaty. The law of treaties cannot itself offer a forum for a decision-making process on the harmonization of treaties because of its specific function. However, the law of treaties is in no way without meaning in this context because its rules are needed to determine the existence, application and termination of treaties. Within the framework of the law of treaties, easier procedures for amending treaties or permitting majority decisions regarding binding interpretations of treaties could enhance the role of the law of treaties in the coordination of conflicting agreements.

D. Cooperation and International Environmental Governance

(Matz)

I. Issues of Governance and Cooperation

Because the law of treaties cannot provide a forum for the coordination of the content of treaties, different approaches must be considered. Elements of an international environmental governance process might provide more realistic and effective chances of success. In particular, mechanisms of cooperation between different international institutions must be taken into account in this context. As a substantial element of the further discussion of such mechanisms it is also necessary to take into consideration the fact that any approach involving the cooperation between States, treaty organs, organizations and other institutions cannot be based upon a one-time event but must involve a continuous process.[336]

1. Reasons for Cooperation in International Environmental Law

The increasing general collaboration of States after World War II and particularly the enhanced cooperation in environmental matters is one of the most important developments in international relations.[337] The reasons why States found a shift from mere coexistence to cooperation necessary are, *inter alia*, reflective of the emergence of transboundary risks with potentially very grave consequences for the international community. These transboundary risks include long-range weapons of mass destruction, but with respect to the treaties at issue in this study,

---

[336] On a systematic approach to a continuous coordination process see UNEP/IGM/2/5 (4 July 2001), para. 7.

[337] P.-T. Stoll, "The International Environmental Law of Cooperation", in: Wolfrum (note 179), 39 et seq.

global environmental dangers such as the destruction of the ozone layer or the depletion of natural resources are especially significant.

In light of increasing international interrelations and interaction, especially characterized and fueled by globalization, the pressure to engage in institutional cooperation continues to rise.[338] This may apply to international environmental law even more than to other fields of international political and legal interest. Only international environmental law can respond on an international level to global environmental damage and the growing awareness of the global interdependence of ecological factors. Global cooperation of States is a necessity in order to successfully address, in a coöperative manner, the need to protect the ozone layer or to prevent climate change. Even if States could approach these global environmental issues unilaterally, cooperation with other States enhances the efficiency of the efforts.[339] In many cases, however, a process leading to better environmental protection must be initiated as a cooperative effort. It is unlikely, for example, that many States would feel obliged to reduce or terminate polluting activities in an international watercourse if the other riparian States were not also willing to change their behavior.[340] Encouraged by modernity's significant risks and often broad cooperation, international environmental law has, in this new climate, undertaken the setting of environmental standards, the establishment of institutions and the development of respective regulations.[341]

---

[338] Ipsen/ Epping (note 266), chapter 2, § 6, para. 1.

[339] In favor of a cooperative linking of issues, particularly in the field of international trade, S. Charnovitz, "Linking Topics in Treaties", *Univ. Penn. J. Int'l Economic L.* 19 (1998), 329 et seq. (335), lists four reasons: (1) the increase of efficiency of policies; (2) the rebalancing of policies; (3) international coalition building and (4) the achievement of economies of a certain scale.

[340] In particular concerning the issue of the conservation and management of international watercourses, the cooperation of riparian States led to significant efforts and several international instruments on the protection of rivers, e.g. the Rhine, the Sambezi river, the Niger and the Amazon as well as the more general Convention on the Protection of Transboundary Watercourses and International Lakes 1992, BGBl. II (1994), 2333 et seq.

[341] Stoll (note 337), 41.

Although States have a common interest in the cooperative problem solving, their interest in cooperation is not of an altruistic nature.[342] As already mentioned in regard to many issues, international cooperation is the only possibility for solving most environmental problems. States are more willing to cooperate because the most pressing environmental problems evade unilateral attempts at a resolution. Ultimately, the necessity of cooperation in order to achieve environmental objectives has itself been enshrined as a principle in international environmental law: (1) by principle 24 of the Stockholm Declaration, 1972;[343] (2) by Agenda 21, which also recognizes the importance of enhanced international cooperation; and (3) by the Rio Declaration, which stresses international cooperation as a prerequisite for the pursuit of its aims in principle 27.

2. *Forms of Cooperation and Their Relevance*

The principle of cooperation in environmental matters is now the fundamental basis of international environmental law.[344] Institutional cooperation in international environmental law refers to two aspects of cooperation: (1) the cooperation of States in the work of international institutions, and (2) cooperation between different institutions. Not only in the ordinary use of the term, but also as used in international legal terminology, cooperation is a broad and not very precisely defined concept. Normally, cooperation in international law is considered to be the voluntary and coordinated action, of two or more subjects of international law, that has a joint objective as its aim.[345]

Effective structures of cooperation in international environmental law cannot, however, be limited to cooperation between recognized subjects of international law. Because of the growing influence of organs and sub-organs of international environmental treaties and NGOs, such a restriction would be inappropriate. Cooperation with regard to international environmental law must involve the cooperation of: (1) States,

---

[342] On the relevance of the common interest in regard to international environmental law and cooperation see J. Brunnée, "Common Interest – Echoes from an Empty Shell?", *ZaöRV* 49 (1989), 791 et seq. (particularly 794 et seq.).

[343] *ILM* 11 (1972), 1416 et seq.

[344] Kilian, "Environmental Protection", in: R. Wolfrum (ed.), *United Nations: Law, Policies and Practice* (1995), vol. 1, 487 et seq., para. 9.

[345] R. Wolfrum, "International Law of Cooperation", *EPIL* II (1995), 1242.

(2) international organizations, (3) organs of international treaties, and to a growing extent (4) non-governmental organizations. Although the institutional cooperation of States (with other States) within the framework of international organizations continues to gain relevance,[346] the significance of cooperation in international environmental law is not limited to such forms, since information and cooperation structures are developing between all of the above identified actors. Consequently, cooperation in international environmental law now comes in a wide-range of different forms.

The coordination of the activities of international environmental organizations through enhanced cooperation is a particularly important development with respect to efforts to prevent overlapping competences and activities. Without the coordination that results from enhanced cooperation, the significant problems that result from conflicts between international agreements finds its equivalence in the overlap of and conflict between the activities of international environmental organizations.[347] Both phenomena (conflicts between treaties and disputes between organizations regarding conflicting competences) are closely connected by the fact that international organizations often prepare and develop international treaties. Furthermore, modern environmental agreements create and consist of institutionalized structures and organs that resemble organizations.

Furthermore, the cooperative relationship between international environmental treaties, as between different treaties and as between treaties and other actors (international organizations) plays an important role in international environmental law. Cooperation between States was traditionally an important factor of transboundary environmental law, e.g. for the clarification and regulation of neighborly relations. It is still the precondition for the negotiation and adoption of multilateral environmental agreements, though its significance with respect to the harmonization of environmental law is declining with the rise in collaboration between other international structures. In this respect, the cooperation of States that leads to the adoption of agreements can be seen as an "initial" form of cooperation. State-based, initial cooperation must be followed, however, by a form of on-going cooperation that takes place

---

[346] W. Hoppe/ M. Beckmann/ P. Kauch, *Umweltrecht* (2000), § 3, para. 7.

[347] See also the remark of P. Haas, "Global Environmental Governance", in: Commission on Gobal Governance, Issues in Global Governance – Papers written for the Commission on Global Governance (1995), 333 et seq. (357 et seq.).

between: (1) the organs created by an individual treaty; (2) organs of different treaties; and (3) distinct institutions. This on-going cooperation makes it possible to coordinate the implementation, interpretation and development of international environmental treaties. With respect to the harmonization of international environmental agreements, close cooperation on two levels seems particularly important: (1) between the organs of international environmental agreements; and (2) between the agreements and responsible international organizations and institutions.

3. Institutional Cooperation and Loss of State Sovereignty

A potential obstacle to institutional cooperation is the perception on the part of States that institutional cooperation will erode the national sovereignty of the participating States. The limitation of State sovereignty and the transfer of power to other decision-making mechanisms and forums are important aspects of international cooperation in environmental law. On the one hand, a limitation of sovereignty by the transfer of powers of enforcement and compliance assistance to international institutions can strengthen international environmental law. On the other hand, the necessary transfer of sovereignty constitutes an obstacle to the development of international law because States, jealously guarding their sovereignty, resist the creation of institutions with expansive competences.

Both aspects, the efficiency of environmental regulations and their enforcement as well as skepticism concerning a loss of sovereignty, are particularly relevant if international institutions are granted decision-making powers that involve majority voting. States object to the possibility of treaty modifications or the creation of binding interpretations based on majority voting.[348] While the acceptance of international environmental agreements and the institutional structure of treaties generally reflects the international community's will to actively collaborate on an interstate level, traditional perceptions of State sovereignty continue to hamper international cooperation for the protection of the environment.[349]

---

[348] Beyerlin (note 303), para. 58, notices a special sacrifice of sovereignty by States.

[349] Ibid, para. 59.

II. The Institutional Structure of International Environmental Agreements

1. Modern Treaties and International Organizations

Modern environmental treaties have in common the fact that they establish different organs. In this respect, modern agreements resemble international organizations, although technically they do not fulfill some of the requirements necessary for qualification as international organizations in international law. The institutionalization of treaties is based upon the understanding that the challenges of modern environmental law require the continuity of cooperative, institutional structures.[350]

Because of the similarities between international organizations and the institutional structures created by modern environmental agreements, authors sometimes refer to international environmental agreements as "small-scale" environmental organizations.[351] At times the discussion does not even distinguish between the two entities, e.g. when "organizations" created by international environmental treaties are listed as a third group of international organizations, following the UN and its sub-organizations as the first group and regional organizations outside the UN as the second group.[352] Primarily, international environmental agreements differ from international organizations in that they lack independence from the will and interest of the member States that created them.[353] Institutionalized treaties also lack legal personality in international law and cannot enter into international treaties themselves. The treaty organs can, however, agree on Memoranda of Understanding[354]

---

[350] A. Kiss/ D. Shelton, *International Environmental Law* (2000), 82.

[351] Beyerlin (note 303) para. 165.

[352] Sands (note 18), 65, who lists *inter alia* the Convention on Biological Diversity, the Framework Convention on Climate Change and the Basel Convention on the Transboundary Movement of Hazardous Wastes as examples.

[353] T. Gehring/ S. Oberthür, "Internationale Regime als Steuerungsinstrumente der Umweltpolitik", in: Gehring/ Oberthür (note 162), 9 et seq. (17).

[354] Memoranda of Understanding or Memoranda of Cooperation are documents negotiated and adopted by institutions, e.g. treaty organs, to clarify issues of common political interest and to set out general agreement on cooperation. While these memoranda are not legally binding, and in many cases worded in rather vague terms, they are the common instrument for formalizing relations and cooperation between institutions. In this respect they can play a sig-

with other organs and thereby engage in some forms of cooperation leading to the harmonization of treaties.

2. *Treaty Organs and Their Functions*

Usually international environmental treaties provide for: (1) a Conference of States Parties (also Meeting of States Parties) as the main decision-making organ, (2) a Secretariat for administrative functions, and (3) a subsidiary body for scientific and technical advice. Additional subsidiary bodies and working groups, e.g. concerned with the implementation of the agreement or special questions, can be established by the Conference of the Parties to provide for the more efficient implementation of the treaty. There is a common need, on the part of most environmental treaties, to provide scientific and technical advice to States and treaty organs. There is also a common need for a decision-making organ that attempts to balance the sovereign rights and obligations of the members, environmental protection, and the administration and cooperative integration of the treaty into the international political and legal system.[355] Because these needs are common to international environmental treaty regimes, most treaties are organized in a similar manner in regard to the organs they create and the functions they assign to these organs.

Five different categories of functions performed by treaty organs can be distinguished: (1) consultation and coordination, (2) setting of rules and regulation, (3) compliance assistance, (4) monitoring, and (5) dispute settlement.[356] However, a strict categorization in the sense that a treaty establishes different organs for each of these activities cannot be found in international environmental law. Usually, at least the Conference of

---

nificant role concerning institutional means for a coordination of agreements. See also further below in section D. III. 3.

[355] J. Werksman, "The Conference of Parties to Environmental Treaties", in: J. Werksman (ed.), *Greening International Institutions* (1996), 55 et seq. (57 et seq.) adds to the first two issues the differentiation of obligations in accordance with the economic capacity of States Parties. However, such a differentiation alone does not influence the organizational structures unless a committee monitors compliance and grants assistance to developing countries or the treaty employs a fund as a compliance assistance mechanism.

[356] See U. Beyerlin, "State Community Interest and Institution-Building in International Environmental Law", *ZaöRV* 56 (1996), 613.

the Parties to an agreement performs several of the listed functions assisted by the Secretariat.

(a) The Conference of the Parties

The Conference of the Parties, also called Meeting of States Parties,[357] is the main organ of modern environmental treaties and is explicitly created by the treaty text.[358] Executive organs and Commissions of certain environmental agreements[359] are in fact similar to Conferences of the Parties.[360] Although the specific functions assigned to this organ by the respective treaties can vary, the Conferences of the Parties have certain functions in common. Generally, the Conference of the Parties is responsible for the interpretation of the treaty, its development and implementation by further decisions and for other activities related to the implementation of the agreement.[361]

In addition to the functions assigned to the Conferences of the Parties that are set out in detail in the agreements, many treaties additionally provide for the general competence to make decisions on all those issues that appear to be relevant for the implementation and performance

---

[357] V. Röben, "Institutional Development under Modern International Environmental Agreements", *UNYB* 4 (2000), 369, points out that the term Conference of the Parties refers to the main organ of framework agreements, whereas the main organ of protocols is named Meeting of Parties. While this is the case in regard to many treaties and protocols, e.g. considering the Framework Convention on Climate Change and its Kyoto Protocol, the terminology is by no means a necessity.

[358] Article 22, para. 2 of the Convention to Combat Desertification calls the Conference of the Parties the "supreme body". So does article 7, para. 2 of the Framework Convention on Climate Change as well as article 13, para 1 Kyoto Protocol. In contrast thereto the Convention on Biological Diversity does not explicitly emphasize the position of the Conference of the Parties in its article 23. However, its function as the main decision-making organ become clear by the listing of its far-reaching competences.

[359] E.g., the executive organ of the Convention on Transboundary Air Pollution and the Commissions of OSPAR and the Helsinki Convention respectively.

[360] See Beyerlin (note 348), para. 165 in footnote 221; different Röben (note 357), 369 et seq. and 431 et seq., who distinguishes between the institutions and their relevant functions.

[361] On the different functions see Röben, ibid, at 369 et seq.

of the treaty.[362] The Conference of the Parties, with its substantial catalogue of powers and an additional competence on all issues related to the implementation of a treaty, is the main reason why modern institutionalized treaties can be compared with international organizations.

The most important function of the Conference of the Parties is the development and implementation of a treaty. Besides monitoring and compliance control, implementation also involves the interpretation and, if necessary, the modification and amendment of the treaty. In this respect, the Conference of the Parties is also the organ responsible for the implementation of decisions regarding the coordination of different agreements that are related to the treaty. However, the mere competence to decide on a modification of an agreement does not give any indication as to the process by the decision regarding the means of coordination will be made. To reach agreement on questions related to two or more international environmental agreements, cooperation with the organs of other treaties and, if necessary, international organizations and institutions is essential. Only by a multilateral process can decisions be reached that are, in the first instance, acceptable to all concerned institutions, and that, in the second instance, can be implemented by the interpretation or modification of the Conferences of the Parties.

Cooperation with organs of other treaties or with international organizations can also be explicitly assigned to the Conference of the Parties. Article 13, para. 4, (i) Kyoto Protocol provides that the Meeting of the Parties shall, if appropriate, cooperate with as well as make use of the services and information provided by competent international organizations and transnational and non-governmental institutions. Even if cooperation with other institutions is not explicitly mentioned in a treaty, it is likely that the authority to cooperate could be based upon a general competence to deal with issues necessary for better implementation of an agreement. Generally, cooperation with other independent institutions is a question of the more efficient implementation of an agreement,[363] e.g. to clarify competences, save financial resources or solve conflicts. The concrete form of cooperation is subject to the discretion of the treaty organs and will be dealt with in greater detail below.

---

[362] See e.g. article 23, para. 4, (i) CBD or article 13, para. 4, (j) Kyoto Protocol.

[363] Röben (note 357), 387.

(b) The Secretariat

Two types of treaty Secretariat can be distinguished, in regard to function: (1) a Secretariat that prepares and organizes the meetings of the Conference of the Parties and the subsidiary bodies, also being responsible for coordinating cooperation with other institutions; and (2) a Secretariat that, in addition to these functions, also implements programs and projects on a regional or national level.[364] UNEP administers the Secretariats of many international environmental agreements. Recently, however, there has been a trend toward the establishment of Secretariats that are independent of UNEP.[365] Another option for newly adopted instruments is that UNEP carries out the Secretariat function on an *interim* basis until the contracting parties have set up an autonomous Secretariat.

The Secretariat can play an important role concerning a treaty's implementation and compliance control. For those treaties that lay down reporting obligations the Secretariat is responsible for the collection of national reports. In many cases the Secretariat not only collects the reports and forwards them to the Conference of the Parties, but it also provides for a synthesis of national reports and other information. Such papers can then serve as a background to meetings held by the Conference of the Parties or subsidiary bodies.

Secretariats can also support States Parties in the implementation of a treaty by coordinating mechanisms of technology transfer and capacity building, or, as an aide to States Parties, by initiating such processes and other measures of implementation and compliance. The Secretariat of the Basel Convention, for example, has collected national legislation and has, based upon their experiences, prepared a model law and technical guidelines on the safe handling of wastes. These guidelines and the model law can be of considerable help to States that are having difficulties with implementation and compliance.[366] As another example, the Secretariat to the Washington Convention on Trade with Endangered Species has issued guidelines regarding the implementation of the treaty and offers technical support as well as analysis of national legislation.

---

[364] Doc. UNEP/IGM/2/INF/3, para. 14.

[365] The Secretariats UNEP administers include the Secretariat of the Convention on Biological Diversity, the Secretariat of the Basel Convention and the Secretariat of the Washington Convention on International Trade in Endangered Species *inter alia*.

[366] See Kiss/ Shelton (note 350), 128.

Another function of the Secretariats serving modern international environmental treaties is closely connected with the better implementation of treaties. Secretariats can be used as a platform for the exchange of information, i.e. an information clearing house. While some agreements, e.g. the Convention on Biological Diversity, have established a specific Clearing House Mechanism, in other cases, e.g. in the case of the Montreal Protocol, the Secretariat collects and disseminates data and information to States Parties and treaty organs. The systematic exchange of information is important for cooperation and coordination with other agreements, particularly if organs of other treaties and international organizations are allowed to participate in such a process.

(c) Scientific and Technical Subsidiary Organs

The greatest variety of fields of activity and functions can be found in regard to the subsidiary treaty bodies. Such organs are created according to a treaty's specific need for additional structures, including working groups focused on certain subjects relevant to the implementation of the treaty.[367] Many agreements have established an expert body charged with providing advice regarding technical, technological and scientific matters. The specific functions of these expert committees are often regulated directly in the treaty.[368] Another group of subsidiary bodies consists of organs that are primarily responsible for the implementation of the agreement, e.g. so called implementation committees. These can either be provided for by the treaty, e.g. by article 10 FCCC, or can later be established by a decision of the Conference of States Parties.

If expert committees are also responsible for methodological questions arising out of the efforts to achieve a more efficient implementation of treaties, they have the possibility to systematically examine the conflicts that exist between their parent treaty and other agreements. This could lead to the development cooperative structures. Furthermore, cooperation with other technical and scientific subsidiary bodies for the development of joint strategies is possible and important for the harmoniza-

---

[367] Many agreements have assigned the competence to their respective Conference of the Parties to decide on the creation of further subsidiary bodies subject to its discretion, see e.g. article 23, para. 4, lit. (g) CBD, article 7, para. 2, (i) FCCC, article 22, para. 2, lit. (c) CCD.

[368] See e.g. article 25 CBD, article 9 FCCC or article 24 CCD.

tion of treaties. The Joint Programmes of Action of the Convention on Biological Diversity and the Ramsar Convention on Wetlands are an example of the intense involvement of scientific bodies in the collaborative efforts of two treaty regimes. In this example, the respective expert committees contributed substantially to the creation of the Joint Programmes.

III. Means of Cooperation between Agreements

1. Introduction

Although the specific objectives as well as the forms of cooperation can differ, the reasons for inter-treaty collaboration are, in principle, the same. Primarily, member States and treaty organs hope to improve the efficiency with which the treaties are implemented. To pursue this objective, the most commonly established mechanisms are the facilitation of information exchange, the adoption of Memoranda of Understanding and joint programs of action. The decision of a treaty organ to enter into cooperation with the organ of another treaty can constitute both a means to achieve an objective and the end (cooperation) itself. According to the Report on the Third Conference of the Parties to the Convention on Biological Diversity, member States aimed to create mechanisms of cooperation to facilitate the exchange of information, facilitate working programs and to initiate an exchange on the issue how other treaties could contribute to the implementation of the Convention on Biological Diversity.[369]

Regarding cooperation between the organs of different environmental agreements, the treaty texts provide almost no concrete regulations. Article 23, para. 4, lit. (h) CBD, for example, provides that the Conference of the Parties shall:

> "Contact through the Secretariat, the executive bodies of conventions dealing with matters covered by this Convention with a view to establishing appropriate forms of cooperation with them (...)".

This competence, granted to the Conference of the Parties and, more indirectly, the Secretariat of the Convention on Biological Diversity, provides no explicit guidance in determining which agreements should be the subject of cooperative relations or how, once this determination

---

[369] Doc. UNEP/CBD/COP/3/29.

is made, such cooperation shall be designed. The general provisions allow greater flexibility but the lack of concrete guidance does nothing to ensure that collaboration between treaty organs will be established, and if so, that it amounts to something more than a mere formality. The gaps left by the generalities regarding cooperation must be filled-in by the later activities and decisions of treaty organs. With the growing sense of the importance of inter-treaty cooperation, as regards the effective implementation of international environmental agreements, the respective treaty organs have become increasingly occupied with their relationships with other agreements. This is not limited to a specific class of treaty organs but involves the Conferences of the Parties as well as the Secretariats and the subsidiary bodies.

2. *The Exchange of Information between Treaty Organs*

An exchange of information is a necessary prerequisite for the coordination of treaties. As a consequence, mechanisms for the exchange of information constitute the most important forms of cooperation. They are the basis of all other means of cooperation between the institutions of various treaty regimes. Generally, the exchange of information places no great strain on the treaty organs. However, the shared information only provides opportunities for the harmonization of different agreements, provided that treaty organs and member States not only desire the collaboration between treaties but also use the shared information towards this end. The mere exchange of information, without more, is not sufficient to lead to better coordination, although it is a necessary precondition.

If States forwarded to the Secretariats, not only those pieces of information they are obliged to provide because of the treaty's reporting requirements, but also other data on the implementation of the agreement, Secretariats could make this more comprehensive body of information available through a common exchange mechanism. If supplemented with data gathered by other institutions, e.g. by the organs of other agreements or international organizations, this would be an important step towards building the foundation necessary for a comprehensive harmonization of implementation policies and the avoidance of conflicts between agreements. At the very least, such a comprehensive exchange of information could help States, treaty organs and international organizations identify conflicts and decide upon priority issues for future activities.

The design of information exchange mechanisms is extremely variable. Information exchange structures can relate to systematic, permanent forums of exchange or other permanent relations, e.g. based upon Memoranda of Cooperation. Information exchange structures can also arise out of one-time events, such as joint studies or workshops on specific topics. There are three primary approaches to the coordination of information exchange: (1) the creation of a joint, harmonized institution for the exchange of information between all participating conventions; (2) the harmonization of national reporting obligations; and (3) the development of a joint network to facilitate the exchange of experiences.[370]

Observation of the meetings of the institutions and organs of other agreements is another viable and widely practiced means exchanging information. However, the shortage of financial and human capacity constitutes a serious restriction to the systematic participation of the observer missions in the meetings of the receiving treaty organs. The participation of observers at all meetings of relevance to a certain environmental agreement is almost impossible because of the growing number of agreements and the large number of meetings. This is even more true if an agreement touches upon a variety of issues as in the case of the Convention on Biological Diversity, e.g. nature conservation, indigenous peoples and trade. The same would be the case for the Convention on the Law of the Sea, which would have to send observers to meetings concerned with subjects as far afield as the safety of navigation, nature conservation and fisheries. A better coordination of meetings, both in time and in location, could partially improve this significant obstacle.

A study of the World Conservation Monitoring Center offers valuable insights with respect to the exchange and management of information relevant to biodiversity treaties.[371] The study was supported by UNEP, the Secretariats of the Convention on Biological Diversity, the Washington Convention on the International Trade in Endangered Species, the Ramsar Convention on Wetlands and the World Heritage Convention. The Ministry for the Environment of Belgium supported the project on behalf of the Bonn Convention on the Conservation of Migrat-

---

[370] WCMC (T.H. Johnson/ I.K. Crain/ M.V. Sneary), Feasibility Study for a Harmonised Informations Management Infrastructure for Biodiversity-related Treaties (1998), at page 3. The paper is available at <http://www.wcmc.org.uk/convent/treaties.htm>, last visited 23 January 2002.

[371] Ibid.

ing Species. These five treaties understand themselves to constitute the group of biodiversity-related treaties and, hence, they are viewed as partner agreements. The partnership does not only refer to the analysis and improvement of information flows between the treaties and their organs, but also to some joint activities. Another example involved a workshop attended by the representatives of the Framework Convention on Climate Change and the Convention to Combat Desertification, in recognition of the fact that the coordination of information management is also relevant between the so-called Rio Conventions. These partnerships are an example of the institutional efforts undertaken to promote a harmonization of treaties.

3. *Memoranda of Understanding or Cooperation*

To a growing extent, organs of environmental treaties employ Memoranda of Understanding or Memoranda of Cooperation to clarify and coordinate their relations with other institutions. As already mentioned above, Memoranda of Understanding are not legally binding treaties but are only politically binding upon the participating institutions. Due to the fact that treaty organs and programs like UNEP lack legal personality, Memoranda of Understanding or other political documents are the only means available for formalizing relations. As a consequence, a significant weight is attached to these Memoranda even if they are not legally binding. Memoranda of Understanding can be employed to enhance cooperation between two agreements. In the realm of the Open-ended Intergovernmental Group of Ministers on International Environmental Governance (Ministerial Working Group on Environmental Governance) UNEP has declared that the growing number of Memoranda within the last two years reflect the increasing political will to implement environmental agreements in a coordinated manner.[372]

Depending upon the agreement reached therein, Memoranda of Understanding can provide guidance for the harmonization of two agreements and set the stage for continuous further cooperation and coordination. A form of overarching coordination, by e.g. an international organization of a greater number of international agreements, might, however, be more viable than bilateral Memoranda. Memoranda of Understanding have, to this point, only been concluded bilaterally and, while po-

---

[372] International Environmental Governance – Report of the Executive Director, Doc. UNEP/IGM/1/2, para. 60.

tentially effective for the coordination of two agreements, they cannot serve as a forum in which a larger number of treaties can be harmonized. Harmonizing treaties in a bilateral manner could, theoretically, establish new and different conflicts. Nevertheless, the contribution these Memoranda of Understanding can make to the coordination of international environmental law, even by only addressing conflicts between specific treaties must be acknowledged.

In principle, all Memoranda of Understanding are only as suitable to the task of formalizing relationships between two agreements as the mechanisms for which the Memoranda provide. This applies in particular to means created for the harmonization of the contents of the relevant treaties. In this respect, some Memoranda constitute little more than a first step in the right direction, falling well short of the theoretical possibilities for effective cooperation and coordination. The flow of information between two agreements seems a good candidate for resolution in Memoranda of Understanding. Unfortunately, many Memoranda in the environmental context do not regulate the issue.[373] Examples of an approach that reaches further and intensifies the relations established by Memoranda of Cooperation are joint programs of action. The most prominent examples of such an approach are the two Joint Programs of Action by the Convention on Biological Diversity and the Ramsar Convention on Wetlands.

4. Partnerships and Joint Activities of Treaties

The Joint Programs of the Convention on Biological Diversity and the Ramsar Convention on Wetlands, as well as efforts concerning a partnership of biodiversity-related agreements, have already been subject to some consideration. Such partnerships seem particularly well-suited for the establishment of forums for the coordination of environmental agreements. Some factors that influence the potential outcome of such partnerships are the number of participating treaties and the issue addressed by partnerships. While joint activities performed by treaties concerning exactly the same or very similar issues can rather easily avoid a doubling of efforts and conflicts, partnerships between the in-

---

[373] The Memoranda of Understanding between the Convention on Biological Diversity and both the Ramsar Convention and the Bonn Convention do not address the issue. See also WCMC (note 370), 13.

stitutions created by the agreements seem particularly valuable in providing for a coordination of a larger scale cooperation.

The Collaborative Partnership on Forests (CPF) is an example. This partnership is built on two treaties, the Convention on Biological Diversity and the Convention to Combat Desertification, both represented by their Secretariats and a number of UN and other institutions.[374] The partnership, however, is more an example of cooperation between international organizations than an instrument of cooperation between treaties.

The creation of mechanisms for the cooperation and coordination, not only of treaties but also of treaties and different international organizations, must be a focus of future activities because of the chance that such cooperation can lead to the establishment of forums in which a significant number of environmental players can meet and coordinate their activities and interests. Partnerships between treaties as well as between treaties and international organizations, especially the efforts undertaken by UNEP in the realm of international environmental governance, are valuable approaches to that extent. The following sections on cooperation by international organizations will further discuss relevant structures and the potential for feasible mechanisms.

IV. Cooperation by International Organizations

1. A Coordinating Function of International Organizations

International organizations are a means of State cooperation for those issues that go beyond the competence and capacity of single States.[375] International organizations gain particular relevance for the regulation of and solutions for international environmental problems because of the transboundary and global challenges of environmental damage. For the same reasons, the importance of international non-governmental organizations dealing with environmental matters has also grown. In

---

[374] At the moment ten institutions are members of the CPF, which was established in April, 2001, in Rome. For more information and documentation of CPF meeting access < http://www.un.org/esa/sustdev/unffcpf.htm >, last visited 23 January 2002.

[375] M. Bothe/ H. Hohmann, "Internationale Umweltorganisationen", in: O. Kimminich/ H. Lersner/ P.-C. Storm, *Handwörterbuch des Umweltrechts* (1994), Vol. 1, 1113.

contrast to international organizations, those organizations described as "non-governmental" are not mechanisms of State cooperation but transboundary assemblies of individuals or of private associations that aim to influence processes of international decision-making concerning a variety of issues.[376]

The lack of a superior "World Environment Organization" or a comprehensive environmental administration makes voluntary cooperative structures between international organizations and between organizations and treaties the only path towards more coherence in international environmental law and environmental policy on an institutional basis.[377] The respective activities carried out by organizations at the moment are probably not sufficient, despite the growing efforts within the last years. A clarification of areas of competence in regard to different environmental organizations has not lost relevance as an important objective of international environmental policy.[378]

2. *The Role of the United Nations*

The United Nations is the organization with the broadest mandate and the greatest organizational support from special organizations and subsidiary bodies. The almost universal participation of States in the United Nations is another important factor establishing the incomparable political weight of the organization. The field of international environmental policies and law is not excepted from the controlling stature of the UN. The conservation of the environment is a topic that has been on the agenda of the United Nations for a long time and its development is reflected, e.g. by the UN Conferences in 1972 and 1992, by the creation of UNEP, and by other activities. Different bodies that deal with matters concerning the protection of environmental resources and sustainable development are gathered under the roof of the United Nations. The coordination of activities of UN institutions as well as the coordination of treaties is regularly on the UN's agenda.

The coordination of the activities of the different organizations and organs within the United Nations is the responsibility of the Administra-

---

[376] Although in some cases States can become members of international non-governmental organizations, e.g. at IUCN, this does not turn the respective organizations to a genuine means of State cooperation.

[377] Kiss/ Shelton (note 350), 84.

[378] Bothe/ Hohmann (note 375), 1131.

tive Committee on Coordination (ACC). As far as the coordination of activities concerning sustainable development is concerned, since 1992, the work of the ACC is supported by the recommendations of the Inter-Agency Committee on Sustainable Development (IACSD).[379] Since 1994 the Inter-Agency Committee on Environment (IACE) has also had a coordinating function in the inner structure of the United Nations.

(a) Decisions of the UN General Assembly Regarding the Coordination of International Environmental Law

Due to the priorities existing after World War II, the Charter of the United Nations focused on the avoidance and peaceful settlement of conflicts and did not explicitly adopt rules on the conservation of the environment in its text. The modern interpretation of the Charter, however, includes environmental issues.[380] As a consequence, the General Assembly can deal with environmental topics and regularly uses its competence to adopt resolutions and recommendations on these matters.[381] The Agenda 21 emphasizes the central role that the General Assembly plays and should continue to play in the development of international environmental policies within the United Nations system.

In regard to the need for better coordination of international environmental law, the General Assembly has not only issued several specific resolutions but has also referred to the problem in the realm of other subjects and has furthermore promised general support to the coordination of environmental treaties.[382] In general, the Assembly recommendations have rather political than legal weight. They do not have legally binding force outside the organization and they are not sufficiently concrete. Only in regard to other bodies of the UN, i.e. within the inner organization of the UN, are General Assembly recommendations binding and, if they are precise enough, their implementation can

---

[379] On the structures so also Sands (note 18), 69 et seq.

[380] V. Röben, "Institutions of International Environmental Law", in: Morrison/ Wolfrum (note 145), 71 et seq. (73).

[381] As an example of an important document of environmental policy see the World Charter for Nature, Resolution 37/7, 28 October 1982, *ILM* 22 (1983), 455 et seq. but also the call for a moratorium on fishing with long driftnets in Resolution 44/225, Doc. A/RES/44/225.

[382] On the last mentioned issue see Doc. A/54/468, 9.

be monitored. However, the guidance developed by the General Assembly in respect to treaty organs and other institutions is neither binding nor substantially concrete.

The following sections sketch out some UN General Assembly decisions on the coordination of environmental law, drawing a distinction between decisions that refer to the coordination of international environmental law in general and decisions that address specific organs of environmental treaties in regard to the treaty's relations to other agreements and their institutions.[383] The coordination of the so-called "Rio Conventions," i.e. the Convention on Biological Diversity, the Framework Convention on Climate Change and also the Convention to Combat Desertification, have frequently been the subject of General Assembly decisions. At times, however, all international institutions are called upon by General Assembly decisions to promote the coordination of environmental agreements.[384]

In the last two years two Resolutions have been issued by the General Assembly concerning the enhancement of the complementary relationship between international instruments.[385] The Assembly urged all treaties and institutions, UNEP in particular, to support the goal of cooperation, to enhance cooperation in general and to jointly promote the implementation of international agreements on an international, national and regional level. Detailed suggestions included the temporal coordination of meetings of Conferences of the Parties and the alignment of national reporting obligations. In Resolution 54/217 the General Assembly suggested that scientific analysis be undertaken by relevant institutions, e.g. UNEP, the Secretariats or scientific bodies, in order to identify activities with multiple advantages for different objectives and, consequentially, a better coordination of activities. Suggestions for a joint, or at least better coordinated, implementation of envi-

---

383 In particular the cooperation between the Convention on Biological Diversity and the Framework Convention on Climate Change and the Convention to Combat Desertification are subject to treaty related proposals. See e.g. the two Resolutions on the Convention on Biological Diversity: Resolution 54/221, 22 December 1999, Doc. A/RES/54/221 and Resolution 55/201 20 December 2000, Doc. A/RES/55/201.

384 E.g. Resolution 54/217, 22 December 1999, Doc. A/RES/54/217; Resolution 54/222, 22 December 1999, Doc. A/RES/54/222 and Resolution 55/198, 20 December 2000, Doc. A/RES/55/198.

385 Resolution 54/217, 22 December 1999, Doc. A/RES/54/217 and Resolution 55/198, 20 December 2000, Doc. A/RES/55/198.

ronmental agreements on a national level was also mentioned in the respective Resolutions.

In Resolution 53/186 the General Assembly specifically calls upon the Conferences of the Parties and the Secretariats of the Framework Convention on Climate Change, the Convention on Biological Diversity and the Convention to Combat Desertification to adopt measures for better coordination and the scientific evaluation of ecological interdependencies between the treaties.[386] All these proposals can also be found, to a differing extent, in the recent work of UNEP, particularly in the documents of the Ministerial Working Group on International Environmental Governance.

(b) Other UN Institutions Dealing with Environmental Matters

In addition to the General Assembly, the United Nations includes other organs and institutions with mandates concerning or touching upon environmental matters. One has to distinguish between institutions that are independent international organizations in a legal sense, UN Special Agencies, and those UN bodies lacking such an independent legal character. Those institutions that must come first when discussing a potential coordinating function are UNEP and eventually the CSD. Those two bodies are the international institutions that manage to keep an overview of environmental and on sustainable development issues.[387] Neither of the two institutions was founded by an international treaty. A General Assembly decision created UNEP and an ECOSOC decision founded the CSD. As a consequence, they lack at least one of the elements needed in order to be qualified as international organizations. It follows that they are subsidiary bodies of the UN without being autonomous subjects of international law.[388] Nevertheless, at least UNEP enjoys a superior role when it comes to the coordination of environmental treaties.

---

[386] Resolution 53/186, 2 February 1999, Doc. A/RES/53/186.

[387] See e.g. the report by L.A. Kimball, "Institutional Developments", *YIEL* 10 (1999), 137 et seq.

[388] As a consequence UNEP cannot be a party to international treaties and usually regulates its relations to other institutions by Memoranda of Understanding e.g. in regard to the agreement with the FAO, ILO, OECD, UNIDO, WHO and UNEP concerning the establishment of the Inter-Organization Programme for the Sound Management of Chemicals, *ILM* 34 (1995), 1311 et seq.

The relevant literature lists the following UN General Assembly specialized agencies as global international organizations with a field of activity that at least partially concerns environmental issues:[389] (1) the UN Organization on Education, Science and Culture (UNESCO), (2) the Food and Agriculture Organization (FAO), (3) the World Health Organization (WHO), (4) the World Meteorology Organization (WMO), (5) the International Atomic Energy Agency (IAEA), (6) the International Maritime Organization (IMO), (7) the International Labor Organization (ILO), and (7) the International Civil Aviation Organization (ICAO). As part of the sphere of activity of the UN on a regional basis, the Economic Commission for Europe (UNECE) is also quite active in environmental matters, often more so than its counterparts for other regions.[390]

The capacity of international organizations to adopt and become parties to treaties has not become relevant in the international practice.[391] However, organizations often provide a forum for the negotiation of treaties. That applies to the UN in general, e.g. in the case of the Convention on the Law of the Sea as well as for special organizations such as the IMO or the FAO and for regional organizations such as UNECE. Acts of secondary legislation in the form of decisions, which are binding for members, are another contribution to the development of international law. However, this contribution has been rather modest in regard to the development of environmental matters.[392]

The organizations mentioned in this context possess a mandate that charges them with concern only for specific subjects. The conservation of the environment is, in most cases, only of marginal importance. None of the said organizations has a general mandate on the coordination of international environmental law and the relevant treaties. The exchange of information between existing global and regional organi-

---

389 For further details see Kiss/ Shelton (note 350), 85-101.

390 Other regional organizations that are not affiliated with the UN and that are also concerned with environmental questions are the Organization for Economic Cooperation and Development (OECD), the Council of Europe (CE), the Organisation of American States (OAS), the regional Organizations of the South Pacific, and the recently terminated Organization of African Unity (OAU). Further institutions with fields of activity that include environmental protection are the European Union (EU) and the Organization for Security and Cooperation in Europe (OSCE).

391 Beyerlin (note 303), para. 62.

392 Ibid, para. 162.

zations, with a view to better coordinating the international protection of the environment, is necessary to avoid the overlap of areas of competence, the doubling of efforts and to generally streamline decision-making. The UN General Assembly, in several documents, has referred to the necessity of adopting measures for the improvement of relations between international organizations.[393] Many UN institutions have already become more active in cooperating with other bodies. The participation of the FAO, the UN Department for Economic and Social Affairs, UNEP and the UNDP in the Collaborative Partnership on Forests is a good example of closer cooperation on certain issues.

V. The Role of UNEP with Respect to the Coordination of International Environmental Agreements

The UN Environment Programme is a subsidiary organ of the United Nations that was created by UNGA Resolution 2997(XXVII) after the Stockholm Conference on the Human Environment in 1972.[394] UNEP's internal organization consists of three main organs: the Governing Council, the Secretariat with a Executive Director and the Environment Fund. In addition to these organs the Programme's work is assisted by a number of functional and regional offices.[395] The identification of synergies amongst international environmental conventions is assigned to the UNEP Division on Environmental Conventions that was established in 1999. The following section analyses UNEP's function and competences concerning the coordination of international environmental treaties from a legal and to some extent a factual perspective.

1. The UNEP's Potential Mandate to Coordinate Agreements

The different tasks assigned to UNEP by Resolution 2997(XXVII) and later by Agenda 21 establish UNEP as the principal institution for steering and guidance in international environmental law. Concerning the relationship between different organizations, UNEP is supposed to

---

[393] See inter alia A/RES 55/198, 20 December 2000.

[394] Doc. A/8730 (1972).

[395] On the organizational structures see Beyerlin (note 303), para. 145 et seq.

function as a catalyst for specific activities.[396] Consequently, the Programme should perform a coordinating function on the inter-organizational level. Although the extent of UNEP's role concerning the preparation and development of new environmental agreements is frequently subject to discussion,[397] the coordination of agreements calls instead for administrative and not legislative activities. UNEP should, however, perform all its activities concerned with international environmental agreements in total cooperation with the relevant Conferences of the Parties, thereby respecting their independence.[398]

The original catalogue of powers does not explicitly grant a mandate for UNEP to provide for or promote the coordination of international environmental treaties, although certain coordinating functions were assigned to UNEP from the beginning. According to Resolution 2997(XXVII), the promotion of international environmental cooperation is one of UNEP's three priorities. Yet this function does not necessarily include the coordination of environmental treaties. An explicit assignment regarding the coordination of international environmental agreements only related to programs and activities of the United Nations.[399] A product of the Earth Summit in 1992, Agenda 21 placed an emphasis on the potential function of UNEP as a coordinator of the growing number of environmental treaties.[400] However, Agenda 21 does not specify which measures UNEP can, or should, adopt in making use of its competence regarding the coordination of agreements. Neither can Agenda 21, as a political non-binding declaration, grant a legal mandate to UNEP or widen its competences in this respect.

---

396 Kiss/ Shelton (note 350), 87; also Haas (note 347), 343, who not only perceives UNEP as a catalyst but also as the "environmental conscience" of the United Nations.

397 See Haas (note 347), 348; A. Timoshenko/ M. Berman, "The United Nations Environment Programme and the United Nations Development Programme", in: Werksman (note 344), 38 (41).

398 The General Assembly confirms this view in each of its documents and resolutions dealing with institutional cooperation, see e.g. the Report of the Secretary General on "International institutional arrangements related to environment and development", Doc. A/54/468, para. 4.

399 The Inter-Agency Committee on Sustainable Development (IACSD) supports UNEP in performing this task.

400 Chapter 38, 22 (h) Agenda 21; see also Timoshenko/ Berman (note 397), 42 and Ipsen/ Heintschel von Heinegg (note 266), chapter 14, before § 57, para. 6.

On several occasions UNEP itself has affirmed its competences to coordinate environmental agreements, e.g. in the Declaration of Nairobi[401] and recently in the Malmö Declaration.[402] In addition to other aspects of coordination, the 1997 Nairobi Declaration mentions in para. 3, lit. (b) that UNEP aims to further develop international environmental law and that this development includes the establishment of coherent relations between existing environmental agreements. Again, this declaration does not have any legal effects concerning UNEP's mandate other than filling the legal frame established by Resolution 2997(XXVII) with political content. The Governing Council, during its special session on the reform and strengthening of UNEP, confirmed that the coordination of environmental treaties would be a priority in a strengthened and effective Environment Programme.[403] This has also been affirmed by UNGA Resolution 53/242, 28 July 1999.[404] This Resolution states that the General Assembly promotes the coordination of environmental treaties and stresses the necessity of supporting UNEP with the means necessary to perform its function in this respect. The report by the General Secretary on institutional structures in the field of the environment and development also mentions UNEP's mandate to develop international environmental law, *inter alia* by creating coherent links between existing environmental agreements.[405]

The most recent UNEP declaration stressing its function to politically coordinate environmental law is the Malmö Declaration, which was adopted within the framework of the first Global Ministerial Environment Forum in May, 2000. This meeting was based on General Assembly Resolution 53/242, which called for a conference at the ministerial level to identify priority issues concerning environmental matters and

401 See Nairobi Declaration: <http://www.unep.org/Documents/Default.asp?DocumentID=111&ArticleID=1728>, last visited 23 January 2002.

402 See Malmö Declaration: <http://www.unep.org/malmo/malmo_ministerial.htm>, last visited 23 January 2002.

403 See the Decision of the Governing Council SS.V/2, 22. May 1998. The UNEP Governing Council Decisions 20/17, 5 February 1999, as well as 20/18 and 20/28, both dating from 4 February 1999 concern the strengthening of UNEP's role in regard to the coordination of treaties and the promotion of cooperation of organs of multilateral environmental agreements.

404 As early as 1997, the General Assembly had referred to the necessary strengthening of UNEP in order to enhance the Programme's capacity in coordinating international treaties, A/RES/S-19/2, Annex, para. 123.

405 Doc. A/54/468, para. 34.

to decide upon guidelines for future activities. In paragraph 3 of the Malmö Declaration the ministers requested a coherent and coordinated approach to support the developing framework of international environmental law.

Two slightly different aspects to UNEP's coordination of treaties can be distinguished. The first aspect concerns the monitoring of contradictions and potential conflicts to existing treaties when a new agreement enters the negotiation phase. The second aspect concerns the coordination of those treaties already in existence. Both aspects are necessarily very closely related. If UNEP initiates or promotes the negotiation and adoption of new multilateral treaties, the Programme should also ensure, during the development of the agreement, that it harmonizes with existing environmental law. The Agenda 21 favors such a role of UNEP. Its text seems to refer to the development of international environmental law when sketching out UNEP's coordinating functions.[406]

However, the development of the content of new treaties and the active steering of the treaty-making process as far as the content of treaties are concerned are not part of UNEP's legal mandate. This restriction is one aspect why UNEP does not and cannot engage more progressively in the development of new treaties and their substantial coordination in the phase of their negotiation. The question of legal independence of UNEP as an institution is closely related to this issue. If UNEP were a fully fledged international organization instead of a Programme it would have the legal capacity to develop treaties and have them adopted by the member States according to the rules set by the organization's statute. This independence is denied to UNEP being only a subsidiary institution of the UN General Assembly.

This also prevents UNEP from concluding binding secondary law e.g. as (binding) guidance concerning the coordination of treaties during the negotiation of new agreements or concerning the coordination of existing treaties. In this respect the lack of independence is a restriction of the potential role UNEP could play in this context. However, whether States would grant UNEP the mandate to adopt binding secondary law on the coordination of treaties or to intervene in the treaty-making process if UNEP were an international organization is a distinct question. Even if States favored a strengthening of UNEP, its legal mandate and extent of competences concerning the coordination of treaties and other issues will give rise to controversies.

---

[406] Timoshenko/ Berman (note 397), 43.

Furthermore, UNEP's limited structural, human and financial capacities, even if the coordination of the contents of treaties during the phase of their making were legally assigned to UNEP, limit the Programme's ability to actively engage in and influence the negotiation of environmental treaties.[407] For the given reasons, not the streamlining of new treaties with existing ones but the coordination of existing treaties is the focus of UNEP's respective activities in international environmental law. Nevertheless, this function is to some extent also restricted by the same reasons concerning the limited legal mandate of UNEP and its actual capacity.

UNEP's confirmation of its own mandate, and similar, general declarations of support from the General Assembly, do not substantially contribute to the coordination of treaties because they are little more than political declarations of good intent providing no concrete guidelines for action. Such declarations do not identify fields of conflict and they do not suggest approaches for the resolution of contradictions. In this respect they do not reach further than Agenda 21, which also calls for the coordination of environmental agreements by UNEP without providing for more substantial guidance. As a consequence, UNEP enjoys a wide margin of independence and discretion as long as the Programme respects the autonomy of the Conferences of the Parties and Secretariats of the treaties it aims to coordinate.[408] In any event, UNEP lacks the authority to override decisions made by treaty organs because it lacks standing as a subject of international law and therefore cannot make decisions that are legally binding upon other international institutions.[409] For five years UNEP's role as a catalyst for and coordinator of developments in international environmental law was to be facilitated and supported by the Inter-Agency Environment Coordination Group (IAEG), which was founded in 1994. After the IAEG had been dissolved the task to assist with the coordination of different environmental and other issues within the UN has been transferred to the UN Environmental Management Group (EMG).

---

[407] Beyerlin (note 303), para. 152.

[408] This limitation is frequently emphasized by the UN General Assembly, *inter alia* in Resolution 53/242.

[409] Beyerlin (note 303), para. 114.

2. *UNEP's Activities Concerning the Coordination of Agreements*

UNEP maintains that its activities concerning the coordination of international environmental treaties suffered from a lack of conscious and overarching strategies before it established the Open-ended Intergovernmental Group of Ministers on International Environmental Governance.[410] It is too soon to tell whether the new strategies under the framework of the Ministerial Group will be successful.

(a) The Coordination of the Secretariats

One opportunity for the promotion of cooperation and coordination is created by the fact that UNEP acts as a Secretariat for different conventions. UNEP administers the Secretariats for different environmental agreements. In regard to this function UNEP performs all the administrative and other tasks assigned to the secretariat by the respective treaty. As has been mentioned above assignments range *inter alia* from the preparation of the meetings of the Conferences of the Parties to the exchange of information among States parties and the cooperation with other institutions. In this respect the secretariats do not differ from those administered by the agreements themselves or by other institutions. The secretariat also when administered by UNEP remains a treaty organ and by no means a (subsidiary) organ or division of UNEP. Otherwise the functional independence of the treaty regime from the UN would not be granted. The secretariats are as a result not accountable to UNEP but to the Conference of the Parties.

However, since the secretariats can perform an important function when it comes to the coordination of treaties by enhancing cooperation with the organs of other conventions UNEP as the administration of different secretariats can play a vital role. This is furthermore so because the fact that a single institution is the organizational roof for different secretariats can theoretically lead to improved cooperation. This consideration bases upon the potential for spatial and personal proximity. Nevertheless, one has to emphasize again that UNEP in its function as a secretariat for an environmental convention is by no means independent. However, the potential for an easier exchange of information between secretariats administered by the same institution shall be given some further attention.

---

[410] Proposal for a Systematic Approach to Coordination of Multilateral Environmental Agreements, UNEP/IGM/2/5, para. 2.

Functional and spatial correspondence in regard to Secretariats is a viable means to improve the flow and exchange of information. As a result of this improved information structure conflicts can be more easily identified and brought to the attention of the Conferences of the Parties. If treaty organs aim at a harmonization by Memoranda of Understanding, cooperation and negotiation between the respective Secretariats is also facilitated when they are located within the same institution. The internal organization of UNEP will determine the extent to which the coordination of treaties will improve as a result of these structural advantages. The location of the Secretariats of international environmental agreements in a common place is a frequent suggestion for the improvement of cooperation and coordination.[411] However, not even UNEP, with its formal unity, realizes the potential of this suggestion. The Secretariats over which UNEP has authority are not centrally located to one another but sit in, e.g. Montreal, Geneva and Bonn.

UNEP's potential functions envisaged by Agenda 21, however, not only concern the coordination of Secretariat activities but the coordination of the international environmental law-making and standard-setting process in general.[412] In accordance with this approach, UNEP has recently changed its attitude to the coordination of international environmental law and, particularly in the realm of the environmental governance process, has begun to explore different means of coordination. Nevertheless, the coordination of Secretariats remains quite important, especially if the coordination of Secretariat activities can be strengthened, improved and brought into a more systematic form. The Ministerial Group on International Environmental Governance also calls for this and other means of coordination.

Concerning the coordination of different environmental agreements[413] UNEP has so far held nine conferences for Secretariats of international environmental agreements.[414] A priority in this respect is the identifica-

---

[411] This suggestion has been made repeatedly by the General Assembly, e.g. in the program on the further implementation of Agenda 21, A/RES/S-19/2, Annex, para. 118 et seq.

[412] Timoshenko/ Berman (note 397), 43.

[413] I.e. not only those for which UNEP provides the Secretariats.

[414] The ninth Meeting on Coordination of Secretariats of Environmental Conventions took place on 11 and 12 February 2001 in Nairobi. The Secretariats of 13 global and 3 regional environmental agreements participated. As list of participants can be found in the report "International Environmental Govern-

tion of subjects that would benefit the most from enhanced coordination of activities. The results of these meetings now play an important role in determining the activities of other institutions, e.g. the activities by the Ministerial Group on International Environmental Governance.

(b) UNEP's Activities Concerning International Environmental Governance

In April, 2001, the first meeting of the Ministerial Group on International Environmental Governance took place in New York, a second meeting followed in July, 2001, in Bonn and a third one on 9-10 September 2001 in Algiers. This process encompasses all international environmental efforts and arrangements within the United Nations system, including at the regional level, and is not restricted to UNEP.[415]

The coordination of environmental treaties plays a special role for this working group because multilateral agreements are a particularly important element of international environmental governance.[416] The working group has given priority, in this respect, to an evaluation of the status of existing environmental agreements as well as the future direction of the development of international environmental law. The coordination of agreements as part of the future development of coherent structures of international environmental law has been stressed throughout the working papers and documents in the environmental governance process.[417] The work of the group is closely related to the

---

ance: Multilateral Environmental Agreements (MEAs)", UNEP/IGM/2/INF/3, 10 July 2001, para. 3.

[415] This report takes into account the development of the Ministerial Group on IEG and relevant documents until December 2001.

[416] Four different levels of international environmental governance can be distinguished. Decision-making processes form the highest level, the next lower level is constituted by the international institutional architecture, one step lower is the policy management. The coordination of the implementation of international governance decisions on a national level is the lowest level; see UNEP/IGM/2/INF/3, para. 5.

[417] The proposals made in the two papers issued by the Ministerial Group on International Environmental Governance: "Improving international environmental governance among multilateral environmental agreements: negotiable terms for further discussion", UNEP/IGM/2/4, and "Proposals for a systematic approach to coordination of multilateral environmental agreements",

conferences on Secretariat coordination and to some extent build upon the results reached during these meetings.

Particularly relevant for the initiation of specific activities, in contrast to the purely political value of most declarations and resolutions, are the proposed "Concrete short-term actions for enhancing coordination among multilateral environmental agreements."[418] According to the suggestions on the solution of conflicts between agreements, regular meetings on a political level shall be held by the bureaus of the Conferences of the Parties as well as by the scientific and technical bodies. Another proposal that is particularly far-reaching and concrete is the creation of a mechanism that monitors decisions adopted within the frameworks of international environmental treaties in order to quickly identify conflicts.[419] UNEP has explicitly offered to provide for such a mechanism and to forward the results of monitoring activities to Conferences of the Parties and Secretariats.

It has been suggested that the Global Ministerial Environment Forum of UNEP (GMEF) should exercise greater authority as a kind of environmental policy forum within the United Nations system, which could also provide broad overarching policy advise to other entities. This would, however, require a clearly defined authority of the GMEF relative to independent and autonomous decision-making bodies such as conferences of States Parties. Before GMEF can act with the authority to review the overall development of environmental policy within the United Nations system and to make cross-cutting recommendations to other bodies it is necessary that all autonomous bodies, in particular the Conferences of Parties take a decision to that extent. It is to be hoped that further developments in this respect may flow from the World Summit on Sustainable Development.

The approach so far, pursued is promising although difficult to realize. Any attempt to provide for a more institutional solution such as the establishment of a new international organization will meat with more resistance.

A new process has also been initiated with the Consultative Meetings of Multilateral Environmental Agreements on International Environmental Governance. These meetings provide a useful link between

---

UNEP/IGM/2/5, give valuable guidance for future development of coordination strategies.

[418] UNEP/IGM/2/4, para. 14 et seq.

[419] UNEP/IGM/2/4, para. 27 et seq.

UNEP's coordination conferences for treaty Secretariats and the Ministerial Group on International Environmental Governance. To date, three conferences have been held for Secretariats participating in the process.

(c) The Coordination of Biodiversity-related Agreements by UNEP

The Convention on Biological Diversity plays a special role concerning the coordination of Secretariats because the second Conference of the Parties instructed the Convention's Secretariat, which is provided for by UNEP, to coordinate its activities with the other relevant biodiversity-related[420] treaties.[421] With respect to biodiversity-related treaties, UNEP has undertaken, *inter alia*, collaboration with the World Conservation & Monitoring Center. In this respect, cooperation aiming at the harmonization of treaties is also an example of collaboration between international institutions and non-governmental organizations in this field.[422] Measures for the exchange of information and information management by biodiversity-related treaties are at the center of the collaboration between UNEP and WCMC. Projects like the Feasibility Study[423] have been supported by the Secretariats of the involved conventions. They are another concrete contribution to improved coordination within the group of biodiversity-related conventions. The same applies to the exchange of information via the UNEP-WCMC Forum on the Conservation of Biological Diversity and Biodiversity-related Agreements.

---

[420] According to the perception of the participating treaties, biodiversity-related treaties include the Convention on Biological Diversity, the Washington Convention on the International Trade in Endangered Species, the Bonn Convention on Migratory Species, the Ramsar Convention on Wetlands of International Importance and the World Heritage Convention.

[421] UNEP/CBD/COP/2/19 Add. 1.

[422] The World Conservation and Monitoring Centre was originally a non-governmental organization. Since July, 2000, UNEP took over the Centre. The status of the new UNEP World Conservation and Monitoring Centre is unclear.

[423] See WCMC (note 370).

UNEP has identified so-called clusters of closely related conventions[424] that can perform an active role in coordinating such treaties. To some extent, as mentioned above, it has already done so for biodiversity-related treaties.[425] A more active role on the part of UNEP would also be natural with respect to those treaties that are part of the UNEP Regional Seas Programme. If related treaties were formed into groups and internal strategies were developed to solve contradictions between the treaties constituting these groups, the number of relevant actors in international environmental law could be reduced. Instead of several hundred free-standing treaties, a much more limited number of treaty groups would have to negotiate conflicts between the respective groups. The creation of clusters and umbrella conventions,[426] potentially supported by UNEP, are important issues for thematically related treaties. However, such considerations still need clarification in regard to structures and the powers of the institutions involved.

(d) Conclusions

The recent activities undertaken by UNEP promise to provide for a greater harmonization in international environmental law. In particular, those strategies and activities envisaged as part of the environmental governance process can prove valuable for the coordination of treaties because they provide a forum for decision-making as well as for developing and implementing strategies for the monitoring of the treaties being coordinated. This potential medium for resolving conflicts, employing environmental governance approaches, contrasts sharply with efforts to solve conflicts according to the law of treaties.

---

[424] Groups can be created according to (1) a sectoral basis, as is the case for biodiversity-related treaties; (2) a functional basis, e.g. for trade issues; or (3) on a regional basis; see Doc. UNEP/IGM/2/5, para. 12 or Doc. UNEP/IGM/2/INF/3, para. 151 et seq.

[425] See the projects on information management by UNEP in collaboration with the World Conservation Monitoring Centre e.g. the already mentioned study by the WCMC (note 370).

[426] This is another suggestion for enhanced coordination made by the Ministerial Group on International Environmental Governance, see Doc. UNEP/IGM/1/2, para. 144.

VI. The Role of the CSD in Regard to the Coordination of Treaties

The Conference on Environment and Development 1992 led to the creation of the Commission on Sustainable Development. The Commission is an organ for the promotion and control of the implementation of Agenda 21. The establishment of the Commission as a control organ is often regarded as one of the most important outcomes of the conference.[427] Since the promotion of sustainable development is a multi-dimensional project, the Commission is also concerned with the coordination of issues and the codification of responses to those issues. It is not clear, however, whether the CSD has a function that is comparable to UNEP's mandate concerning the political coordination of environmental agreements. In general, it is not desirable to assign similar competences to two different institutions in order to avoid uncertainty in regard to areas of competence and the contradictions resulting therefrom.

1. The Mandate of the CSD

As already mentioned the creation of the CSD is not based upon an international treaty but upon a resolution by the Economic and Social Council of the UN (ECOSOC).[428] As a subsidiary organ of ECOSOC, the Commission has to address its recommendations to the Council which forwards them to the General Assembly. To fulfill administrative duties the Commission has a Secretariat and is assisted by the Department for Policy Coordination and Sustainable Development (DPCSD).[429] This Department is mainly responsible for activities concerning organization and documentation.

According to Agenda 21, the Commission is primarily responsible for the collection of data relevant to the implementation of the Agenda as

---

[427] C. Mensah, "The United Nations Commission on Sustainable Development", in: Werksman (note 355), 21.

[428] Resolution 1993/207.

[429] Together with the Administrative Committee on Coordination, the Inter-Agency Committee on Sustainable Development and the Inter-Agency Committee on Environment, this Department is the fourth UN institution responsible for the coordination of activities by organizations and subsidiary bodies within the United Nations.

well as for certain more general coordination processes.[430] Altogether, the mandate of the CSD aims to ensure an effective follow-up of the Rio-Conference. The fact that the General Assembly has called upon the CSD to prepare the summit planned for the tenth anniversary of the Rio-Conference exemplifies the CSD's role in this respect.[431]

The most important functions of the CSD, from an environmental perspective, are: (1) the monitoring of the implementation of Agenda 21 and the integration of environment and development; (2) the evaluation of information by national governments including regular reports; (3) the assessment of information regarding the implementation of international agreements submitted by the Conferences of the Parties; and (4) the competence to make recommendations to the General Assembly of the UN on the implementation of Agenda 21.[432] The coordination of environmental treaties is not an explicit part of the CSD's mandate.

Some authors include the coordination of international instruments when describing the Commission's coordination responsibilities.[433] However, the CSD's coordination of activities is primarily concerned with actions taken by the bodies and institutions of the UN.[434] In contrast to the coordination of international treaties, such a competence concerns the coordination of internal rather than of external structures. As part of the preparations of the Rio + 10 summit the Commission will suggest ways to strengthen the institutional framework for sustainable development. On this point, the institutional framework to which CSD refers need not be limited to UN institutions. It is not clear whether, in this context, the CSD will also deal with the coordination of environmental treaties as part of an institutional framework for sustainable development.

[430] Agenda 21, para. 38.13; see also Beyerlin (note 303), para. 154.

[431] See Resolution 55/199, 20 December 2000, Doc. A/RES/55/199.

[432] Sands (note 18), 74 et seq.

[433] Mensah (note 427), 21.

[434] The General Assembly has affirmed this role during the Rio + 5 process in its program for the further implementation of Agenda 21 dating 28 June 1997, see Doc. A/RES/S-19/2, Annex, para. 117.

2. The Relationship between the CSD and UNEP

The final document of the UN Special Session in June 1997 (Rio + 5 Process) calls for a better cooperation between CSD and UNEP and a clearer definition of their respective areas of competence.[435] During its 18th session, UNEP's Governing Council also dealt with its relationship to the CSD and to other UN institutions, non-governmental organizations and the private sector. According to the Governing Council, the CSD shall be the political forum for discussions concerning the implementation of decisions and recommendations made at the UNCED; UNEP is responsible for providing for the environmental dimension of the debate. In this context UNEP shall advise the CSD on issues of concerned with the global environment and support the work of the Commission by providing scientific, technical and environmental policy information.[436]

Although precise criteria for marking the areas of competence concerning UNEP and the CSD have not yet been developed, the coordination of international environmental agreements has explicitly been assigned to UNEP and not to the CSD. The Commission on Sustainable Development is neither explicitly called upon to coordinate agreements nor is the coordination of treaties an inherent part of its functions. Furthermore, according to the Programme of the Special Session of the General Assembly from 1997, an overlap of areas of competence must be avoided. Since UNEP plays the role of the coordinating power for international environmental agreements pursuant to its functions agreed upon in Agenda 21, a potential dispute over competence in this area appears to favor UNEP. As a consequence, the efficiency of the future coordination of treaties depends to a large extent upon UNEP's performance. Improved efficiency might, however, also include the improvement of structural and organizational conditions to enable UNEP to better fulfill its tasks.

VII. Joint Financial Mechanisms as a Means of Coordination

A rather specific aspect of the institutional coordination of environmental treaties concerns the financial links that exist between interna-

[435] This can be concluded from the description of the different bodies' functions and particularly from para. 131, Doc. A/RES/S-19/2, Annex.

[436] Doc. A/RES/S-19/2, Annex, para. 124.

tional environmental agreements. While many agreements have established independent operational funds, some treaties make use of external, previously existing financial mechanisms.[437] In some cases, several treaties make use of the same financial mechanism. Because of the importance of financial mechanisms for the implementation of and ensuring compliance with treaties, shared financial mechanisms represent an important link between treaties. The fact of cooperation at this level bears the potential for better coordination between agreements, as long as internal structures avoid inconsistent funding decisions. Conflict would result from the sharing of these financial mechanisms only if an institution supports a project within the framework of one environmental agreement, with funds from the shared source, that contradicts projects within being pursued by one of the other participating treaties.

1. The Role of the GEF

The best, and in it its form a quite unique, example of a joint use of a financial mechanisms by different treaties is the Global Environment Facility (GEF). The GEF is the financial mechanism for both the Convention on Biological Diversity and the Framework Convention on Climate Change. As between these treaties, the GEF so far only makes a limited contribution to greater coherence and compatibility. The primary function of the GEF is not to streamline the substance of the treaties it provides the financial mechanism for but to fund projects for each treaty according to this agreement's criteria and guidance. However, as a shared mechanism of different treaties the GEF has at least in theory the possibility to actively contribute to the coordination of treaties. The ranges of such a function depends upon the balance of independence and accountability. There lies the main difficulty concerning an extension of the GEF's powers in this respect: States parties to the involved treaties must be expected to be most reluctant to transfer competence to the GEF to coordinate the substance of the agreements.

Nevertheless, lessons learned from the GEF experience could pave the way for comparable mechanisms between different sets of treaties or on a more universal scale. Furthermore, by the GEF's engagement in other cooperative processes, e.g. as a member to the Collaborative Partner-

---

437 On this issue see also N. Matz, "Environmental Financing: Function and Coherence of Financial Mechanisms in International Environmental Agreements", *UNYB* 6 (2002), 473 et seq.

ships on Forests, the GEF supports institutional cooperation and coordination on different levels. These experiences might also be used in the context of the coordination of treaties. While other agreements also make use of existing mechanisms or institutions;[438] the structures cannot be compared to the cooperation between GEF and the organs of the treaties that have chosen the GEF as their financial mechanism.

In 1994, the participating States made institutional and substantial modifications with the adoption of the Instrument for the Establishment of the Restructured Global Environment Facility.[439] Afterwards, the implementing agencies, i.e. the UN Development Programme, the UN Environment Programme and the World Bank, formally adopted the Instrument.[440] The acceptance of the GEF as the interim financial mechanism for the Convention on Biological Diversity and the Framework Convention on Climate Change followed this considerable restructuring of the original GEF pilot scheme.[441]

(a) Function and Organization of the GEF

The GEF's main function is to support activities and projects aiming at global environmental benefits within four GEF focal areas: global climate protection, biological diversity, international waters and the ozone depletion.[442] GEF funding should enable developing countries to bear incremental costs arising out of the implementation of environmental protection measures. Incremental costs are those "extra" costs that result from activities that are environmentally beneficial as opposed to

---

[438] The Convention to Combat Desertification has, after long considerations, chosen the International Fund for Agricultural Development (IFAD) as host for its Global Mechanism; see Decision 10/Cop.3, Doc. ICCD/COP(3)/20/ Add. 1, 37; the respective Memorandum of Understanding is contained in Annex, para. 38-42.s

[439] *ILM* 33 (1994), 1283 et seq.

[440] The respective decisions of the implementing agencies are reprinted in *ILM* 33 (1994), 1279 et seq. Annex D of the Instrument on a Restructured GEF (note 439), 1304 et seq. assigns specific responsibilities to the different implementing agencies.

[441] See article 39 CBD and article 21, para. 3 FCCC.

[442] For further background information see J. Werksman, "Consolidating Governance of the Global Commons: Insights from the GEF", *YIEL* 6 (1995), 27 (48 et seq.); Sands (note 18), 736 et seq.

either not perform a protection measure at all or to perform an activity without the necessary environmental safeguards at lower costs. This can be explained by the following example. If a developing State uses substances in industrial processes that deplete the ozone layer and agrees to substitute these substances with others that do not have harmful effects on the ozone layer but are more expensive, the difference between the higher costs for non-depleting substances and the costs for using ozone-depleting substances would be incremental costs.

On the one hand, the GEF is a treaty-specific financial mechanism. On the other hand, the GEF supports projects in its rather very broad and generally defined focal areas. The support granted by the GEF can include the promotion of a State's compliance with international standards or obligations, but also assistance as States prepare in an initial phase to become a member to an international treaty.[443]

The institutional composition of and cooperation within the GEF are unique not only because of the cooperation between Bretton-Woods institutions and the United Nations, but also because of their overall innovative design.[444] The financial elements of the GEF are located at the World Bank which serves as a trustee of the GEF's financial resources. The central role concerning the identification, preparation and implementation of sponsored projects lies with the implementing agencies.[445]

(b) The Relationship between the GEF and Environmental Agreements

The relationship between both conventions (the Framework Convention on Climate Change and the Convention on Biological Diversity) and the GEF the subject to lengthy and difficult negotiations. Even after the restructuring of the GEF the potential for tensions has by no means been abolished. Both conventions required assurances from the World Bank, as the GEF's main implementing agency, that GEF-funded

---

[443] Sands (note 18), 784.

[444] See L. Boisson de Chazournes, "The Global Environment Facility Galaxy: On Linkages among Institutions", *UNYB* 3 (1999), 243 (254 et seq.); on a detailed account of the innovative elements of the cooperation see S.A. Silard, "The Global Environment Facility: A New Development in International Law and Organization", *Geo. Wash. J. Int'l L. & Econ.* 28 (1995), 607 (645 et seq.).

[445] C. De Klemm, "Die Global Environment Facility", *RIW* (1998), 921 (923).

projects would be in conformity with the policies and guidelines established by the respective Conference of the Parties.[446] The Framework Convention on Climate Change and the Convention on Biological Diversity have very similar provisions regarding financial mechanisms.[447] Both make the convention's financial mechanism accountable to the COP, which will also decide on the policies, program priorities and eligibility criteria. However, the Convention on Biological Diversity requires that the mechanism "function under the authority and guidance of ... the Conference of the Parties," whereas reference to the authority of the Conference of the Parties is lacking in article 11(1) FCCC. While legally binding relations, e.g. treaties, cannot be concluded with the GEF because it lacks international legal personality,[448] both conventions formed their relationship with the GEF by way of Memoranda of Understanding.

The GEF's function as a treaty-specific tool for the Convention on Biological Diversity and the Framework Convention on Climate Change is governed by elaborate rules concerning the treaties' organs' guidance and the implementation of the guidance given. The overarching principle is that the GEF is bound by the guidance of the Conferences of the Parties. This guidance is incorporated in different operational instruments of the GEF. The Operational Strategy that lays the foundation for GEF activities in the four focal areas incorporates guidance from the Convention on Biological Diversity and the Framework Convention on Climate Change as far as strategic considerations for the two focal areas are concerned. More specifically, the Operational Programs serve as the tools of implementation of the conventions' guidance.[449] The Conferences of the Parties at their meetings decide upon guidance to the GEF.[450] In a second step the GEF establishes the Operational Programs, which then serve as the basis for funding of proj-

[446] C. Di Leva, "International Environmental Law and Development", *Georgetown Int'l Env. L. R.* 10 (1998), 501 (513).

[447] See article 11 (1) FCCC and article 21 (1) CBD.

[448] The legal status of the GEF has not been finally settled or defined, yet it is the common understanding that it lacks the ability to legally bind itself.

[449] Currently there are 13 Operational Programs. Five concern biological diversity, four relate to climate change, three to international waters and the OP on integrated ecosystem management is considered to relate to a multifocal area.

[450] See for example decision VI/7 of the Conference of the Parties to the CBD, Doc. UNPE/CBD/COP/6/20, 196 et seq.

ects. Accountability of the GEF requires reports to the Conferences of the Parties. As a consequence they can review and modify guidance to the GEF. This system of checks and balances shall safeguard that projects funded by the GEF are consistent with the treaties in the respective focal areas.

In general UNEP, as an implementing agency, provides environmental expertise and monitors the consistency of projects with existing environmental treaties. Due to the multitude of multilateral environmental agreements this is a difficult task. Furthermore, if treaties are inconsistent the GEF would in general have to make sure that a project implementing one of the agreements does not infringe the provisions of the other – inconsistent – treaty. Such a scenario might well arise in the context of tensions between the Convention on Biological Diversity and the Framework Convention on Climate Change. If the building of sinks by monocultures of alien tree species would be funded by the GEF as part of its activities in the climate change focal area this would contradict the principles and objectives of the Convention on Biological Diversity. However, it is the primary responsibility of the organs of the treaties involved to solve such contradictions rather than the GEF's since the latter is more of an implementing tool than a policy-maker. The GEF can only safeguard that the Operational Programs are not openly inconsistent with one another i.e. if contradictory guidance given by different treaty organs shall be implemented in Operational Programs the issue must be brought to the attention of the conventions' organs. Insofar the detection of potential tensions and potential conflicts should be promoted and, if realized, be immediately communicated to the treaty organs before conflicts originating from contradictory treaties are further implemented by contradictory Operational Programs.

The Montreal Protocol on Substances that deplete the ozone layer also has a formalized link to the GEF. The GEF serves to fund projects for States with economies in transition i.e. the former socialist Eastern European States, while the Montreal Protocol Multilateral Fund funds projects in developing countries. The formalization of the relationship serves to avoid an inconsistent practice of funding. The Memorandum of Understanding explicitly calls for the avoidance of a doubling of efforts and conflicts within the regime on ozone layer protection. The participating institutions have a vital interest in seeing that the activities by the GEF do not compete with those of the Montreal Multilateral Fund. It is intended, rather, that the two mechanisms supplement one another. The GEF Operational Strategy confirms that the political guidelines issued concerning ozone protection projects will be consistent with the Montreal Protocol.[451] Although these issues do not concern the coordination of two or more different treaties, the coherence of mechanisms within a thematic regime is a fundamental aspect of the solution of conflicts in international environmental law. The formalization of cooperation is one aspect that contributes to the creation of a system of international environmental law that is free of conflicts. Whether the GEF can manage to coordinate activities that concern distinct subjects in order to solve conflicts, as it does within the singular ozone regime, remains an open question.

(c) The Coordination of Projects within the GEF

The Instrument on the Restructured GEF does not explicitly mention the coordination of GEF funded projects. The Memoranda of Understanding concluded between treaty organs and the GEF Council only deal with the relations between these institutions and are not concerned with the coordination of the activities of other treaties making use of the GEF. One possibility for providing for enhanced coordination of international environmental law in the terms of the Memoranda would have been to require regular meetings of the CBD Secretariat, the FCCC Secretariat and the GEF Secretariat. In the context of such conferences joint guidelines on funding of projects could be adopted to decrease the risk of contradictions during the implementation of the respective agreements. A potential argument against such meetings is that the complex system of GEF's organization as a treaty financial mechanism would be further complicated. Nevertheless, while the competence to give binding guidance to the GEF as an implementing tool shall generally remain with the treaty organs, joint meetings can assist the clarification of priority issues concerning the coordination of environmental law in the areas involved.

The GEF Operational Strategy is more detailed as far as the coordination of activities on different issues is concerned. One strategic guideline requires the planning and implementation of GEF activities in a way that avoids the transfer of negative environmental impacts between the four GEF areas of interest. However, the Operational Strategy does

---

[451] This is part of the first principle out of ten operational principles of the Operational Strategy of the Global Environment Facility, see <http://www.gefweb.org/public/opstrat/ch1.htm>, last visited 23 January 2002.

not give any indication as to the means by which this aim is to be achieved. Since UNEP is the GEF implementing agency responsible for the environmental aspects of project planning and implementation, the question of coordination lies within its area of competence.

In this context UNEP is not only responsible for a general expertise in environmental questions but must particularly consider the issue of conflicts between funded projects and international environmental agreements. As a consequence UNEP is responsible for the political coordination of international environmental law on different levels: as part of its general mandate and as part of its GEF activities. UNEP can promote the coherent implementation of treaties through its GEF functions, although this opportunity is primarily limited to those treaties that deal with the issues addressed by the four project areas of GEF activities. In addition to the Convention on Biological Diversity and the Framework Convention on Climate Change, UNEP could bring its GEF authority (and thereby enhanced coordination) to bear on: (1) treaties dealing with the conservation of international waters; (2) the instruments concerned with the protection of the ozone layer; and (3) if projects come under one of the four GEF issues, the Convention to Combat Desertification.

The GEF's authority, as a treaty specific funding mechanism, to promote the coordination of international environmental agreements is limited by the fact that it is subject to directives from the treaty organs. The GEF Council, which is responsible for the assessment and adoption of working programs, the monitoring of the work and evaluation of the GEF's efficiency, is bound by the political guidelines and decisions issued by the respective Conferences of the Parties of the Convention on Biological Diversity and the Framework Convention on Climate Change. If the directives of the different Conferences of the Parties were to be inconsistent as to their contents, the GEF would be obliged to sponsor projects that contradict one another. That means that, in those cases where the GEF acts as a treaty specific financial mechanism, the policy of project consistency can only reach as far as the freedom of discretion granted by the responsible treaty organs.

According to the Memorandum of Understanding between the Framework Convention on Climate Change and the GEF Council, the latter can request advice and guidance from the Conference of the Parties on all questions relevant to its function as the financial mechanism. The identification of conflicts with other agreements when planning or implementing projects would most certainly be such a case. This is especially true because the respective treaty organs frequently underscore their intention to promote cooperation between their organs and other treaty regimes. The report issued by the GEF Council regarding cooperation with environmental agreements does not, however, refer to relations between different treaties which are linked by the GEF. Instead, it only assesses the bilateral relations between the GEF and individual agreements.

The last aspect of the potential enhancement of coordination of international environmental law within the financial framework of the GEF relates to the Integrated Ecosystem Management Programme.[452] This program identifies cross-cutting issues and synergies. Although the Programme identifies interdependencies between environmental factors and environmental damage, the GEF review does not consider the coordination of different agreements when suggesting activities and strategies. To make use of the Management Programme as a means of coordination of international environmental law, joint meetings of the treaty organs and the GEF, especially aiming for the general promotion of the exchange of information, would be necessary. On the basis of its experiences with other environmental areas and treaties, the GEF might wield a greater degree of influence on the political decisions of the Conferences of the Parties. Only by doing so could synergies identified in the project management review be transferred to the level of political decision-making and lead to a more coherent system of international environmental regulations.

2. *Conclusions*

The GEF's potential as an institution for the coordination of international environmental agreements has not yet been fully exhausted. However, the assignment of a more active role to the GEF or comparable institutions would require a strengthening of their respective status. In the case of the GEF this might require further functional restructuring. Whether this would include the organizational setting of a platform for coordination or the inclusion of this function in the Organizational Strategy is a question of how willing States are to assign this function to the GEF. A platform for coordination within the GEF would need to include input from and participation of the organs of the involved trea-

---

[452] See GEF, Operational Programme #12 – Integrated Ecosystem Management, 20 April 2000.

ties. As has been mentioned before such a proceeding might make the already complex structure of the GEF even more complicated.

A first and potentially viable step would be to establish an Operational Program on the issue of the coordination of conventions. Like the OP on the integrated ecosystem management such a Program would be multifocal. However, according to its function it must be more organizational and lay out additional procedure to be abided by when funding projects as the financial mechanism of environmental agreements. A Operational Program on the issue would be the least far-reaching option, since this would not include a formal strengthening of the GEF's position in relation to the Conferences of the Parties of the involved treaties.

For those treaties using the GEF as their financial mechanisms, a formal strengthening of the GEF's position would most probably be unacceptable because the power to issue binding directives is of central importance in the relationship between the treaties and the Facility.[453] In this respect, consideration of the harmonization of the contents of treaties must take place on the level of the Conferences of the Parties in order to avoid the issuance of contradicting guidelines to the financial mechanism. If GEF strategies on the identification and avoidance of contradictions on a project level are added to the coordination on the treaty organ level the different institutions can mutually reinforce the efforts to achieve greater coherence in international environmental law.

Mechanisms for environmental financing, particularly by joint mechanisms like the GEF, can contribute to the coordination of environmental agreements. An institution that sponsors and monitors concrete projects can, for example, identify conflicts arising out of the implementation of agreements. This role could be further strengthened if the GEF served as the financial mechanism for a greater number of international environmental agreements. However, the harmonization efforts of the GEF would be primarily concerned with special projects and not with broader treaty regulations. Any coordination of treaty provisions would be incidental and out of the GEF's control; left in the hands of the treaty organs. Furthermore, a harmonization of projects only concerns developing countries. For industrialized States a financial mechanism cannot give any indication concerning concrete conflicts of

[453] It is most likely that the loss of power is a particular concern of developing countries because they counter the allegedly Western dominated structure of the GEF with their majority in the Conferences of the Parties of environmental treaties.

implementation. As a consequence, the role of financial mechanisms in promoting the coordination of international environmental law is limited.

VIII. A Coordination of International Treaties by Non-governmental Organizations

The number and size of international non-governmental organizations dealing with environmental matters in the broadest sense of the concept reflect the increasing links, or the increasing consciousness of links, between: (1) divergent environmental issues; and (2) environmental and other issues. The fact that the number of participating NGOs at the Rio Earth Summit exceeded the number of States speaks to the growing number and importance of non-governmental organizations. An estimated 6000 NGOs world wide deal with environmental matters,[454] far exceeding the number of recognized international organizations.

1. Participation of NGOs in International Environmental Law

NGOs can perform different functions in international environmental politics and international law. The extent of their participation and their capacity to influence international processes varies. With respect to international law their participation can be separated into the following categories: (1) initiating law-making, (2) development of law, and (3) monitoring and calling for the enforcement of international law. Primarily, however, non-governmental organizations participate as observers of international processes. NGOs can be and often are accredited as observers at international diplomatic conferences as well as at meetings of treaty organs. The influence these NGOs have on the decision-making processes of international institutions is, with some exceptions, not systematized because international law has not yet developed mechanisms for directly taking account of NGO initiatives, even as an expression of the opinion of civil society.[455]

As a result of the UNCED, the UN General Assembly concluded that for the promotion of sustainable development the continuation and

---

[454] Bothe/ Hohmann (note 375), 1128.

[455] Wolfrum (note 286), 76.

strengthening of a dialog between States and non-governmental actors was a necessity.[456] To implement this guidance the CSD created relatively far-reaching rights for participation for NGOs, which serve as a model for the general participation of NGOs on the international level.[457] Opening the law-making process to non State actors runs contrary to the traditional understanding of international law and reflects increasing flexibility.[458]

Treaty organs increasingly make use of non-governmental organizations' expertise, e.g. by the request for studies or by workshops on specific topics.[459] Another related aspect is the accreditation of NGOs not only as observers but also as advisors at international conferences.[460] Such advisory functions contribute to the development of international law. NGOs can also provide a forum for the exchange of information on certain topics. Depending upon the design of the exchange mechanisms and respective consequences, this function can include the development or monitoring of international environmental law. The vision of a transnational network of NGOs with a central data bank charged with collecting, evaluating, verifying, storing and disseminating[461] environmental information has not been realized to such a sweeping degree.[462] The same applies with respect to the Non-Governmental Earth Council envisaged by Agenda 21 in section 38.45.

Concerning the development of international law and the monitoring of compliance, there is clear evidence of increasingly close cooperation between treaty regimes and NGOs. Such cooperation can also be based

---

456 Doc. A/47/191 (1992).

457 UNECOSOC, Doc. E/1993/14 (1993).

458 Wolfrum (note 286), 78.

459 The various studies done by IUCN are good examples to that extent.

460 E.g. according to article 8, para. 3 World Heritage Convention.

461 See M. Garner, Transnational Alignment of Nongovernmental Organizations for Global Environmental Action, *Vanderbilt J. Transn. L.* 23 (1991), 1057 et seq. (1070).

462 The institution coming closest to such a network is the IUCN. IUCN, an association of, *inter alia*, some 735 non-governmental organizations, 78 States and 112 international organizations. Figures taken from: <www.iucn.org/2000/about/content/index.html>, last visited 23 January 2002. In regard to specific topics, e.g. climate change networks of non-governmental organizations, have also been formed, see H. French, "The Role of Non-State Actors", in: Werksman (note 355), 251 et seq. (253).

upon respective Memoranda of Understanding or cooperation and joint work programs.[463] In some cases treaties explicitly transfer certain functions concerning implementation and compliance control to NGOs. This is the most far-reaching level of participation of non-State actors in international environmental law at the moment. The Convention to Combat Desertification, for example, explicitly recognizes the need to involve relevant non-governmental organizations in the implementation of the treaty on a regional and local level in order to, *inter alia*, increase the participation of and acceptance from the affected public.[464] Another example of a significant transfer of powers from a treaty regime to a non-governmental organization is the appointment of NGOs to serve as the *interim* Secretariat. Such an appointment of the IUCN took place according to article 8 of the Ramsar Convention.

2. *Obstacles Concerning the Role of NGOs and the Coordination of International Law*

A potential difficulty when employing non-governmental organizations as a mechanism for improving the coordination of international environmental law is that they originate out of the private law sector as opposed to the public law sector. In this respect, NGOs also differ from those institutions which, although not being subjects of international law, are nevertheless institutions performing functions in the sphere of public international law, e.g. UNEP. The fact that NGOs are not, in general, subjects of international law, is not the decisive factor with respect to the role they play in coordinating international environmental law. Nonetheless, placing NGOs on equal footing with international organizations would clarify the status of NGOs in public international law.[465] Particularly, if the role of NGOs is to go farther than merely

---

[463] An impressive example is the Ramsar Convention. In addition to its formal relationship to several other agreements the treaty has concluded memoranda with 11 non-governmental organizations, for an overview see <www.ramsar.org/index_mou.htm>, last visited 23 January 2002.

[464] Because of the special role of NGOs, e.g. K.W. Danish, International Environmental Law and the "Bottom-Up" Approach: A Review of the Desertification Convention, *Indiana J. Global Legal Studies* 3 (1995), 133 et seq., uses the term "bottom-up approach" meaning an active participation by non-governmental groups and individuals.

[465] While it is possible to grant to a non-governmental organization the status and rights of a subject of international law this is a rare exception that is

collecting information and giving advice to treaty organs and conferences, the lack of any formal status, beyond that of observer, is problematic. This applies in regard to a potential transfer of powers to non-governmental organizations as well as in regard to the subsequent performance of coordinating functions. For the last years, despite their increasing size, numbers and involvement, there has not been any significant trend toward formalizing the public law nature of NGOs.[466] However, at present the strengthening of NGOs and their role in international law – and particularly international environmental law – is an issue that is broadly discussed and might be seen as a expression of a shift of the role of non-governmental organizations in international law.[467]

Another trend concerning the more active engagement of non-governmental actors in international environmental policies is the holding of Multi-Stakeholders-Dialogues within the framework of the UN, mainly initiated by the CSD, on certain issues.[468] The main aim of such dialogues is to bring stakeholders at one table to more actively form partnerships on certain issues of sustainable development.

---

so far limited to the status of the Committee of the International Red Cross; see also S. Hobe, "Der Rechtsstatus der Nichtregierungsorganisationen nach gegenwärtigem Völkerrecht", *Archiv des Völkerrechts* 37 (1999), 152 et seq. (159).

[466] French (note 462), 257.

[467] See also F. Yamin, NGOs and International Law, *RECIEL* 10 (2001), 149 et seq.; P. Bombay, The Role of NGOs in Shaping Community Positions, *RECIEL* 10 (2001), 162 et seq.

[468] The most prominent example being the multi-stakeholder dialogues held during the PrepComs to the Johannesburg Summit, see e.g. <http://www.johannesburgsummit.org/html/major_groups/multistakeholderdialogue.html>, last visited 17 June 2002. The Multi-stakeholder Dialogue on Sustainable Energy and Transport held at the 9th session of the CSD in 2001 and the Multi-stakeholder Dialogue on Sustainable Agriculture held at the CSD's 8th session in 2000 are examples for the trend within the UN to more actively engage non-governmental actors in this context; for the summary of the chairman see Doc. E/CN.17/2001/19 and Doc. E/CN.17/2000/20 respectively. A recent example for a dialogue not initiated by the UN includes the Stakeholder Dialogue on Sustainable Water Management held in April 2002, for more information see <http://www.iisd.ca/sd/ruschlikon/>, last visited 17 June 2002.

3. Consequences for the Cooperative Coordination of Treaties

Besides the potential for providing specific expertise on certain issues, the coordination of agreements with the assistance of single NGOs does not have any significant advantages in comparison to the coordination with the help of international organizations. The assignment of a coordinating role to one NGO could rather prove particularly difficult, because the current approach to the participation of and cooperation with non-governmental organizations is rather fragmentary. As a consequence, the assignment of coordinating functions and powers to a non-governmental organization would first require a considerable strengthening of its position as well as its international acceptance. This might meet with resistance from States and other international actors. Such a process also might not be considered necessary, when an international organization already has a mandate to coordinate international environmental law in the area or regarding the issue in question.

At the present time there is no single non-governmental organization that explicitly aims to provide for greater coordination of international environmental law and contributes to such an objective with any substantial efforts. As a result of the need for institutional and financial stability as well as comprehensive expertise in international environmental law, there are very few non-governmental organizations with the capacity to perform such a function. A potential candidate from among NGOs that might contribute to a coordination of international environmental law is the IUCN, with its office for international environmental law.

Distinct considerations relate to networks of non-governmental actors and formalized as well as institutionalized models for multi-stakeholder dialogues. The most recent example for a planned formalized forum is found in Decision SS.VII/5 of the Special Session of the UNEP Governing Council.[469] The decision relates to enhancing civil society engagement in the work of UNEP. The process shall be initiated together with the Global Minister Environment Forum. It remains to be seen whether such an approach could lead to an institutional with the necessary strength and acceptance to perform an active role in the coordination of international environmental law. In any case such a multi-actor approach that is initiated under the auspices of UNEP seems much more viable than efforts to engage single NGOs more actively in the process of coordination of international environmental law. However,

---

[469] Doc. UNEP/GCSS. VII/6, 44 et seq.

much will depend upon the agreement of States and treaty organs to generally agree to a coordinating influence of multi-stakeholder institutionalized fora.

E. Conclusions and Outlook

(Wolfrum/Matz)

Treaty based international environmental law has developed probably more progressively over the last centuries than any other branch of international law. Such development was initiated and sustained by several factors, namely: the growing awareness of the need to promote the use of natural resources or the environment which safeguards the options of future generations for further development; a growing insight concerning the impact new technologies and new forms of utilization may have upon the environment; a growing insight into the interactions of different economic activities and their combined effect upon the environment; the acknowledgement that the protection of the environment should not be undertaken from a purely utilitarian point of view but should take the intrinsic value of the environment as well as of its components into consideration.

International treaty law on the protection of the environment has developed following a sector approach and in different stages. This resulted in an overlap of the various international agreements as far as substance is concerned; it further resulted in differing approaches pursued. For example, the protection of the marine environment is covered by several universal international agreements as well as several regional ones. Due to the successive development of the international treaty law on the protection of the environment they are based upon different approaches. For example, the ecosystem approach which is the guiding approach for the Convention on the Conservation of Antarctic Marine Living Resources or the Straddling Fish Stocks Convention does not govern the rules of the UN Convention on the Law of the Sea concerning the conservation and management of marine living resources although some aspects of this regime may be assimilated to the ecosystem approach. Therefore there exist several conflicts between the various regimes which have been identified in this study. Such conflicts may exist on the normative level or on the level of implementation or on both.

As far as there are conflicting rules in various regimes covering the same components of the environment or identical activities this study can only recommend policies to ameliorate the effects of such conflicts. It may, however, be worth while to point out that in future, before engaging in the negotiation of further instruments for the protection of the environment efforts should be undertaken to exhaustively list all existing international norms touching upon the very subject matter or the very activity. The implementation of this recommendation may turn out to be politically more controversial as one may expect. Initiatives for the development of new international norms is more often than not only fueled by consideration that there is an unregulated issue which requires to be regulated but that existing treaty based rules are considered inadequate. Instead of renegotiating already existing international agreements with the view to amend them or, at least, develop a protocol thereto new treaties or new soft law is developed without clarifying the relationship between the new and the already existing law.

The study identifies several mechanisms through which a harmonization of existing international agreements on the protection of the environment may be achieved. They range from mechanisms based upon the Vienna Convention o the Law of Treaties (treaty based option) to options which are institution oriented. The latter either involve the Meetings of States Parties or other international institutions.

The traditional law of treaties does not offer sufficiently effective means to harmonize agreements and to solve arising conflicts between them. This is due to the nature and function of the law of treaties as the settlement of general technical questions that arise in the realm of the creation, application and termination of treaties. As a consequence of this approach, the content of treaties and the question of how contradicting contents of specific treaties can be brought into coherence are not within the realm of the law of treaties.

There exists, however, the possibility in filling blanket provisions, that are provisions that provide for an interpretative margin to take into account the purpose and objective of other international agreements covering the same activity or the same issue. This mechanism is well established in the interpretation of human rights agreements and could be used in the context of international environmental agreements, too. The justification for such an approach rests on the principle how international agreements should be interpreted namely– as far as possible – so as not to undermine established treaty based regimes.

The coordination of the contents of international agreements could be achieved best if a forum would be established that provides for a respective harmonization of either interpreting particular rules or coordinate implementation. In this respect Meetings or Conferences of States Parties may play a viable role. Many of the more recent international environmental agreements provide for such a body whose functions differ significantly. If endowed with the function to progressively develop the respective treaty regime – such a function is exercised by the Meeting of States Parties of the Montreal Protocol, for example, – it would also have the power to initiate a harmonization of that treaty with another one. The disadvantage of that approach is that such Meetings of States Parties look upon the issue from the perspective of one particular international agreement. In spite thereof several Meetings of States Parties have taken up the task of trying to harmonize conflicting international agreements and even have provided for a cooperation with other fora. Such development should be encouraged in spite of its inherent limitations. The main one is that such Meetings of States Parties have only a very limited possibility to alter an existing agreement. In this respect, a reform of the law of treaties is called for to provide for more dynamic regulations on interpretation and amendment of treaties so as to keep up with the general tendency for more dynamic and interactive structures in international law.

While cooperation between the organs of international treaties and between treaties and international organizations must generally be strengthened and streamlined, international environmental institutions show first approaches in this direction. Particularly the attempts by UNEP to coordinate the activities of the Secretariats of international environmental agreements should be further explored, developed and cautiously institutionalized. At the moment UNEP is the only institution with the competence to coordinate international environmental treaties on a political level. However, only rather recently has UNEP started to engage more actively and more comprehensively in activities that promise a certain success in coordinating environmental agreements. The mere concentration on the coordination of the activities of different Secretariats had not been able to significantly reduce the potential for conflicts between agreements, although this approach had been a step in the right direction.

In this context one may, however, question the strength of UNEP's position despite its role as a coordinator of international environmental law. UNEP, in its current form, may be too weak to provide for a satisfactory solution of conflicts between agreements. UNEP cannot decide upon binding guidelines for a comprehensive and substantial harmonization of international environmental law, because treaties and their organs enjoy independence from the decisions of other institutions. This also applies to those agreements for which UNEP performs the function of a Secretariat. Only further reforms and a potential strengthening regarding the competences can turn UNEP into a viable institution for the coordination of international environmental agreements. The discussion of this issue as part of the suggestions made within the Ministerial Group on International Environmental Governance is a beginning in this respect. However, States' sovereignty and the independence of international agreements from UNEP provide for obstacles to such an approach.

Another option, although not as far-reaching as a competent and powerful international institution responsible for the coordination of agreements, might be an international "harmonization conference" that aims to coordinate existing international environmental agreements. Such an approach, however, is not likely to offer any systematic solution for the future harmonization and avoidance of conflicts.

Given the existing structure for the administration of international agreements, programmes and activities it seems not to be recommendable to attempt to develop UNEP into an international organization.[470] Such an international organization would have no competence in respect of other international organizations or institutions. It is difficult to perceive that States would accept a design which places UNEP as such in hierarchical position vis-à-vis other international organizations. The respective Conferences of Status Parties which at the moment have the task to progressively develop the respective agreements and which are quite successful in this respect are not likely to yield parts of their competences. It is, apart from that generally questionable whether it would be prudent to curtail competences of Conferences or Meetings of States Parties since the have developed into viable instruments of the respective international environmental agreements.

However, it is worth while to explore whether international organizations and institutions are willing to establish, by agreement, an institution attached to UNEP and endow it with coordinating functions as to the application of the various international environmental agreements. Such institution should be independent from UNEP although administered through the latter so as to ensure that all the treaty bodies (secretariats or Meetings or Conferences of States Parties) and institutions

---

[470] Different WBGU, Politikpapier, Chancen von Johannesburg: Eckpunkte einer Verhandlungsstrategie (2002), 5.

administering or undertaking environmental programs or activities may participate in its decision making.

Max-Planck-Institut für ausländisches öffentliches Recht und Völkerrecht

Beiträge zum ausländischen öffentlichen Recht und Völkerrecht

Hrsg.: A. von Bogdandy, R. Wolfrum

Bde. 27–59 erschienen im Carl Heymanns Verlag KG Köln, Berlin (Bestellung an: Max-Planck-Institut für Völkerrecht, Im Neuenheimer Feld 535, 69120 Heidelberg); ab Band 60 im Springer-Verlag Berlin, Heidelberg, New York, London, Paris, Tokyo, Hong Kong, Barcelona

---

164 Rüdiger *Wolfrum*, Nele *Matz:* **Conflicts in International Environmental Law.** 2003. XI, 213 Seiten. Geb. € 64,95

163 Adam *Bodnar*, Michał *Kowalski*, Karen *Raible*, Frank *Schorkopf* (Eds.): **The Emerging Constitutional Law of the European Union.** 2003. IX, 595 Seiten. Geb. € 99,95

162 Jochen Abr. *Frowein*, Klaus *Scharioth*, Ingo *Winkelmann*, Rüdiger *Wolfrum* (Hrsg.): **Verhandeln für den Frieden/Negotiating for Peace. Liber Amicorum Tono Eitel.** 2003. XIII, 866 Seiten. Geb. € 129,95

161 Michaela *Fries:* **Die Bedeutung von Artikel 5 (f) der Rassendiskriminierungskonvention im deutschen Recht.** 2003. XIX, 429 Seiten. Geb. € 84,95

160 Helen *Keller:* **Rezeption des Völkerrechts.** 2003. XXXV, 855 Seiten. Geb. € 129,95

159 Cordula *Dröge:* **Positive Verpflichtungen der Staaten in der Europäischen Menschenrechtskonvention.** 2003. XX, 432 Seiten. Geb. € 89,95

157 Thomas *Giegerich:* **Europäische Verfassung und deutsche Verfassung im transnationalen Konstitutionalisierungsprozeß: Wechselseitige Rezeption, konzeptionelle Evolution und föderale Verflechtung.** 2003. LXV, 1534 Seiten. Geb. € 199,95

156 Julia *Sommer:* **Verwaltungskooperation am Beispiel administrativer Informationsverfahren im Europäischen Umweltrecht.** 2003. XXX, 891 Seiten. Geb. € 129,95

155 Frank *Schorkopf:* **Die Maßnahmen der XIV EU-Mitgliedstaaten gegen Österreich – Möglichkeiten und Grenzen einer „streitbaren Demokratie" auf europäischer Ebene.** 2002. XIII, 217 Seiten. Geb. € 64,95

154 Hanri *Mostert:* **The Constitutional Protection and Regulation of Property and its Influence on the Reform of Private Law and Landownership in South Africa and Germany.** 2002. XXV, 643 Seiten. Geb. € 99,95

152 Hans-Joachim *Cremer*, Thomas *Giegerich*, Dagmar *Richter*, Andreas *Zimmermann* (Hrsg.): **Tradition und Weltoffenheit des Rechts. Festschrift für Helmut Steinberger.** 2002. XVI, 1483 Seiten. Geb. € 199,–

151 Nico *Krisch:* **Selbstverteidigung und kollektive Sicherheit.** 2001. VIII, 449 Seiten. Geb. 169,90 DM

150 Beate *Schulte zu Sodingen:* **Der völkerrechtliche Schutz der Wälder: nationale Souveränität, multilaterale Schutzkonzepte und unilaterale Regelungsansätze.** 2002. XXXI, 575 Seiten. Geb. € 99,95

149 Mahendra *Singh:* **German Administrative Law in Common Law Perspective.** 2001. XXXI, 377 Seiten. Geb. 169,90 DM

148 Utz *Remlinger:* **Die Einwirkung des Gemeinschaftsrechts auf die Rückabwicklung rechtswidriger Beihilfeverhältnisse.** 2001. XXVI, 393 Seiten. Geb. 169,90 DM

147 Dagmar Patricia *Stroh:* **Die nationale Zusammenarbeit mit den Internationalen Straftribunalen für das ehemalige Jugoslawien und für Ruanda.** 2002. XXVII, 395 Seiten. Geb. € 84,95

146 Rainer *Grote*, Thilo *Marauhn* (Hrsg.): **Religionsfreiheit zwischen individueller Selbstbestimmung, Minderheitenschutz und Staatskirchenrecht – Völker- und verfassungsrechtliche Perspektiven.** 2001. VIII, 632 Seiten. Geb. 199,90 DM

145 Silja *Vöneky:* **Die Fortgeltung des Umweltvölkerrechts in internationalen bewaffneten Konflikten.** 2001. XXVIII, 593 Seiten. Geb. 199,90 DM

144 Niels *Krüger:* **Anwendbarkeit von Umweltschutzverträgen in der Antarktis.** 2000. XXII, 360 Seiten. Geb. 159,– DM

143 Bettina *Kellersmann:* **Die gemeinsame, aber differenzierte Verantwortlichkeit von Industriestaaten und Entwicklungsländern für den Schutz der globalen Umwelt.** 2000. XXII, 380 Seiten. Geb. 159,– DM

142 Beate *Rudolf:* **Die thematischen Berichterstatter und Arbeitsgruppen der UN-Menschenrechtskommission.** 2000. XXVI, 663 Seiten. Geb. 229,– DM

141 Andreas *Zimmermann:* **Staatennachfolge in völkerrechtliche Verträge.** 2000. L, 960 Seiten. Geb. 298,– DM

140 Christoph *Benedict:* **Sekundärzwecke im Vergabeverfahren.** 2000. XXXII, 323 Seiten. Geb. 149,– DM

139 Clemens *Ladenburger:* **Verfahrensfehlerfolgen im französischen und im deutschen Verwaltungsrecht.** 1999. XXIV, 534 Seiten. Geb. 198,– DM

138 Britta *Specht:* **Die zwischenstaatliche Geltung des Grundsatzes** ne bis in idem. 1999. XXII, 237 Seiten. Geb. 119,– DM

137 Hans-Konrad *Ress:* **Das Handelsembargo.** 2000. XXVI, 532 Seiten. Geb. 186,– DM

136 Georg *Nolte:* **Eingreifen auf Einladung.** 1999. XXXIV, 699 Seiten. Geb. 218,– DM

135 Volkmar *Götz,* Peter *Selmer,* Rüdiger *Wolfrum* (Hrsg.): **Liber amicorum Günther Jaenicke – Zum 85. Geburtstag.** 1998. XXV, 1038 Seiten. Geb. 298,– DM

134 Peter *Rädler:* **Verfahrensmodelle zum Schutz vor Rassendiskriminierung.** 1999. XVII, 454 Seiten. Geb. 148,– DM

133 Volker *Röben:* **Die Einwirkung der Rechtsprechung des Europäischen Gerichtshofs auf das Mitgliedstaatliche Verfahren in öffentlich-rechtlichen Streitigkeiten.** 1998. XXX, 478 Seiten. Geb. 168,– DM

132 Frank *Hoffmeister:* **Menschenrechts- und Demokratieklauseln in den vertraglichen Außenbeziehungen der Europäischen Gemeinschaft.** 1998. XXII, 654 Seiten. Geb. 186,– DM

131 Stefan *Schuppert:* **Neue Steuerungsinstrumente im Umweltvölkerrecht am Beispiel des Montrealer Protokolls und des Klimaschutzrahmenübereinkommens.** 1998. XXII, 297 Seiten, Geb. 128,– DM

130 Jochen Abr. *Frowein,* Thilo *Marauhn* (Hrsg.): **Grundfragen der Verfassungsgerichtsbarkeit in Mittel- und Osteuropa.** 1998. IX, 583 Seiten. Geb. 178,– DM

129 David *Weissbrodt,* Rüdiger *Wolfrum* (Eds.): **The Right to a Fair Trial.** 1997. X, 779 Seiten. Geb. 198,– DM

128 Stefan *Lehr:* **Einstweiliger Rechtsschutz und Europäische Union.** 1997. XXXVI, 693 Seiten (12 Seiten English Summary). Geb. 198,– DM

127 Grace *Nacimiento:* **Die Amerikanische Deklaration der Rechte und Pflichten des Menschen.** 1997. XII, 208 Seiten (14 Seiten English Summary). Geb. 98,– DM

126 Ralf *Alleweldt:* **Schutz vor Abschiebung bei drohender Folter oder unmenschlicher oder erniedrigender Behandlung oder Strafe.** 1996. XXI, 228 Seiten (7 Seiten English Summary). Geb. 98,– DM

125 Rüdiger *Wolfrum* (Ed.): **Enforcing Environmental Standards: Economic Mechanisms as Viable Means?** 1996. VIII, 640 Seiten. Geb. 198,– DM

124 Christian *Walter:* **Vereinte Nationen und Regionalorganisationen.** 1996. XX, 407 Seiten (5 Seiten English Summary). Geb. 128,– DM

123 Gunnar *Schuster:* **Die Internationale Anwendung des Börsenrechts.** 1996. XXV, 729 Seiten (3 Seiten English Summary). Geb. 220,– DM

9 783540 405207

Batch number: 10704041

Printed by Printforce, the Netherlands